Chicago Jewish Source Book

JWB BIENNIAL CHICAGO

MAY 12-16, 1982

Presented by the

Jewish Community Centers

of Chicago

for the library of

Rachel B. Heimovics

Rachel B. Heimovics, author

The Chicago Jewish Source Book

Rachel Baron Heimovics

𝒇 Follett Publishing Company/Chicago

Designed by Sue Lowenstein Doman

Copyright © 1981 by Rachel Baron Heimovics. Cover design copyright © 1981 by Follett Publishing Company, a division of Follett Corporation. All rights reserved. No portion of this book may be used or reproduced in any manner whatsoever without written permission from the publisher except in the case of brief quotations embodied in critical reviews and articles.
Manufactured in the United States of America.

Library of Congress Cataloging in Publication Data

Heimovics, Rachel Baron, 1933–
  The Chicago Jewish source book.

  Includes index.
  1. Jews in Chicago—Societies, etc.—Directories. 2. Jews in Chicago—Directories. 3. Chicago—Societies, etc.—Directories. I. Title.
F548.9.J5H44   977.3′11004924   80-27100
ISBN 0-695-81568-7

First Printing

To Bud

Separate not yourself from the community.
                                    Hillel

It is only when all Jews are together as a community that the whole Torah can be fulfilled.
                                    Jehiel Michael Epstein

Contents

Introduction **9**
1 About Chicago **11**
2 Community Life **17**
3 Religious Life **85**
4 Cultural Judaism **129**
5 Life-Cycle Events **145**
6 Education **157**
7 Health **191**
8 The Arts **201**
9 History **233**
10 Social and Political Concerns **257**
11 Israel and Zionism **277**
12 Publications and Media **295**
13 Goods and Services **301**
Index **331**

Introduction

The Chicago Jewish Source Book is for newcomers and old-timers. For visitors, students, teachers, and program chairmen. For senior adults, preschoolers, women, youths, singles, servicemen. For anyone and everyone who is interested in meeting, joining, and partaking of Jewish Chicago.

The Chicago Jewish community is historic, dynamic, evolving, varied—a rich composite that defies definition and categorization. Therefore, the organization of material in this book, by necessity, is by arbitrary design. Entries have been listed as logically as possible and with few cross references to make usage easier for the reader. Browsing through the pages is recommended.

All entries—whether people or organizations or places—offer something of Jewish substance or ethnic identity or are Jewish community-sponsored services. Artists and performers, whether Jewish or not, are listed only if they create or perform something of Jewish content or for Jewish purpose.

The book provides a broad, objective survey of the community's resources. Listing is not an endorsement nor a recommendation by the author. No one paid for inclusion. Persons and organizations are not included if they did not respond to inquiries, if they asked to be excluded, if their information arrived too late, or if, upon consideration, they failed to meet the author's criteria for inclusion.

The Chicago Jewish community offers a wide variety of religious and secular expressions. The author has attempted to give equal time to all options available and has intentionally eliminated qualifying terms implying bias. There are opportunities for all Jews to strengthen their Jewish identity and commitment and for non-Jews to learn more about Jews and Judaism.

Involvements are listed throughout the book. Nearly all congregations have open membership; nearly all agencies need volunteers; nearly all organizations seek members, particularly young members.

Programming resources and historic references are inserted throughout the pages. Individuals who may be helpful in programming are designated by a box (■). Almost every place and every person included are within the geographic boundaries of the Greater Chicago Metropolitan Area. All addresses listed are for the city of Chicago unless otherwise specified. All telephone area codes are (312) unless otherwise indicated.

Basic information about Chicago is included in the first chapter for the benefit of visitors and newcomers.

A constantly changing community is impossible to freeze upon the pages of a book. People move. Agencies redefine services. New resources arrive. This book represents the best possible effort to present facts accurately. *The Chicago Jewish Source Book* was researched, written, and updated in 1980. Changes inevitably occur. So be careful. Call ahead to check out information!

So many people helped in assembling this book. With each entry, the author sends a thank you for information and permission to include the listing. Many generous and knowledgeable people offered their time, ideas, suggestions, and leads. Most particularly, I am indebted to Janice Feldstein for her inspired editing and counsel.

Special thanks for special help to Rabbi Michael Azose, Rivka Becker, Rabbi and Mrs. Yitzchok Bider, Rabbi Alan Bregman, Dr. Irving Cutler, Bryna Cytrynbaum, Clare Greenberg, Baila Grinker, Michael Karzen, Betsy Katz, Rabbi Daniel Leifer, Sheryl Leonard, Gail Prince, Chana Rosen, Dr. Samuel Schafler, Miriam Schiller, Beverly Siegel, Ralph Siegel, Ruth Silverman, Rabbi Mordecai Simon, Sid Sorkin, Shirley Tatar, Rabbi Nathan Weiss, and Rabbi Harvey Well. Thanks, too, to those with the Jewish Federation of Metropolitan Chicago and its agencies and the many affiliated and independent organizations throughout Jewish Chicago who assisted me.

As for all who expressed their confidence and offered encouragement, I hope that this book fulfills their expectations. I pray that I have presented each one accurately and fully and apologize for any inadvertent omissions or errors. To my family, especially, I bestow my deepest gratitude for their loving support and patience through the many solitary months I spent in researching and writing this book. And, finally, to the Chicago Jewish community, my dedication and trust for ever-increasing abundance and vitality.

1
About Chicago

Chicago is a city of rich and diverse ethnicity. Throughout its 150 years, Chicago has received every imaginable ethnic group. Jews first arrived in the 1830s, became organized in the 1840s with a burial society and congregation, and have since left their imprint upon all segments of community life.

Chicago Jewish Population and Demography

In 1970, the estimated Jewish population for the Chicago metropolitan area was 269,000. Within a few years, a revised estimate indicated that the number was more likely 253,000. For 1981, the estimate of Jewish population will have to await census results and their interpretation by experts.

- **Peter Friedman**
  Director of Research, Jewish Federation of Metropolitan Chicago
  1 S. Franklin St., 60606; 346-6700

An expert on Chicago's Jewish population and demography, Friedman also lectures on the sociology of Chicago and American Jewry. He is a resource for studies from various academic fields pertaining to population and demography.

Geography of Chicago

Chicago covered only one square mile at the time of its first incorporation, 1833. Now the city is over 220 square miles, with 29 miles of lakefront. Chicago has grown as a patchwork of many distinct neighborhoods. Since 1930, the neighborhoods have been grouped into 75 community areas for statistical and research purposes. Today Jews live in many of these community areas, especially West Ridge (basically West Rogers Park), Rogers Park, Lakeview, Lincoln Park, Near North Side, North Park, Lincoln Square, Albany Park, Uptown (Edgewater), and Hyde Park.

Many of these and other community areas (South Shore, Englewood, Austin, Near West Side, Humboldt Park, and so forth) are closely associated with the memories and history of Jewish Chicago. One community area stands out above all others in the history of Chicago Jewry: the community area of North Lawndale.

Jews began moving into North Lawndale, on the West Side, before the 1920s and remained to the 1950s. Over 100,000 Jews lived there at its height, and the old former synagogues-turned-churches now stand like ghosts along Independence and Douglas boulevards. This was the religious, cultural, and political center of Chicago Jewish life, compressed into a single neighborhood in a way that probably can never reoccur.

Meyer Levin described North Lawndale in *The Old Bunch* (New York: Simon & Schuster, 1937), p. 4:

> Now he turned up Douglas Boulevard. Naturally this was a sweller street; most of the buildings were six flats, six-room apartments, red-brick sunparlor fronts. Occasionally there remained a large private residence, built when the Irish ran the neighborhood....
>
> Turning again onto Independence Boulevard was like walking up the last side of a rectangle bounding that world. Almost everybody lived inside that rectangle....[The] half-mile square that he had bounded was somehow warmer, full of life, it was the body containing the guts of the neighborhood though there might be limbs spreading outward.

The "limbs" have now extended to the far reaches of the metropolitan area. Actually Jews have lived in some of the suburbs (and smaller communities now considered suburbs) since the nineteenth century. Residential patterns for Chicago-area Jews are widening, and new congregations have begun in many locales relatively new to Jewish population. Within the city limits, West Rogers Park has the greatest concentration of Jewish population and institutions. Outside the city limits, Jews tend to live in northern and northwestern suburbs, with an increasing number in southern suburbs.

■ **Dr. Irving Cutler**
Chairman, Department of Geography

Chicago State University
995-2186 or 251-8927
An expert on the geography of Chicago and the Chicago Jewish community. Author, lecturer, and tour guide. Dr. Cutler's book, *Chicago: Metropolis of the Mid-Continent*, has been published in several editions since 1973 under the auspices of the Geographic Society of Chicago and Kendall-Hunt Publishing Company.

Pointers for Visitors and Newcomers to Chicago

Some Geographic Facts

All Chicago street numbers start in the Loop at State and Madison and run uniformly block by block in each direction.

This fact was not always true; all street numbering was changed between 1909 and 1911. Cross indexes to old addresses are available in reference libraries and in the front of 1909–11 city directories.

When a Chicago Jew muses about having lived on the "East Side" in his youth, he means that he lived in the Maxwell Street neighborhood, technically the Near West Side, the primary area of first settlement for Jewish immigrants to Chicago between 1880 and 1920.

The old streets in the old neighborhoods are not necessarily safe for a nostalgic stroll or bike ride.

Some Central Area Resources

Religious services are held daily at the Chicago Loop Synagogue (Orthodox) 16 S. Clark (346-7370). This synagogue includes a magnificent Abraham Rattner stained-glass window and sculpture by Henri Azaz.

Near North and North Michigan Avenue congregations are Central Synagogue (Conservative) 30 E. Cedar (787-0450); Kol Ami–The Near North Temple (Reform) with services at Water Tower Hyatt House, 800 N. Michigan (644-6900); and Park Synagogue Shaare Shalom (Orthodox) in the Radisson Chicago, 505 N. Michigan (467-5928).

The Spertus Museum of Judaica is at 618 S. Michigan (922-9012) one block south of the Pick Congress Hotel and one block north of the Conrad Hilton.

Centrally located public art and sculpture, historic and architectural landmarks, and other sites of Jewish interest are noted throughout this book.

Agudath Israel offers Travelers Assistance at 588-5078 to Orthodox Jews visiting the Chicago area.

14 *The Chicago Jewish Source Book*

Jewish Institutions Along Douglas and Independence Blvds. and Other Nearby Major Facilities—1948

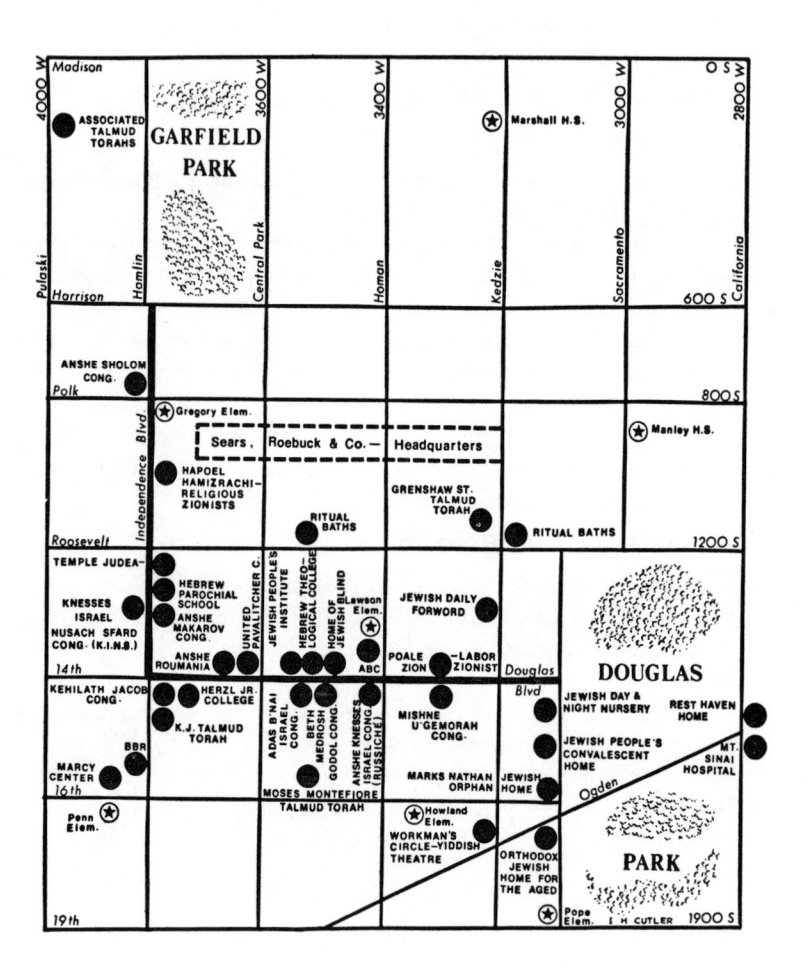

From "The Jews of Chicago: From Shtetl to Suburb" by Dr. Irving Cutler, *Ethnic Chicago*, © 1981 by William B. Eerdmans Publishing Company. Used by permission.

About Chicago 15

Major Jewish Institutions of West Rogers Park in 1979

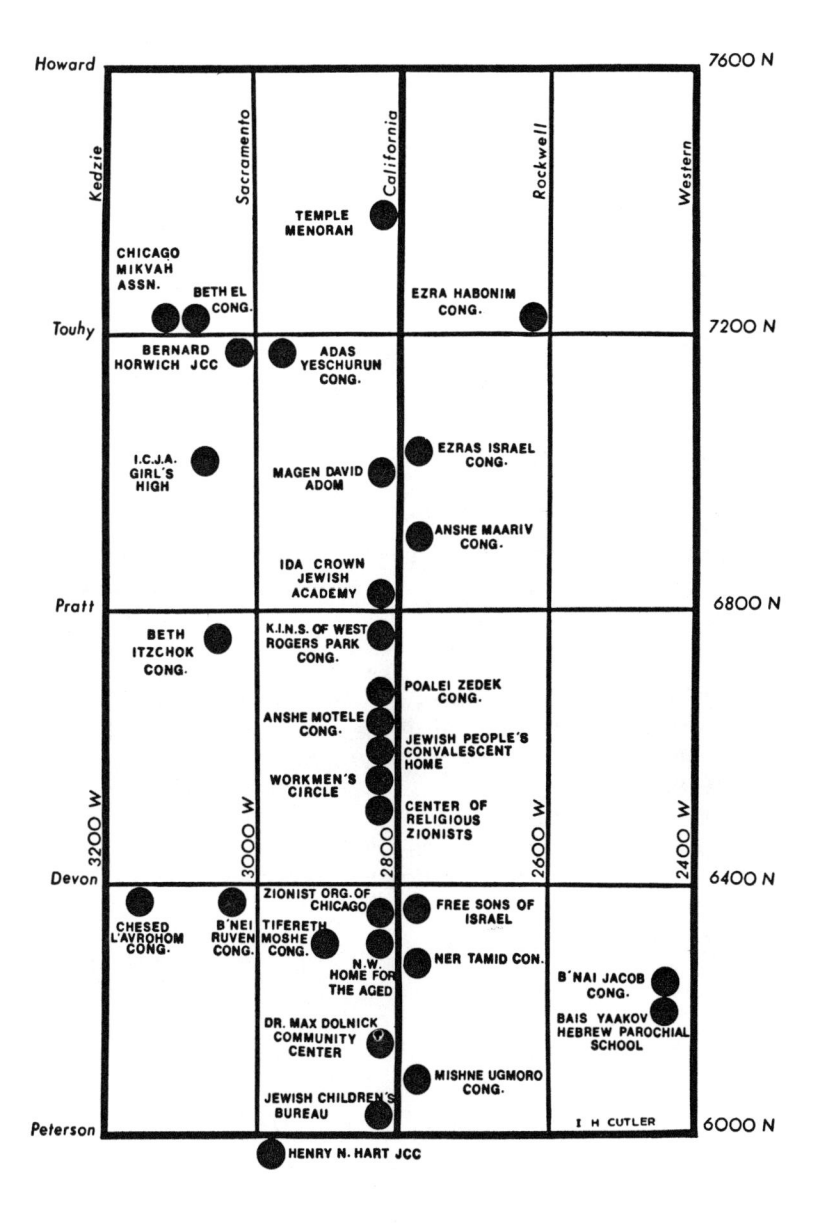

From "The Jews of Chicago: From Shtetl to Suburb" by Dr. Irving Cutler, *Ethnic Chicago*, © 1981 by William B. Eerdmans Publishing Company. Used by permission.

Des Plaines, Illinois

Myrna and Jeffrey Buckman
296-1977
Sherwin and Barbara Pomerantz
297-4354

An unusual free service is provided by the Buckmans and Pomerantzes, who supply information about Jewish resources in Des Plaines to anyone interested, especially those who are looking for a new community in which to settle. Information is provided about the local congregation, religious schools, bus service to Jewish day schools, preschools, and availability of housing.

ZIP Code Key

ZIP codes are used throughout *The Chicago Jewish Source Book*. A Chicago ZIP code map appears in the annual *Red Book* that is issued by Illinois Bell Telephone Company and published by Reuben H. Donnelley.

Here is a key to some frequently used ZIP codes in this book:

60601 through 60606 are in the greater Loop area, north to the Chicago River, south to Roosevelt Road, east to Lake Michigan, and west to Ashland.
60610 and 60611 are North Michigan Avenue, and north to North Avenue, east to the lake and west to Halsted.
60613 and 60657 are in the Lakeview community area.
60615 and 60637 are in South Kenwood and Hyde Park and include the University of Chicago.
60625 is Albany Park.
60626 is (East) Rogers Park.
60640 and 60660 are Uptown-Edgewater.
60645 and 60659 are West Rogers Park and southward.

2
Community Life

Specialized Services

Adoption

The Jewish Children's Bureau Placement Services
1 S. Franklin, 60606; 346-6700
The local agency for Jewish couples seeking to become parents through adoption.

Chicago Rabbinical Council
2735 W. Devon Ave., 60659; 764-0259
Through its Conversion and Adoption Committee, the CRC will take adopted children through the process of conversion when natural parentage is not known to be Jewish.

Bikur Cholim Societies and Projects (Visiting the Sick)

Bickur Cholem Lodge
c/o Irwin Lapping
Barnett Joseph & Son, 1400 S. Des Plaines Ave., Forest Park 60130
Still functioning well, this fraternal lodge, which celebrated its 100th anniversary in 1973, serves its members through visits to the sick, care for widows and orphans, and funeral and burial services.

AFTA (Association for Torah Advancement)
2852-D W. Touhy, 60645; 338-2575
AFTA's Bikur Cholim committee provides weekly Shabbat and holiday visits to Jewish patients in Edgewater Hospital and Skokie Valley

Community Hospital. Also assists certain hospitals in making Kosher-for-Passover TV meals available to patients requesting them.

Lubavitch Chabad of Greater Chicago
2014 Orrington, Evanston 60201; 869-8060

Makes weekly Shabbat visits to Jewish hospital patients, leaving candlesticks, chala, and a small, sealed bottle of wine.

Neshei Chabad
Women's organization of Lubavitch Chabad of Greater Chicago, 869-8060

Visits are made to Jewish patients at St. Francis Hospital, Evanston.

North Side Chaplaincy Committee
c/o any of constituent sisterhoods or congregations

The NSCC, over 30 years old, is composed of members of the sisterhoods of Beth Israel, Menorah, Sholom, and Emanuel congregations and women of Beth Emet. Holiday celebrations, dinners, and parties are offered to patients connected with Chicago-Read Mental Health Center, 4200 N. Oak Park Ave. The NSCC works with the Jewish chaplain at Read, Rabbi Harry Shapiro.

North Suburban Synagogue Beth El
Couples Club Bikur Cholim Project
c/o Gloria Taussig, 433-2181

Makes Shabbat visits, with candles, to Jewish patients in Highland Park Hospital. Will also blow shofar at Rosh Hashannah time for any patients who request this service. Approximately 100 couples are in the club, and hospital visits are rotated. Candles taken to patients are battery operated.

B'nai B'rith Hillel Foundation
University of Chicago
752-1127

Hillel students visit patients at Billings Hospital.

The Blind and Visually Handicapped

Association of the Jewish Blind of Chicago
Home and Recreation Center
3525 W. Foster Ave., 60625; 478-7040

Founded in 1932 by self-sufficient blind Jewish men and women and located until 1943 on W. Douglas Blvd., this strictly kosher shelter includes a synagogue on the premises, a staff that speaks Yiddish and German, therapy, medical and nursing care, social and cultural activities, and room and board. Open to all faiths. Also provides a sheltered workshop where blind work for wages and an organized recreational program for the blind. Supported by seven auxiliaries as well as by public aid and private bequests.

Blind Service Association
127 N. Dearborn, 60602; 332-6767

Founded in 1924, this nonsectarian organization has been dedicated to furthering self-sufficiency of the blind. In 1940 the BSA affiliated with Mount Sinai hospital. Most recently it has supported that hospital's Touhy Satellite screening program for eye disabilities among recent Soviet immigrants to Chicago.

B'nai B'rith Opportunities Unlimited
c/o B'nai B'rith Council
8 S. Michigan, Rm. 2301, 60603; 346-8555

Opportunities Unlimited—a singles group of 35- to 60-year-olds—sponsors a Sing-a-Long for the blind.

Philip H. Cohen Institute for the Visually Handicapped
5200 S. Hyde Park Blvd., 60615; 752-2770

Formerly called Hoffman House Institute, this service provides the blind with books in braille and large type, records, and tapes as well as machines to play the records and tapes. All services and equipment are supplied free to the recipient.

Johanna Bureau for the Blind and Visually Handicapped
30 W. Washington, Rm. 1600, 60602; 332-6076

Offers braille and tapes for the blind and visually handicapped—as well as for the physically handicapped who are unable to hold books. Supported by the Johanna Lodge. Open Monday through Friday.

Camps

Overnight Camps

B'nai B'rith Beber Camp
8 S. Michigan, Suite 2301, 60603; 782-4766

Kosher, Jewish-content camp in Mukwonago, WI, for boys and girls 8 to 16.

Camp Chi
1 S. Franklin, 60606; 346-6700

Operated by the JCCs, this Wisconsin-based, kosher-style camp has winterized year-round facilities. For 4th graders through high schoolers. (*Chi* is an acronym for the Chicago Hebrew Institute, original name of the JCCs.)

Camp CHUSY
72 E. 11th St., 60605; 939-2353

Postcamp for members of any United Synagogue Youth (USY) group or member. Unaffiliated youth may attend by joining USY. For high school age, but qualified 8th graders may attend. At Camp Ramah, Conover, WI.

Camp Gan Israel
2014 Orrington, Evanston 60201; 869-8060

Kosher camp operated by the Lubavitch Chabad, for boys 10 to 15.

Habonim Camp Tavor
c/o Gayle Shavit, 433-0512; Stephanie Grossman, 729-9226

Labor Zionist Youth movement camp, located in Michigan. Kosher. For boys and girls 10 to 16.

Camp Henry Horner
30 W. Washington, 60602; 726-8891
Camp telephone: 546-4435

Young Men's Jewish Council's overnight camp in Round Lake, IL; year-round winterized facilities. Kosher style. For ages 9 to 15. Also sessions for mentally handicapped.

Camp Menorah
8 Blackhawk Hills Dr., Rock Island, IL 61201; (309) 786-1866

Private kibbutz-style, kosher-style Jewish Folk Arts camp, limited to sixteen boys and girls, ages 11 or 12 or beginning 6th or 7th grade. At Folklore Village, Dodgeville, WI. Nina Segal, M.S.W., Director. One two-week session.

Camp Moshava
6500 N. California, 60645; 338-2871

The camp of Religious Zionists–B'nei Akiva, located in Wild Rose, WI. Kosher. Ages 9 to 16.

Olin-Sang-Ruby Union Institute Camp
100 W. Monroe, Rm. 312, 60603; 782-1477

Five camps in one (Kibbutz, Moshava, etc.) operated by Union of American Hebrew Congregations. Kosher-style, year-round facilities in Oconomowoc, WI. For 4th graders through high schoolers.

Camp Ramah
72 E. 11th St., 60605; 939-2393

Kosher camp of the Conservative movement. For girls and boys 11 through 17; located in Conover, WI. Also operates Tikvah Camp for youths with learning disabilities.

Camp Shomria
c/o Israel Aliyah Center
205 W. Wacker Dr., Rm. 516, 60606; 332-2709
Canadian-based camp of the Hashomer Hatzair Zionist youth organization. On Lake Otty, Perth, Ontario.

USY on Wheels
72 E. 11th St., 60605; 939-2353
Actually a caravan rather than a camp, for 14½- to 18-year-olds and chaperons, touring the United States by bus, visiting Jewish landmarks and communities. Kashrut and Sabbath observed.

Camp Yehudah
6328 N. California, 60659; 262-5949
Sponsored by Masada, youth group of the Zionist Organization of Chicago and Zionist Organization of America, in Leonides, MI, for 9- to 14-year-olds.

Camp Young Judaea
4155 Main, Skokie 60076; 676-9790
Michigan-based kosher camp sponsored by Hadassah for 8- to 14-year-old girls and boys.

Special Overnight Camps

Michael Reese Hospital and Medical Center
791-2000
Sponsors a one-week camp in its Pediatric Kidney Dialysis Program for children who are able to use portable dialysis. Camp held at Camp Chi.

Camp Henry Horner
30 W. Washington St., 60602; 726-8891
Young Men's Jewish Council sponsors precamp and postcamp programs for mentally retarded from ages 16 to 60.

Tikvah Program of Camp Ramah
72 E. 11th St., 60605; 939-2393
Tikvah Program is an eight-week, Jewish educational camp program for the teenage boy and girl (ages 13 to 18) with learning disabilities. No previous Jewish education is required. Staff, camper ratio is 1:2.

Judith Krassner
Student Camp and Trip Adviser
564-1845
Free referral to private Jewish-content camps in several regions of the country, including one offering bar/bat mitzvah preparation for children with learning disabilities.

Day Camps

Agudath Israel
3540 W. Peterson, 60659; 588-5078
Operates separate day camps for boys and girls.

Associated Talmud Torahs
2828 W. Pratt, 60645; 973-2828
Cosponsors day camp Givat Ran with Bernard Horwich JCC, which offers Jewish-content, five-day program for 6- to 11-year-olds. Separate sections for boys and girls.

Sponsors summer session for preschoolers at Lavin Educational Center in Northbrook: Gan Yadodin.

Board of Jewish Education
72 E. 11th St., 60605; 427-5570
Cosponsors Shraga Arian Camp Medurah with the Mayer Kaplan JCC and North Suburban JCC. Kaplan JCC serves boys and girls from West Rogers Park to Glenview; North Suburban, northern suburbs through Highland Park. A Northwest Suburban Unit also functions through the North Suburban JCC for children from Arlington Heights, Wheeling, Buffalo Grove, Palatine, Mt. Prospect, and Prospect Heights. Attendance may be for three or five days a week for four or eight weeks.

Jewish Community Centers
1 S. Franklin, 60606; 346-6700
In addition to camps cosponsored with the Associated Talmud Torahs and the Board of Jewish Education, the JCCs have a wide range of day camps for preschool through junior high school age. For specific day camp opportunities, contact the following:

Anita M. Stone JCC, 799-7650
Bernard Horwich JCC, 761-9100
Henry N. Hart JCC, 275-8445
Hyde Park JCC, 268-4600
Lincoln Park–Lakeview JCC, 871-6780
Mayer Kaplan JCC, 675-2200
North Suburban JCC, 272-2267
Rogers Park JCC, 274-0920

Lubavitch Chabad of Greater Chicago
2014 Orrington, Evanston 60201; 869-8060
Gan Israel Day Camp, for ages 4 to 13, includes transportation and lunches. Open to Soviet children; Associated Talmud Torahs provides

tutorial assistance to Soviet Jewish boys and girls within the larger camp structure. Separate preschool camp for 2- and 3-year-olds.

Union of American Hebrew Congregations
100 W. Monroe, Rm. 312, 60603; 782-1477
UAHC operates Camp Shalom in the west suburbs of Oak Park and Lombard for Jewish children who have no other Jewish day camp opportunities. For boys and girls 6 to 10 years old.

Young Men's Jewish Council
30 W. Washington St., 60602; 726-8891
Sunflower Day Camp, for children 3 to 5, is coordinated through Parent and Child Care Centers in Highland Park, Lincoln Park, and Niles. Day camps for children 5 to 11 are located in Lincoln Park, Morton Grove, Highland Park, Hoffman Estates, and Arlington Heights. Tween Camp, for 11- to 14-year-olds, serves children in Arlington Heights, Buffalo Grove, and Highland Park.

Child Abuse

To report child abuse, call (800) 25-ABUSE

Jewish Children's Bureau
1 S. Franklin, 60606; 346-6700
Lake County: 210 Skokie Valley Rd., Highland Park 60035; 831-5630
The JCB is the child-welfare agency of the Jewish Federation. Crisis intervention and counseling are provided by JCB in matters of child abuse. Other offices of the JCB that may be contacted:
120 W. Eastman, Arlington Heights 60004; 255-4410
5050 Church St., Skokie 60077; 675-2200
6014 N. California Ave., 60659; 761-8366

Jewish Family and Community Service
1 S. Franklin, 60606; 346-6700
North Suburban District Office, 210 Skokie Valley Rd., Highland Park 60035; 831-4225
Handles child-abuse referrals; provides counseling.

Michael Reese Hospital and Medical Center
29th St. and Ellis Ave., 60616; 791-2000
Operates a state-aided program for child abuse and neglect.

Child Abuse Prevention Speakers' Bureau, Inc.
P.O. Box 265, Dolton 60419; 841-5414 or 841-5419
Diane Kreiman, Executive Director

CAPSB, a nonprofit organization, began in 1973 as a project of B'nai B'rith and B'nai B'rith Women with 45 volunteers. It was originally called CASE (Child Abuse Service and Education). A 1975 reorganization led to independent status and change of name. Currently, there are nearly 400 volunteers, 250 of whom are speakers. Many of these men and women are from B'nai B'rith chapters. CAPSB will provide speakers on child abuse and the new legislation concerning child abuse for any group in the state and will give guidance to those who wish to set up similar speakers' bureaus. CAPSB has worked closely with the National Committee for the Prevention of Child Abuse.

Board of Jewish Education
72 E. 11th St., 60605; 427-5570
Marvell Ginsburg, Director, Early Childhood Jewish Education

The drop-in mother-and-child program at Early Childhood Centers is a joint effort with the Virginia Frank Child Development Center, which strives to prevent child abuse. Professionals are able to monitor stress situations and offer preventive counseling.

Mount Sinai Hospital Medical Center
California Ave. at 15th St., 60608; 542-2000

Sponsors a Child Protection Team that deals with all forms of child abuse—physical, psychological, and sexual.

National Council of Jewish Women
53 W. Jackson, Rm. 724, 60604; 663-9400

Several sections of Chicago area NCJW participate in the Agency Monitoring Project with the Cook County Juvenile Court–Foster Care. Volunteer women are trained to monitor records of children placed by the court into foster care and report to the court their findings as to the needs of individual children. Project is under the supervision of the chief deputy probation officer for juvenile court.

City Clubs

Jewish-sponsored city clubs (and country clubs as well) provide a significant base for local fund raising, for the development of philanthropic leadership, and for identification with the Jewish community throughout the world.

The Covenant Club
10 N. Dearborn, 60602; 782-9474

Originally founded by B'nai B'rith (thus the name Covenant, B'rith). In the early days membership in B'nai B'rith was the only prerequisite for membership. Today the Covenant Club is a private social club with limited recreational facilities for both men and women as well as a library and a ballroom. The club welcomes organizations to use its kitchen and dining room. Kosher catering is available.

The Standard Club
320 S. Plymouth Ct., 60604; 427-9100

A private social and recreational club, the Standard Club has permanent and transient residents. Founded in 1869, the club published a good history, with many illustrations, in honor of its centennial. An early clubhouse at 13th and South Michigan Ave. was used by General Philip Sheridan as his headquarters when martial law was established following the Great Chicago Fire of 1871. A later clubhouse, designed by Adler and Sullivan, stood at 24th and South Michigan. It was a fine specimen of their tall-building architecture.

Country Clubs

Jewish-supported country clubs (like city clubs) form a significant base in local fund raising. The annual Country Club Day, sponsored by JUF in June 1980, included these eleven clubs: Birchwood, Briarwood, Bryn Mawr, Green Acres, Highland Park, Hillcrest, Idlewild, Northmoor, Ravinia Green, Ravisloe, and Twin Orchard.

Lake Shore Country Club, just south of the northern boundary of Glencoe on Sheridan Road, has the distinction of being the oldest Jewish organization in the North Shore suburbs. Founded in 1908, it preceded the founding of the first congregation by twelve years.

Couples Clubs

B'nai B'rith and the American Jewish Congress are just two of the organizations with new units for young-adult couples—these clubs seem to be the way of the eighties.

Mayer Kaplan JCC Couples Clubs
5050 Church, Skokie 60077; 675-2200

Two clubs: one for couples in their twenties and thirties; the other, for those in their forties and fifties.

Lincoln Park-Lakeview JCC
524 W. Melrose, 60657; 871-6780

This young-adult couples club meets on the second Sunday of each month and is open to nonmembers of the JCC.

Cults

Response Center
Inter-Agency Project on Cults
7457 N. Western Ave., 60645; 338-2292

Response Center provides information, counseling and supportive services, and referrals for families of current cult members and for former cult members themselves. Will provide parents of cult members with list of dos and don'ts. Offers speakers to community groups, schools, and religious organizations. Has assembled resource library of articles, books, and pamphlets about the cult phenomenon. The Response Center is studying Jewish involvement in cults as well as other aspects.

■ Edward M. Levine
Professor of Social Psychology, Department of Sociology
Loyola University
Contact through university or at 828 Oakton St., Evanston 60202 (home)

Professor Levine is a resource on the subject of cults as well as a lecturer. He is interested in establishing a network of people who will work to prevent youths from entering cults. A number of his articles on the subject of cults have appeared in professional journals.

■ Howard Richter
930 Cedar St., Deerfield 60015; 948-5138

Lecturer, teacher, resource person on comparative religion and on Jewish high school students and the cults.

Day Care

Akiba-Schechter Jewish Day School
5200 S. Hyde Park Blvd., 60615; 493-8880

Day care in association with the day school.

Mayer Kaplan Jewish Community Center
5050 Church, Skokie 60077; 675-2200

This JCC has several day-care plans. The program for 3- to 5-year-olds incorporates nursery school, hot kosher lunch and nap, gym, swimming, trips, and participation in special activities, 7:30 A.M. to 6 P.M. year-round. Pearl Goodman Schoen Preschool and Day Care Center.

The After Kindergarten Day Care Program operates 11:30 A.M. to 5:30 P.M. Mondays through Thursdays and 11:30 A.M. to 5 P.M. Fridays. Transportation can be provided for extra fee. Recreational activities include swimming, gym, and art.

Rogers Park Jewish Community Center
7101 N. Greenview, 60626; 274-0920

Day care for 3- to 5-year-olds, 8 A.M. to 5 P.M., includes hot kosher lunch.

Tri-Con Child Care Center
425 Laurel Ave., Highland Park 60035; 433-1450

One of the major sponsoring organizations of this day-care center is the National Council of Jewish Women, North Shore Section.

Young Men's Jewish Council
Operates three Parent and Child Centers that offer day care, five days a week to 5:30 P.M., in Highland Park, Niles, and the Lincoln Park area of Chicago. For information, call

Highland Park, 433-5495
Niles, 470-1540
Lincoln Park, 281-2533

The Deaf and Hearing Impaired

Congregation Bene Shalom of the Deaf
4435 Oakton, Skokie 60076; 677-3330
Rabbi Douglas H. Goldhamer

Full congregational program includes religious education for deaf, hearing-impaired, and hearing Jews. Services, auxiliaries, religious school, bar and bat mitzvah, social functions, and a special funeral plan.

Jewish Family and Community Service
5050 Church St., Skokie 60077; 675-2200
Telecommunication number: TTY 679-5992

A unique program in which the full range of JFCS services is made available to the hearing impaired. Interested persons may call for an appointment by voice by calling 675-2200 and asking for JFCS, or by TTY 679-5992, or by visiting Niles District office of the JFCS, 5050 Church, Skokie.

Original Weinstein and Sons, Inc., Funeral Home
3019 W. Peterson Ave., 60659; 561-1890
TTY 561-0655

Funeral director Robert A. Weinstein has developed a unique program for serving the funeral needs of deaf and hearing-impaired family members.

Piser Memorial Chapels
679-4740
TTY 674-5900
The first funeral home in Illinois to purchase Porta-telecommunicator-TTY for purpose of serving the hearing impaired.

Foundation for Hearing and Speech Rehabilitation
Michael Reese Hospital and Medical Center, 791-2900
An auxiliary supporting research and services at Michael Reese.

David T. Siegel Institute for Communicative Disorders
Michael Reese Hospital and Medical Center
3033 S. Cottage Grove Ave., 60616; 791-2900
Siegel Institute is a comprehensive diagnostic and treatment center for persons with hearing, language, and speech disorders. It also houses a state center for evaluation of deaf-blind children and for psychiatric services to the deaf and their families.

Divorce and Separation

- **Rabbi Mordecai Rosen**
  Beth Judea Congregation, Buffalo Grove 60090; 634-0777
  Rabbi Rosen has made a specialty of assisting persons coping with divorce. He does one-to-one counseling and lecturing, leads support groups and one-time discussions. All avenues dealing with the subject of divorce are open to him. Call him in care of his synagogue office.

- **Joanne H. Saunders**
  One IBM Plaza, Suite 1414, 60611; 467-1414
  An attorney who has had experience not only with the legal aspects of divorce but also with leading a support group of divorced parents at Temple Sholom. Her expertise has been used by the Family Education Association of the Board of Jewish Education in a review of the needs of the growing number of Jewish divorced parents and their school-age children.

Jewish religious divorce is handled by the courts of arbitration, the Beth Din Zedek of the Chicago Rabbinical Council (Orthodox) and the Bet Din of the Chicago Region of the Rabbinical Assembly (Conservative).

Drug Abuse

Response Center
7457 N. Western, 60645; 338-2292

Jewish Children's Bureau
1 S. Franklin, 60606; 346-6700

These two agencies dealing with problems of adolescent drug abuse are both under the umbrella of the Jewish Federation of Metropolitan Chicago.

Emergency Food

The Ark
3509 W. Lawrence Ave., 60625; 463-4545

The Ark operates an emergency food pantry available on a limited-time basis and also a Kosher Meals-on-Wheels program, primarily for short-term convalescents and persons 60 and older. Sliding-scale fees up to $2 a meal; one meal a day, five days a week. Food stamps accepted.

The Ark also distributes Shabbat baskets of food to needy families. Sisterhoods, congregations, and other organizations may assist with this program.

Moes Chitim Committee of Greater Chicago
55 E. Washington St., Suite 1505, 60602

Passover food boxes distributed to needy families who may register for this assistance at such places as the Ark, the Religious Zionists of Chicago, and Congregation Beth Sholom of Rogers Park. For information, call the Ark (463-4545).

Council for Jewish Elderly
1015 W. Howard St., Evanston 60202; 973-4105

Various food-service programs for the elderly are coordinated by CJE, including kosher home-delivered meals as well as noontime programs at several sites jointly sponsored by the JCCs and the Chicago Office for Senior Citizens and Handicapped.

Employment Agencies and Services

Hire-a-Teen
Hyde Park Jewish Community Center
268-4600

A job bank for teens, age 13 and older.

Jewish Vocational Service
1 S. Franklin, 60606; 346-6700

Provides placement for persons who for one reason or another ordinarily have difficulty in finding a job, including senior adults, Soviet Jews, Indo-Chinese and other refugees, and the handicapped. Provides a summer placement program for temporary jobs for college students. Registration takes place in spring. Senior Employment Unit is a free, nonsectarian service specializing in the placement of persons 65 and older. Neither the job seeker nor the employer pays for this service. Call 973-3800 for information.

National Council of Jewish Women, Chicago Section
53 W. Jackson, Suite 1511, 60604; 987-1927
This NCJW section has two employment agencies:
JOY (Job Opportunities for Youth), 1791 W. Howard St., 60626; 973-2190. Open 9:30 A.M. to 5 P.M. Mondays through Thursdays; places youth 15 to 18 years of age.
Senior Employment Opportunities, same address, 274-4950. Places persons 55 years old and over with no fees to clients or employers.

National Council of Jewish Women, North Shore Section
Youth Employment Service
1811 St. Johns Ave., Highland Park 60035; 433-4090; 441-5514
Founded in the early 1960s. Provides free job referrals to high school students in ten northern suburbs. Highland Park office open 10 A.M. to 5 P.M. weekdays (except Wednesday) during the school year and 9 A.M. to 4 P.M. summers.

Families

American Jewish Committee
55 E. Jackson, Rm. 1870, 60604; 663-5500
Both the Chicago Task Force on Jewish Family Life and the Task Force on Single Parent Families are coordinated by AJC.

Board of Jewish Education Department of Family Education
72 E. 11th St., 60605; 427-5570
Moshe Samber, Director
BJE's central resource for materials on Jewish education and the family. Issues the *Family Education Newsletter*. Assists the United Synagogue of America in sponsoring the Parent Education Program (PEP) dealing with adolescents and parent-child studies. The Family Education Association is a lay affiliate.

Jewish Family and Community Service
1 S. Franklin, 60606; 346-6700
Assists families through family counseling and problem solving. Professional Family Life Educators available to speak to organizations and set up workshops dealing with specific areas of stress and concern in family life.

Family Planning and Sex Education

The following agencies sponsored by the Chicago Jewish community provide family-planning and sex-education counseling and programs.

Jewish Children's Bureau
1 S. Franklin, 60606; 346-6700
Unmarried-parent services.

Jewish Family and Community Service
1 S. Franklin, 60606; 346-6700

Michael Reese Hospital and Medical Center
29th St. and Ellis Ave., 60616; 791-2850
Serves the needs of pregnant adolescents and adolescent mothers.

Mount Sinai Hospital Medical Center
California Ave. at 15th St., 60608; 542-2000
A professional staff services the Response Center.

Response Center
7457 N. Western Ave., 60645; 338-2292
A major resource for assistance to adolescents in family planning and sex education. Individual or family counseling.

Financial Assistance

Lending money at no interest has historically been considered a function of the Chicago Jewish community—through free loans, Bikur Cholim, mutual-aid societies, and fraternal organizations. The following agencies are resources for direct financial aid or for information about loans.

AFTA (Association for Torah Advancement)
338-2575
AFTA's G'Milus Chesed Fund has provided short-term free loans since the early 1970s. Of the more than 100 borrowers, none has defaulted. To qualify, applicant must provide reliable cosigners. Repayment is by monthly installments, and loans are limited to a maximum of $1,000.

The Ark
463-4545

Chicago Board of Rabbis
427-5863

Jewish Family and Community Service
346-6700

Jewish War Veterans of the United States, Department of Illinois
372-0262 (9 A.M. to 1:30 P.M. weekdays)
Maurice Lepavsky, Adjutant

JWV assists servicemen and servicewomen and their dependents with obtaining the benefits due them. This service is provided on a nonsectarian basis.

Foster Care

Jewish Children's Bureau
1 S. Franklin, 60606; 346-6700

JCB is the agency of the Jewish Federation that handles the placement of children in foster homes when that seems to be the wisest option for the care of children who are unable to live with their families.

JCB also provides placement in its own residential facilities for children in need of specialized care. Persons interested in being foster parents are encouraged to call the agency. There is a Jewish Children's Bureau Foster Parents Association.

Fraternal Organizations

Fraternal organizations, for women as well as men, were very popular among Chicago Jews of the nineteenth and early twentieth centuries. They provided social and mutual aid to members and, as did the folk groups, administered cemeteries and funeral insurance plans.

But only those fraternal organizations that provided something more than mutual aid tended to survive. B'nai B'rith is the most notable example. Although it was once a fraternal organization, it is no longer regarded as one because of the diversity of its programs.

Among the national social and mutual benefit organizations classified as such in the *American Jewish Yearbook*, the following have chapters in Chicago: the Free Sons of Israel, Jewish Labor Bund, United Order True Sisters, and the Workmen's Circle. Local fraternal organizations are the Bickur Cholem Lodge; Shomrim, an organization of Jewish police officers; and Israelite Portuguese Fraternity, the Sephardic Congregation.

Fraternities and Sororities

Vestiges of the once-popular Jewish college fraternities and sororities may be found in the Chicago area, although these groups vary in the depth of their Jewish identity.

At Northwestern University, Evanston, there are chapters of Alpha Epsilon Phi, Sigma Delta Tau, and Zeta Beta Tau. There is an Alpha Epsilon Pi chapter at the Illinois Institute of Technology and a Sigma Alpha Mu chapter at the University of Illinois–Chicago Circle.

Alpha Omega, the Jewish dental fraternity, has chapters in the dental schools of Northwestern University, Loyola University, and the University of Illinois in Chicago. Unlike the undergraduate Greek societies, Alpha Omega has maintained a strong Jewish profile by founding and supporting professional dentistry training in Israel.

Gay Jews

Or Chadash
656 W. Barry, 60657; 248-9456

This congregation has outreach to Jewish lesbians and gay men. Shabbat services are held at 8:30 P.M. the second and fourth Fridays of the month at the Second Unitarian Church. Services or celebrations are also held on all Jewish holidays, including a Passover seder. For information, call anytime and leave your name and telephone number on the tape recorder.

The Handicapped

Aids to Motor Handicapped Children
Jean Holzman Weiss, President

This organization, founded 40 years ago, raises money specifically for motor-handicapped children's programs at Michael Reese Hospital and in Israel through AKIM.

Jewish Vocational Service
1 S. Franklin, 60606; 346-6700

JVS has a multifaceted program assisting persons with mental and physical disabilities to remain or become employable. In addition to programs of general rehabilitation, special projects include training for employment as messengers and clerical workers. The JVS Research Development Unit tests and investigates methods for mainstreaming handicapped persons into productive occupations.

Sampson-Katz Center, 2020 W. Devon, 60659; 761-9000
Vocational Adjustment Center, 320 N. Dearborn, 60610; 828-9700
Self-Actualization Center, 325 W. Huron, 60610; 440-1107

Mayer Kaplan Jewish Community Center
5050 Church, Skokie 60077; 675-2200

Kaplan JCC has a homebound program cosponsored with the Maine/Niles Association for Special Recreation. On Mondays door-to-door bus service brings persons ordinarily homebound to the JCC for social, cultural, and educational programs and services.

Michael Reese Hospital and Medical Center
29th St. and Ellis Ave., 60616; 791-2000
A comprehensive medical center with a wide range of services for the physically, mentally, emotionally, and multiply handicapped, including the following four programs:

Department of Rehabilitation Medicine
791-2430
Total rehabilitation services for adults and children who are physically disabled.

David T. Siegel Institute for Communicative Disorders
3033 S. Cottage Grove Ave., 60616; 791-2900
State center for diagnostic evaluation and treatment of blind-deaf children.

Neural-Muscular Disabilities Program
791-4233
A multidisciplinary program for both children and adults with neural-muscular disabilities.

Dysfunctioning Child Center
791-4233
Evaluation, diagnosis, treatment, respite care, and continuing health care for developmentally disabled and multihandicapped persons. DCC services include a five-day-a-week preschool nursery for retarded children with organic dysfunctions, designed to prepare them for eventual placement in community schools; a program for children with neurological handicaps and learning disabilities who are already in school; and programs for children who are nonverbal, have stopped developing, or display other manifestations of organic dysfunctions. An auxiliary supports this center.

Home-Care Services

Council for Jewish Elderly Housekeeping Division
1015 W. Howard, Evanston 60202; 973-4105
Provides assistance with household chores. There is a charge for this service, which requires a social and health assessment by CJE. Geographic area served is Broadway to Lake Michigan, Howard St. to Bryn Mawr Ave.

Jewish Family and Community Service
1 S. Franklin, 60606; 346-6700

Will send trained homemakers to tide over until other arrangements can be made in cases of convalescence, death of the homemaker, or other crises. JFCS also provides consultants in all aspects of home economics—budget planning, nutrition, and so forth.

Care Unlimited, Inc.
864-1244

This agency, under kosher operation, provides professional health care, including nurses, where and when needed. Although the services are absolutely nonsectarian, Care Unlimited is run by several women with a long association with the Chicago Jewish community who understand the kosher dietary needs of Jewish patients. This service is designed to be an alternative to the nursing home.

Home Care and Nursing Services
111 N. Wabash Ave., 60602; 346-0260

Provides home care and nursing services 24 hours a day in any area of Chicago and surrounding suburbs to which there is public transportation. Office personnel speak Yiddish. Kosher dietary laws and needs are understood and will be observed. Yiddish- or Russian-speaking therapists, including a Soviet Jewish masseuse who will provide home-care massages, are available.

Both Mount Sinai and Michael Reese hospitals provide home-care services in certain situations.

Immigrants

The Chicago Jewish community is assisting not only Jewish immigrants but also refugees from Indochina and Cuba. The Jewish Vocational Service, Jewish Family and Community Service, and other agencies of the Jewish Federation of Metropolitan Chicago have been part of citywide and even nationwide programs providing emergency services to these newcomers. HIAS (Hebrew Immigrant Aid Society) and the Anti-Defamation League have also played major roles in these efforts. Many congregations and organizations have aided by assuming some of the financial and humanitarian needs of the refugees. See the section on Soviet Jews in Chicago for information about specific immigrant services.

- **Joanna Spilman**
  Coordinator of Immigrant Services
  Bernard Horwich JCC, 3003 W. Touhy, 60645; 761-9100

A resource person for all Jewish immigrants to Chicago; will assist in directing persons to appropriate programs and social services. She is especially interested in encouraging newcomers to become integrated into the community, the Jewish community in particular, by joining groups and programs that are not limited to immigrants.

Jewish Communal Service

**B'nai B'rith Hillel Foundations Jewish Federation
College Age Youth Services**
1 S. Franklin, 60606; 346-6700

Offers a summer intern program in Jewish communal service for college students. The program includes eight weeks of placement, with pay, in a social-service agency within the family of Federation agencies, seminars in Judaica and social work, and an opportunity to work with some needy segment of the population.

Spertus College of Judaica
618 S. Michigan, 60605; 922-9012

Offers a Master of Arts in Jewish Communal Service.

Jewish Marriage Encounter

Jewish Marriage Encounter
c/o Gloria and Morris Wolin, Coordinators
7411 N. Karlov, Skokie 60076; 673-3681

This couple provides assistance for individuals and groups interested in setting up or attending a Jewish Marriage Encounter weekend at a hotel or a motel in the Chicago vicinity. Weekends are led by a rabbinical couple and take place about once a month. Marriage Encounter is not a form of counseling; it is designed to improve communication and provide enrichment in the marriage relationship.

Karaites

Karaites are a Jewish sect dating from the eighth century. In their religious practice, they were regarded as fundamentalists and outside mainstream Judaism. Chicago's small Karaite community came from Cairo in the 1960s. They were led by Jacques Mangoubi who, prior to his death in 1976, incorporated the Chicago group as the "Jewish Karaite Community of America." According to an article in *Hadassah Magazine* (March 1979), the Chicago Karaites have held High Holiday services. Recently, one of Mangoubi's sons indicated the group still meets and has a location for activities and services.

Leadership Training

The Jewish community recognizes that the development of leadership is of prime concern. The following programs are examples; there are many more.

B'nai B'rith Council of Greater Chicago
346-8555
B'nai B'rith Women Land of Lakes Region
679-6077
Sponsor a Young Leadership Unit of young adult singles and marrieds who meet through the year to discuss significant issues confronting the American and world Jewish community.

Board of Jewish Education
72 E. 11th St., 60605; 427-5570
Among several programs for developing leadership are the Institute for Jewish Leadership and the School Board Leadership Institute. The latter offers special sessions for those already serving on congregational religious-school boards.

Chicago Jewish Youth Council
3003 W. Touhy, 60645; 761-9100
One of the functions of the CJYC is the sponsoring of leadership-training programs.

Young Leadership Division of Jewish United Fund
1 S. Franklin St., 60606; 346-6700
One of two divisions of JUF that is represented on the Public Affairs Committee (the other is the Women's Division). Although YLD does have social functions, its primary business is to develop leadership in the Jewish community. It is organized into several subdivisions: Career Women, Singles, etc.

JUF Dialogues Group
For information, contact Robert and Sue Mednick
936 Rollingwood Rd., Highland Park 60035
A two-year leadership-development program series that may be unique among Jewish Federations in major American cities. Its purpose is to educate and raise the consciousness of a core of young people who may well become the future leaders of JUF. At the present time four groups are functioning, and there is a waiting list to get into one. Several past groups have continued to meet and learn into a third and a fourth year. The Mednicks are leaders of one group.

Legal Resources

American Jewish Congress
22 W. Monroe St., Suite 2102, 60603; 332-7355
Sponsors forums on legal concerns and handles civil-rights and civil-liberties issues. Staff lawyer. Cosponsors Chicago Jewish Immigrant Legal Services Clinic at Rogers Park JCC.

Anti-Defamation League of B'nai B'rith
222 W. Adams, Rm. 1449, 60606; 782-5080
Lawyer on staff.

The Ark
3509 W. Lawrence, 60625; 463-4545
Offers legal assistance to clients.

B'nai B'rith Council of Greater Chicago
8 S. Michigan, Rm. 2301, 60603; 346-8555
Lodge #2837, the Justice Lodge, is composed of lawyers, judges, and policemen.

Council for Jewish Elderly
1015 W. Howard, Evanston 60202; 973-4105
Provides legal assistance.

Most legal-assistance programs need volunteer lawyers.

Decalogue Society of Lawyers
180 W. Washington, 60602; 263-6493
This organization, whose membership of about 1,600 consists largely of Jewish lawyers, provides a variety of social and professional services for its members. It also maintains the Lawyer Referral Service, which is administered as a free public service by (Ret.) Judge David Lefkovits. Volunteer lawyers who speak Yiddish, Hebrew, Polish, Russian, or German are available for consultation. Referral is made to a lawyer with experience in the appropriate field of law. Hours are from 10:30 A.M. to 3:30 P.M. Mondays, Wednesdays, and Thursdays. Call for an appointment.

Student chapters in Chicago law schools operate in conjunction with the Decalogue Society and the Jewish Federation. There is also a Women's Auxiliary.

Jewish Family and Community Service
1 S. Franklin, 60606; 346-6700
Offers legal consultations to clients.

Jewish Federation and Jewish United Fund of Metropolitan Chicago
1 S. Franklin, 60606; 346-6700
An informative *Handbook for Lawyers* is published from time to time that includes up-to-date tax tables and other information relevant to the legal aspects of contributions to tax-exempt organizations.

Jewish Immigrant Legal Services Clinic
Rogers Park JCC
7101 N. Greenview, 60626; 274-0920
Cosponsored by the American Jewish Congress, the clinic provides free legal services to Jewish immigrants whatever their national origin. Appointments are necessary. Call ahead.

Men's Clubs

National Federation of Jewish Men's Clubs Midwest Region
72 E. 11th St., 60605
Men's clubs of the Conservative movement.

National Federation of Temple Brotherhoods
100 W. Monroe St., 60603
Men's clubs of the Reform movement.

The Mentally Retarded

Associated Talmud Torahs
2828 W. Pratt, 60645; 973-2828
Offers Jewish religious education to residents of the Glenkirk Home in Lake Forest, for mentally retarded children aged 6 to 21.

Deborah House
7428 N. Rogers Ave., 60626; 761-0395
Chicago Association for Retarded Citizens
343 S. Dearborn, 60604; 922-2202
A residential facility for developmentally disabled adults over 18. Although Deborah House was originally started by parents of the disabled who had an association with the Young Men's Jewish Council, that connection no longer exists. Jewish residents are provided with celebrations for Jewish holidays—as are persons of other religions with their holidays. Deborah House is a recipient agency of the Chicago Woman's Aid.

Bernard Horwich Jewish Community Center
3003 W. Touhy, 60645; 761-9100
Tripsters/Seekers is a weekly social-skills program for adult retardates who plan their own programs and activities.

Jewish Vocational Service
1 S. Franklin, 60606; 346-6700
Has a wide variety of programs for persons with many forms of disabilities.

Michael Reese Hospital and Medical Center
29th St. and Ellis Ave., 60616; 791-2000

Many services, programs, and facilities serving the developmentally disabled.

Young Men's Jewish Council
Center for Enriched Living
9301 Gross Point Rd., Skokie 60076; 679-8490

The only full-time social center in Illinois for mildly and moderately retarded children, teens, and young adults. Nonsectarian. Provides sports, recreation, consumer education, creative arts, sociability to persons between 8 and 35. A Married Couples Club for those who have attended the center meets to discuss problems and share thoughts. The first center opened in 1975 in Albany Park. Transportation is provided to and from Albany Park on weekends.

YMJC also runs a precamp and postcamp for the mentally retarded, ages 16 to 60, at Camp Henry Horner, Round Lake.

Prisoners

Jewish Prisoners' Assistance Foundation
Marshall Zeidman, Contact, 644-6900

A nonprofit organization founded in 1979 that helps Jewish prisoners and ex-offenders throughout the United States. Counsels not only prisoners but their families as well. Volunteer legal staff protects civil rights of Jewish prisoners within the hostile prison environment and of ex-offenders who are illegally denied employment or are victims of police harassment. Gives assistance to Jewish ex-offenders in finding employment and suitable housing to prevent them from returning to crime. Seeking volunteers and donations.

B'nai B'rith Council of Greater Chicago
8 S. Michigan, Rm. 2301, 60603; 346-8555

B'nai B'rith has stepped in on occasion to rectify problems affecting Jewish prisoners locally.

Reunions and Alumni

AZA and BBG
B'nai B'rith Youth Organization
4432 W. Oakton Ave., Skokie 60076; 675-9260

An alumni group for both AZA and BBG is in formation.

B'nai Bezalel Sisterhood
Thelma Dobkin, Contact
966-1768

B'nai Bezalel Congregation closed its doors in 1969, but the sisterhood still meets monthly, bringing together about 40 women who live in various parts of the metropolitan area. At the end of the year, a large closing luncheon is held. The funds that are raised go to Magen David Adom and other good causes.

B'nai Bezalel Congregation was founded in 1910 and moved to its last location, 7549 S. Phillips in South Shore, in 1957. That synagogue and an earlier one on S. Champlain, in Woodlawn, still stand.

B'nai Israel Men's Club
Harry Karpen, Contact
973-4465

Today the Men's Club of B'nai Israel of Austin numbers less than 20 members. The group meets six to eight times a year. One of the members is the former rabbi of the congregation, Rabbi Shlomoh Z. Fineberg. Each July 4th the Men's Club gets together with the B'nai Israel Social Club—the former sisterhood—for a brunch. Congregation B'nai Israel of Austin closed in 1967. It was founded in 1922. For over 40 years its synagogue was at 5433 W. Jackson.

B'nai Israel Social Club
Yetta Karpen, Contact
973-4465

Formerly the Sisterhood of B'nai Israel of Austin, the B'nai Israel Social Club meets about six times a year. These gatherings are entirely social, but a small contribution is made at year's end to agencies like the Ark. Members of the B'nai Israel Men's Club and the Social Club are scattered in different parts of the Chicago area.

B'nai Shalom Friendship Club
Esther Perlowsky, Contact
334-7551

The nucleus for the B'nai Shalom Friendship Club is the sisterhood of former B'nai Shalom Congregation, on Ainslie and Sawyer in Albany Park, which was dedicated in 1929 and closed in 1972. Today there are about 100 members in this club; two-thirds are newcomers. The one-third nucleus of B'nai Shalom Sisterhood members includes four former sisterhood presidents. The club meets on the second Monday of each month at the Zionist Organization of Chicago building. It supports Jewish education and the Jewish Home for the Blind.

Chicago Home for Jewish Orphans
Roy Klowden, Contact
6517 N. California Ave., 60645; 764-6288

In 1978, Roy Klowden organized the first reunion of the CHJO since its closing in 1943. Hundreds of "alumni" and their families attended the spectacular party on Sunday, September 3, at the Dolnick Center on N. California. Klowden keeps in touch through newsletters and an updating of the alumni roster. Any Aitchkays (H-K means "home kid") who have never reported their current whereabouts are urged to do so.

Deborah Boys Club of Division Street
Dr. William W. Friedman, Contact
7442 N. Western Ave., 60645

The alumni of this boys' club currently number 700. This includes a West Coast alumni group in California with about 100 members. Reunions are held every five years, but there are also annual picnics. According to Dr. Friedman, "The ties have never been severed in the last 50 years. The vehicle of kinship is now into the second and third generation."

Former Members of Congregation Shomre Hadas of Roseland
Mrs. Morris (Esther) Eisenberg, Contact
2341 Carroll Parkway, Flossmoor 60422; 799-7472

Mrs. Eisenberg has organized an informal group of former members of this historic congregation, which closed January 1, 1974. The former synagogue stood at 11445 S. Forest.

Frank Heidenreich Memorial Reunion
Edwin Hokie Goldstein, President

Men who attended the Lawson School Playground as youths meet biennially at a dinner to honor the memory of Frank Heidenreich, playground director from 1918 to 1950. The first reunion was held in 1953 as a tribute to Heidenreich. Since his death a decade ago, the men have awarded an annual scholarship in his memory to a Jewish athlete. The scholarship is administered by the Sportsmen's Lodge of B'nai B'rith.

Hadassah-Chicago
111 N. Wabash, 60602; 263-7473

Although they are not in fact alumni or reunion groups, some Hadassah groups from old neighborhoods still maintain continuity. Austin Hadassah, with 113 members, still meets regularly in the headquarters office at 111 N. Wabash. Albany Park Hadassah meets in West Rogers Park. Northwest Hadassah, from the old Humboldt Park neighborhood, meets at B'nai David Shaare Zedek congregation on Foster.

High School of Jewish Studies
Board of Jewish Education
72 E. 11th St., 60605; 427-5570

BJE is interested in forming an alumni organization for graduates of the High School of Jewish Studies.

Lawson School Class of 1938 Club
Goldie Finfer Bulgatz, Contact
5831 Main St., Morton Grove 60053; 966-7473

The big reunion for this class was held October 5, 1975, but because of the excitement generated by the celebration, they are still meeting. The women of the class meet regularly, and there are socials with men from the class twice a year. Twenty-two members of the class are unaccounted for. Anyone who has not yet responded should contact Goldie Finfer Bulgatz.

Lawson School Reunion of June 1941 Graduating Class
Syke Capsuto Berg, Chairman
7238 W. Crain, Niles 60648

Stimulated by the success of the 1938 class reunion, the 1941 class alumni, led by Syke Capsuto Berg and Bernard (Butch) Radin, held theirs. Members of the class of '41 should contact Syke Berg.

Marks Nathan Alumni Foundation
Allan Mack, Contact and Newsletter Editor
945 Elm St., Winnetka 60093; 446-2993

The alumni of Chicago's Orthodox Jewish orphanage have a regular membership organization that was established in 1970. The alumni have held reunions in 1966, 1974, and 1979. An annual Passover seder is held at the Sovereign Hotel. There is a directory of members. The organization supports a scholarship fund.

Olin-Sang-Ruby Union Institute Alumni Association
Adrianne Daskal, Contact
1020 North Ave., Deerfield 60015

The first alumni association of OSRUI camp was organized in 1979. Attempts are still being made to contact the more than 10,000 alumni of the camp. The organization would like to hear from all alumni over 18 years of age. The group has three purposes: to get together socially, sometimes at the camp; to provide services and support to the staff for special events; and to assist the camp financially.

Pincus Rosenberg Family Society
Ira Rosenberg, President
465-2938

This family society is probably the most enduring of the hundreds of Jewish family societies in Chicago. In 1984, the 65th reunion will be held. For the 60th, in 1979, 150 direct descendants of P.R., who died on Chicago's Northwest Side in 1919 at the age of 109, assembled at Congregation Ezras Israel. Rosenberg's last wish was for the family to keep together. Large gatherings are held every five years. Local cousins meet monthly.

Most of Chicago's Jewish family societies are no more. They have been forgotten by all but a few descendants. Anyone with information about any Jewish family circle or cousins' club should contact

- Sidney Sorkin
  Board Member, Chicago Jewish Historical Society
  8343 S. Kenwood, 60619; 221-4096

Runaway Youth Counseling

Response Center
7457 N. Western Ave., 60645; 338-2292
Martha Chernov, Director
Counseling to youth and to parents.

Chicago Board of Rabbis
72 E. 11th St., 60605; 427-5863
Rabbi Mordecai Simon, Executive Director
A useful source for contacts in other cities who may be helpful to parents.

Scouting

Jewish Committee on Scouting, Area III State of Illinois
Marvin Charak, Chairman, 498-3250 or 433-0022
The Jewish Committee on Scouting is part of a national network, all volunteer, except for one staff person in the New York area. The committee administers the Jewish-content awards in the Cub Scouts and the Boy Scouts: the Aleph Program for Cub Scouts, the Ner Tamid Award for Boy Scouts, and the Shofar Award for Adults in Scouting. The Ner Tamid and the Aleph awards require a lengthy series of projects, including study, volunteer service, and religious observance. The Shofar Award for Adults in Scouting, a silver Ner Tamid Pendant, is awarded in recognition of outstanding service by adults in the promotion of scouting among Jewish boys. An additional contact:

Philip Lapin, Chairman
Northeast Illinois Council Jewish Committee on Scouting
241 Ridge Rd., Highland Park 60035; 831-4850

One of the functions of the Jewish Committee on Scouting is to coordinate the visit to Chicago made by Israeli Scouts each summer.

Chicago Metro Jewish Girl Scout Committee
Shirley Kaplan, Contact
251-7775

Administers the Menorah Award—the Jewish Girl Scouting Award requiring basic Jewish knowledge, observance, and service. Also participates with the Jewish Committee on Scouting to coordinate the visit of Israeli Scouts each summer.

Senior Adult Resources

Agencies

Council for Jewish Elderly
1015 W. Howard St., Evanston 60202; 973-4105
Ronald Weismehl, Executive Director

One of the youngest agencies of the Jewish Federation, founded in 1972, CJE offers a broad social-service program: drop-in centers, medical services, household help, social services, home-delivered kosher meals, a variety of housing alternatives, legal counseling, social centers (cosponsored in a few cases with the JCCs) and meal programs. The Friends of CJE is the agency's auxiliary. Drop-in centers are at the following locations:

1415 W. Morse Ave., 60626; 973-6065
6400 N. Sheridan Rd., 60626; 973-5570
1345 W. Jarvis, 60626; 973-1559
1751 E. 55th St., 60615; 363-2900

Generally, hours for the drop-in centers are 8:30 A.M. to 5 P.M. Mondays through Fridays.

CJE sponsors independent housing in low- to medium-cost rental apartment buildings at various locations, including the newly completed Swartzberg House, 3101 W. Touhy. Charles A. Weinfeld Residence, a group-living facility, has received national publicity. In this residence, twelve elderly adults share responsibilities and provide support to one another. A second group-living facility, the Robineau Residence, is under construction.

Day services for senior adults with special social or medical needs are offered at Temple Menorah, 2800 W. Sherwin, 8 A.M. to 5 P.M. Mondays through Fridays.

A major new facility, the Jacob and Marcelle Lieberman Residence, is under construction at Golf and Gross Point roads, Skokie. This $11.5-million project, which is scheduled for completion in late

1981, will provide housing for those who need 24-hour medical supervision. There will be 240 units.

The Park View Home, 1401 N. California, 278-6420, now provides long-term care.

Senior Adult Department of the Jewish Community Centers
3003 W. Touhy, 60645; 761-9100
Leon M. Woolf, Executive Director

This department administers many programs for senior adults—educational, social, and recreational—through centers and clubs, sometimes in cooperation with other agencies. Special events and travel programs are offered to all regardless of affiliation. The centers, which function four to six days a week, are as follows:

Devon-Sheridan JCC
6400 N. Sheridan, 60626; 764-3090

B'nai Zion (CJE and JCC)
6759 N. Greenview, 60626; 764-6191

Fisher Center JCC
5821 N. Broadway, 60660; 728-1215

Henry N. Hart JCC
4850 N. Bernard, 60625; 478-6766

Mayer Kaplan–Chicago
3003 W. Touhy, 60645; 761-9100

Mayer Kaplan Skokie Senior Adults
5050 Church, Skokie 60077; 675-2200

South Side (CJE and JCC)
1642 E. 56th St., 60637; 667-7373

The following JCC Clubs meet once or twice a week and provide meetings, programs, luncheons, and one-day trips:

Anshe Emet (Tuesdays)
3760 N. Pine Grove Ave., 60613

B'nai Emunah (Tuesdays)
9131 Niles Center Rd., Skokie 60076

B'nai Zion (Mondays)
6759 N. Greenview, 60626

Del Prado (Tuesdays)
1642 E. 56th St., 60637 (Windermere Hotel)

Dempster Club (Wednesdays)
4747 Dempster, Skokie 60076

Edgewater (Wednesday nights)
5445 N. Sheridan, 60640

Henry Hart (Mondays, Wednesdays; Tuesdays, Thursdays)
2961 W. Peterson, 60659

Kenmore Plaza (Tuesdays)
5225 N. Kenmore, 60640

Leisure Time Club (Tuesdays, Thursdays)
3480 N. Lake Shore Dr., 60657

Loyola (Wednesdays)
7050 N. Sheridan Rd., 60626

Ner Tamid (Mondays)
2754 W. Rosemont, 60659

Oakton (Mondays)
8001 Lincoln, Skokie 60077

River Park (Tuesdays)
5100 N. Francisco, 60625

Rodfei Zedek (Wednesdays)
5200 S. Hyde Park Blvd., 60615

Shaare Tikvah (Wednesdays)
5800 N. Kimball, 60659

Group meetings are sponsored in the following condominiums:
Hollywood Towers
5701 N. Sheridan Rd., 60660

Shoreline Towers
6301 N. Sheridan Rd., 60660
5757 N. Sheridan Rd., 60660

The following three programs are also under the auspices of the Senior Adult Department of the Jewish Community Centers:

Open University
3480 N. Lake Shore Dr., 60657; 975-8375
Continuing-education opportunities for adults 55 and older.

Florence Weiss Perlstein Park Resort
Lake Delton, Wisconsin Dells
For information, contact Shirley Tatar, 761-9100
A resort for men and women 55 years old and older. Accommodations are modern and climate controlled, with private bath, gourmet kosher meals, and a variety of activities. Daily or weekly rates.

Seniors' Alert
Senior Adult Department, 761-9100
The advocacy program of the JCC Senior Adult Department, a group that takes action on local and state issues in support of legislation to improve the quality of life for older adults.

Additional Housing Resources

Council for Jewish Elderly
1015 W. Howard St., Evanston 60202; 973-4105

The Housing Resource Center helps older persons find suitable housing in East Rogers Park and acts in behalf of the elderly in landlord/tenant conflicts. The Family Support Program assists the elderly person who would like to share an apartment or other living accommodations with another individual or family, and is also for persons of all ages who have homes to share with senior adults. Screening and matching are handled by CJE.

Drexel Home
6140 S. Drexel Ave., 60637; 643-2384

Has rendered service to the Jewish elderly since 1893. Provides health and social services within a personalized, creative Jewish group-living environment to aged and chronically sick who cannot continue independent living in the community. Drexel Home also enables elderly persons to stay in the home temporarily if their family is planning to be away on a vacation. Short-term admissions and short-term stays for posthospital care and other special situations can be arranged. This is a Reform Jewish home and is not kosher. Drexel Home is an agency of the Jewish Federation.

George J. Goldman Memorial Home for the Aged
6601 W. Touhy, Niles 60648; 647-9875

A nonprofit, kosher home for the Orthodox aged, founded in 1950, and in its Niles location since 1978. Provides total health-care services, 24-hour medical staff. Resident synagogue offers daily services. There are many amenities. Golden Day Care provides day-care services for senior adults who are not residents.

Northwest Home for the Aged
6300 N. California, 60659; 973-1900

A nonprofit, kosher retirement home, founded in 1944. Around-the-clock nursing care available. A synagogue is on the premises. Many members of the Yiddish cultural community of Chicago and many auxiliaries support this home. It was once located just north of Humboldt Park; the new facility was opened in 1973.

Selfhelp Home for the Aged
908 W. Argyle St., 60640; 271-0300
Rolf A. Weil, President
Dorothy W. Becker, Director

A home for men and women 62 years old and older, founded by refugees from Hitler's Germany. Efficiency and multi-occupant units. Both Jewish dietary laws and holidays are observed. The home, also called Selfhelp Center, is operated in association with the Selfhelp Home Health Care Facility, which provides temporary nursing care. There is a gift shop at the home.

Other Resources

Board of Jewish Education
72 E. 11th St., 60605; 427-5570
Dr. Irving Skolnick
BJE has junior high school curriculum materials on aging.

Commission on Aging of the United Synagogue of America
72 E. 11th St., 60605; 939-2351

Family Life Education
Jewish Family and Community Service
1 S. Franklin, 60606; 346-6700

Golden Day Care
George J. Goldman Home
6601 W. Touhy Ave., Niles 60648; 647-9875
A day-care service offering social and nursing services to senior adults who might otherwise be alone during the day. Operates 8:30 A.M. to 4:30 P.M. Mondays through Fridays. Transportation arrangements are available. Breakfast, lunch, and afternoon snacks are included. This is a kosher, nonprofit facility.

Golden Diner Program
This program offers inexpensive hot meals, provided by the Chicago Office of Senior Citizens, at some JCC senior adult centers. For information call the Senior Adult Department, 761-9100. Meals are offered at the following:
  Henry Hart Center, Tuesdays and Wednesdays at noon.
  Fisher Center, Mondays, Wednesdays, and Thursdays, 11:45 A.M.
  B'nai Zion, Mondays through Fridays at noon.
  South Side at the Windermere Hotel, Mondays through Fridays at noon.

North Shore Seniors
North Shore Congregation Israel
1185 Sheridan Rd., Glencoe 60022; 835-0724

Senior Club
Emanuel Congregation
5959 N. Sheridan Rd., 60660; 561-5173

Senior Friendship Club
Northwest Suburban Jewish Congregation
7800 Lyons, Morton Grove 60053; 965-0900

Sholom Over-50 Seniors
Anshe Sholom a Beth Torah
20820 Western Ave., Olympia Fields 60461; 748-6010

■ **Irene Nathan**
743-8421

Offers special programs for seniors: A Holistic Approach to Aging covers nutrition, health, physical exercise, combating loneliness, etc.

Single Parents and Single-Parent Families

Beth Emet The Free Synagogue
1224 Dempster, Evanston 60202; 869-4230
Has an ongoing chug for single parents.

Board of Jewish Education Department of Family Education
72 E. 11th St., 60605; 427-5570
Moshe Samber, Director

This department has sponsored several projects that attempt to address the needs of parents and children in single-parent families.

Emanuel Congregation
5959 N. Sheridan Rd., 60660; 561-5173
Has an ongoing group of single parents; some of the activities include children.

Jewish Children's Bureau
1 S. Franklin, 60606; 346-6700
Provides services to single-parent families.

National Council of Jewish Women–South Cook Section
Contact through Anita M. Stone JCC
18600 Governors Highway, Flossmoor 60422; 799-7650

Sponsors a single-parents project at Anita M. Stone JCC. Has published a directory of resources for south suburban single parents, and provides funds for camp scholarships for children of single-parent families.

Temple Sholom
3480 N. Lake Shore Dr., 60657; 525-4707

Sponsors an ongoing support group for divorced or separated single parents.

SPARK (Single Parents Alone Raising Kids)
Mayer Kaplan JCC
5050 Church St., Skokie 60077; 675-2200

Within the Singles Panorama, a varied program, this committee plans activities and programs for single parents and single-parent families. Contact Gail Prince.

Task Force on Single Parent Families
c/o American Jewish Committee
55 E. Jackson, Rm. 1870, 60604; 663-5500

AJC coordinates this joint effort of various local agencies.

Union of American Hebrew Congregations
100 W. Monroe, Rm. 312, 60603; 782-1477

Sponsors an annual Single Parent Family Retreat over Labor Day weekend at Olin-Sang-Ruby Union Institute Camp. Also cosponsors with Reform congregations Friday evening services with an Oneg Shabbat for single parents.

Virginia Frank Child Development Center
3033 W. Touhy, 60645; 761-4550

This agency of the Jewish Family and Community Service has drop-in programs for single mothers and their children during the week and special play-discussion groups for divorced, separated, or widowed fathers and their young children on weekends.

Young Men's Jewish Council
546-4435 or 726-8891

Sponsors Single Parent Weekends at Camp Henry Horner with activities planned for parents and children, separately and together. Weekends begin with Friday dinner and end with Sunday lunch.

Singles

■ Sheryl Leonard
55 E. Jackson, Rm. 1870, 60604

Although her official address is with the American Jewish Committee, Sheryl Leonard is the unofficial Singles Maven of Chicago. A *must* for all singles is Sheryl's weekly column, For Singles Only, in the *Sentinel* (323 S. Franklin, 60606). For information about any of the singles groups listed below for which no specific contact is given, drop a line to Sheryl at the address on E. Jackson.

Combined Jewish singles events take place several times during the year, often in connection with festival celebrations. Read Sheryl Leonard's column for information.

■ **Dr. Stanley Newman**
Professor of Anthropology
Northeastern Illinois University
583-4050

Dr. Newman has been involved with Chicago's singles scene and is a good resource.

Congregations Sponsoring Singles Groups

A. G. Beth Israel Singles
3635 W. Devon, 60659; 539-9060
For 22- to 45-year-olds.

Am Shalom
614 Sheridan Rd., Glencoe 60022; 835-4800
One group for college age to 30; another group for over 30.

Temple Anshe Sholom a Beth Torah
20820 Western, Olympia Fields 60461; 748-6010

Beth Emet The Free Synagogue
1224 Dempster, Evanston 60202; 869-4230
For single parents.

Beth Tikvah
300 Hillcrest Blvd., Hoffman Estates 60195; 885-4545
Tikvah Singles for persons over 35; Young Singles for under 35.

B'nei Ruven
6350 N. Whipple, 60659; 743-5434
For ages 21 to 35.

Central Synagogue Singles
Central Synagogue of South Side Hebrew Congregation
30 E. Cedar, 60611; 787-0450

Chicago Sinai Congregation
5350 S. South Shore Dr., 60615; 288-1600
Singles group for 20- to 40-year-olds. An older group may be starting.

Emanuel Congregation
5959 N. Sheridan Rd., 60660; 561-5173
For single parents.

Etz Chaim
1710 S. Highland, Lombard 60148; 627-3912
Sponsors several singles groups in cooperation with Oak Park Temple: Jaffa Road West, Jewish Singles of the Western Suburbs. Groups for under and over 35 years of age.

Ezras Israel Singles
7001 N. California, 60645; 764-8320

KINS of West Rogers Park
2800 W. North Shore, 60645; 761-4000

Maine Township Jewish Congregation
8800 Ballard Rd., Des Plaines 60016; 297-2006 or 694-4477
Cosponsors some of the singles programs at the Mayer Kaplan JCC.

Northwest Suburban Jewish Congregation Singles Scene
7800 Lyons, Morton Grove 60053; 965-0900

Oak Park Temple
1235 N. Harlem, Oak Park 60302; 386-3937
Cosponsors several singles groups with Etz Chaim serving Jewish singles in western suburbs.

Or Chadash
656 W. Barry, 60657; 248-9456
Chicago's congregation for gay and lesbian Jews.

Temple Sholom
3480 N. Lake Shore Dr., 60657; 525-4707
Sponsors Sholom Singles for college age to 40 and Sholom Fellowship for 40 and older.

Skokie Valley Traditional Synagogue Singles Group
8825 E. Prairie Rd., Skokie 60076; 674-3473

Other Jewish Singles Groups

Anita M. Stone JCC
18600 Governors Highway, Flossmoor 60422; 799-7650
Several singles groups: one for ages 30 to 55, another for ages 20 to 30. The Illiana Young Jewish Singles has members from northwest Indiana as well as from south suburban Cook County.

Bernard Horwich JCC
3003 W. Touhy, 60645; 761-9100
Three singles groups: JASS—Jewish American Singles Society—for 21- to 35-year-olds, has social events plus meetings 8 to 10 P.M. on the

second and fourth Thursdays of each month; Majority of 1's Forum meets Sundays for cultural and educational programs, primarily for 25- to 45-year-olds; Center Singles is for over-45-year-olds.

Lincoln Park–Lakeview JCC
524 W. Melrose, 60657; 871-6780
Sponsors the Photography Group for singles who share an interest in photography and socializing.

Mayer Kaplan JCC
5050 Church, Skokie 60077; 675-2200
Singles Panorama is a collection of singles groups and programs roughly divided into one series for those in their twenties and thirties, another for those in their forties and fifties. Also handles programming for North Shore Jewish Singles. Gail Prince, staff person at the JCC, is the person in charge of singles programming. Call Prince for a rundown.

Rogers Park JCC
7101 N. Greenview, 60626; 274-0920
Tzimmes Singles is for young Jewish singles.

American Jewish Committee
55 E. Jackson, Rm. 1870, 60604; 663-5500
Sponsors Vistas, a program for over-40 Jewish singles that is culturally and educationally oriented. Free to members of the AJC. Meets in various places throughout the year, with one large open meeting held annually.

American Jewish Congress
22 W. Monroe, Rm. 2102, 60603; 332-7355
Sponsors worldwide travel for singles—for groups of those who are 40 and younger and those over 40.

B'nai B'rith Women
7701 N. Lincoln Ave., Skokie 60077; 679-6077
Connection Center, a network of various groups, includes some for singles. New Horizons chapter is for women on their own. Opportunities Unlimited, cosponsored with B'nai B'rith, is for 35- to 60-year-olds.

Chicagoland Jewish Singles
Gerald Hoffman, 549-5015
For singles 25 to 55.

Chutzpah Unlimited, Inc.
P.O. Box 2400, 60690; 248-2661

(7 to 10 P.M. weeknights, 10 A.M. to 5 P.M. weekends)
Eleanor Heather Siegel, Coordinator

Sponsors parties, a dating directory, and some singles travel services. Nonprofit corporation serving Jewish singles of all ages.

Coalition of Single Shabbat Services
Gail Prince, Contact, 675-2200

An organization representing various Jewish singles groups sponsors Shabbat services followed by an Oneg Shabbat. All Jewish singles are invited.

Hadassah-Chicago
111 N. Wabash, 60602; 263-7473

Aviva Hadassah is for professional single women 25 to 45. Simcha Hadassah is for young working women.

Jewish Business and Professional Singles
For singles 22 to 45.

New Perspective
9462 Bay Colony Dr., Des Plaines 60016

Nonprofit, independent singles group aimed at 25- to 50-year-old professionals and executives. Send stamped, self-addressed envelope for information.

Noam
Singles group for young religious Zionists, 20 to 30 years old.

North Shore Jewish Singles
P.O. Box 395, Wilmette 60091

For singles 35 and older. Meets at locations throughout the North Shore suburbs and receives some programming assistance from the Mayer Kaplan JCC staff.

Option II
673-5350

A social and cultural alternative for Jewish singles who have never been married. Founded in 1980.

Pioneer Women–Chicago Council
220 S. State, 60604; 922-3736

Menorah Pioneer Women is for single women in their twenties and thirties. Parties and other activities benefit Pioneer Women's programs in Israel and support social concerns in America.

Union of American Hebrew Congregations
100 W. Monroe, Rm. 312, 60603; 782-1477

In addition to a variety of programs for single parents, the Chicago office of UAHC sponsors an annual singles trip to Israel.

Union of Orthodox Jewish Congregations
c/o Council of Traditional/Orthodox Synagogues
6716 N. Whipple St., 60645; 973-2522

Sponsors Jewish Post-Collegiates, which is a group for 21- to 29-year-old singles.

Young Leadership Division of Jewish United Fund
1 S. Franklin, 60606; 346-6700

The Singles Committee of the YLD engages in fund raising and other activities for 22- to 40-year-olds.

Sisterhoods

Midwest Federation of Temple Sisterhoods
100 W. Monroe, Rm. 312, 60603; 782-1477

The Midwest branch of the National Federation of Temple Sisterhoods of the Reform Jewish movement.

Women's League for Conservative Judaism Central Branch
72 E. 11th St., 60605; 939-2351

The Midwest branch of the national federation of Conservative sisterhoods.

The oldest Jewish women's organization in existence in Chicago is the Sisterhood of KAM–Isaiah Israel. In 1859, the B'nai Sholom Ladies Social Society was formed, later changing its name to Sisterhood. B'nai Sholom, founded in 1852, later became B'nai Sholom Temple Israel, then Isaiah Israel, and, in 1971, KAM–Isaiah Israel.

Yeshiva Women
Hebrew Theological College
7135 N. Carpenter Rd., Skokie 60077; 267-9800 or 674-7750

Though not a federation of sisterhoods, the Yeshiva Women is composed of representatives from Orthodox and Traditional congregation sisterhoods in the Chicago area. They support Jewish education and, in particular, the Hebrew Theological College.

Soviet Jews In Chicago

Between 1971 and 1980 approximately 5,000 Soviet Jews arrived in Chicago.

Agudath Israel
3540 W. Peterson, 60659 (Center)
5621 N. St. Louis, 60659; 588-5078 (Office)

A committee meets with and works with Soviet families on a one-to-one basis. Sponsors day camps for Soviet Jewish children.

American Jewish Congress
22 W. Monroe St., Rm. 2102, 60603; 332-7355

AJAR (Association of Jewish Americans and Russians), a social and supportive group formed by AJC in 1978, meets at the Horwich JCC. Cosponsors the Chicago Jewish Immigrant Legal Services Clinic with the Rogers Park JCC.

Associated Talmud Torahs
2828 W. Pratt Blvd., 60645; 973-2828

Provides a tutorial program for Soviet children that introduces American culture and gives English-language and reading lessons. Mainstreams these children into day schools through grade school and high school. Provides psychological and backup services. Assists day-camp programs for Soviet children. Provides adult education and religious observances. Has held mass bar/bat mitzvah ceremony for Soviet children.

B'nai Zion Congregation
6759 N. Greenview Ave., 60626; 465-2161

Provides many services to Soviet Jews, including tickets for High Holidays. Joint Senior Adult Department JCC and Council for Jewish Elderly programs held with the congregation provide English class for immigrants.

Board of Jewish Education
72 E. 11th St., 60605; 427-5570

BJE is one of the sponsoring agencies in the preparatory program to help Soviet Jewish children attending public school. After-school tutoring is provided. This program is also sponsored by the Associated Talmud Torahs and Jewish Family and Community Service.

Decalogue Society
Lawyer Referral Service
180 W. Washington, 60602; 263-6493

Referral may be made to attorneys who speak the Russian language.

FREE (Friends of Refugees of Eastern Europe)
6418 N. Greenview, 60626; 274-5123
Rabbi Shmuel Notik, Director

Assistance to newly arrived Soviet immigrants. Contributions of clothing and furniture, camp scholarships for children. FREE sponsors Jewish holiday celebrations for Soviets. Founded in 1973, this organization has a strong Orthodox religious commitment. It publishes *Shalom*, a biweekly newspaper in Russian with articles of Jewish content, social-service information, and entertainment. FREE also has a radio program directed to the Soviet immigrant. FREE held a large brit milah celebration in February 1980, honoring 120 Soviet-immigrant men and boys who have undergone circumcision since arriving in this country.

Friends of Soviet Jews in Fine Arts
c/o Rogers Park JCC
7101 N. Greenview, 60626; 274-0920

A group of people, primarily from the North Shore, working out of the Rogers Park JCC to help Soviet immigrants involved in the fine and performing arts find audiences and exhibitions and placement. Chairman is Marlene Breslow.

HIAS (Hebrew Immigrant Aid Society)
1 S. Franklin, 60606; 263-6880

Begins helping the Soviet immigrant by issuing the "Vysov," the official invitation required by the Soviet government. HIAS meets the immigrants when they arrive in Chicago.

Bernard Horwich Jewish Community Center
3003 W. Touhy, 60645; 761-9100

Sponsors social and educational programs for Soviets. English lessons are held during the week. Staff person Joanna Spilman serves as coordinator of Immigrant Services. She is the resource person for all Soviet Jews regarding opportunities to participate in programs, social services, and groups that are not necessarily set up for immigrants. She attempts to get the newcomers to enter into the established Jewish community services.

Jewish Family and Community Service
2710 W. Devon, 60659; 274-1324

It is especially through its Northern District office that JFCS helps the Soviet immigrants—with housing, counseling, and related services. Upon arrival in Chicago, each family is immediately assigned by JFCS to a Russian-speaking resettlement worker who puts the family in contact with the network of other Jewish agencies that will help them get started in their new life. This agency also coordinates volunteer services in behalf of the Soviet immigrants. Anyone interested should contact the Volunteer Coordinator.

Jewish Vocational Service
1 S. Franklin, 60606; 346-6700
Russian Refugee Placement Center
201 N. Wells St., 16th Floor, 60606; 454-0288

Provides a wide variety of tutorial programs, retraining, and specialized job-placement services. Has a triple support program in which volunteers in engineering and related fields offer (1) English lessons for engineers on Tuesday evenings at the Rogers Park JCC; (2) assistance to families in adjusting to their new community; and (3) places where Russian engineers and draftsmen can go to observe American engineering and drafting techniques and to practice their own with assistance from volunteers.

Lubavitch Chabad of Greater Chicago
2014 Orrington, Evanston 60201; 869-8060

Provides open enrollment for Soviet children at the Gan Israel Day Camp.

Maccabi Sport Club
6237 N. Sacramento, 60659; 338-7597
Isaac Glickstein, President

Maccabi is a sports, cultural, and social-work movement for all ages in Israel, and the local chapter has followed that model in organizing athletics for Soviet Jewish youth in Chicago. The program includes about 250 youths.

Michael Reese Hospital and Medical Center
Russian Immigrant Health Care Center
2341 W. Devon, 60659; 338-9080

Opened in 1978, this center provides Soviet immigrants with routine exams and, when necessary, referrals to the medical center. Seven Russian interpreters assist by accompanying patients into exams, explaining procedures to them, and relaying information about health problems to the doctors. Reese has special adult, pediatric, and obstetric clinics for Soviets. Most medical care offered the immigrants is free.

Moes Chitim Committee of Greater Chicago
55 E. Washington St., Suite 1505, 60602

Distributed hundreds of Passover food packages to Soviet immigrants who had signed up through FREE. For information call either the Ark, 463-4545, or FREE, 274-5123.

Mount Sinai Hospital Medical Center
Touhy Satellite
2901 W. Touhy Ave., 60645; 973-7350

Provides many health services to the Soviet Jewish immigrants. One special program concerns eye difficulties. With funding in part from the Blind Service Association, Soviet immigrants receive eye tests and service at this satellite. Medical care is offered to the Soviet immigrants at no charge.

North Shore Congregation Israel
1185 Sheridan Rd., Glencoe 60022; 835-0724

This congregation provides many services to Soviet immigrants. Among special events sponsored by NSCI are Passover parties for immigrants of all ages with food, songs, and a chance to talk about the holiday. The religious school works closely with the Rogers Park JCC.

Rogers Park Jewish Community Center
7101 N. Greenview, 60626; 274-0920

This center pioneered in services to the Soviet immigrants when they began arriving in numbers in 1971. Issues a newsletter and has drop-in programs in the Coach House attached to the center. This JCC sponsors Club Freedom, a social club, and helped establish a Russian-American chavurah. The drop-in center has a library of books in English, Hebrew, Yiddish, and Russian and offers a chance for immigrants to meet with American Jews and other immigrants. Help with English is offered from 7 to 9 P.M. Mondays through Thursdays. Students may drop in during these hours for assistance with homework assignments. The Coach House Crowd welcomes Soviet teens, 7 to 9 P.M., Wednesdays.

Temple Sholom
3480 N. Lake Shore Dr., 60657; 525-4707
Beverly Sontz, Soviet Jewry Chairman, 288-2827

Since September 1979, Temple Sholom has sponsored a Soviet-Jewry Drop-in Center from 1 to 2 P.M. Wednesdays, followed by English lessons sponsored from 2 to 3 P.M. by the Jewish Community Centers. The first hour includes efforts to help the newcomers adjust to life in the United States and specifically to life as American Jews. The Soviet-immigrant population in the vicinity of Temple Sholom tends to be over 55 years of age. More volunteers are needed.

Women's American ORT   Midwest District VIII
111 N. Wabash, 60602; 726-6466

This organization has been closely tied to efforts to assist Soviet Jews here and throughout the world. Various chapters in different regions throughout the metropolitan area have projects. One chapter adopted a family in the Soviet Union and assisted them in their emigration from the USSR, through their arrival in Chicago, and after. ORT members have been involved with programs at the Rogers Park JCC, including the establishment of the Russian-American Chavurah. The Chicago Region has sponsored bus tours for Soviet Jews.

Sports

B'nai B'rith Council of Greater Chicago
8 S. Michigan, Rm. 2301, 60603; 346-8555
Gerald M. Dicker, Executive Director

B'nai B'rith sponsors many community sports events, including baseball and basketball tournaments and bowling leagues. They also sponsor a track and field day for all ages.

Sports Lodge of B'nai B'rith #2458
Mark Pearlstein, Contact
925 Spring Hill Dr., Northbrook 60062; 498-2451

This lodge, which is made up of men who have had careers in sports or are supporters of sports, awards annual scholarships to men and women graduating from high school who have shown outstanding talent in athletics, academics, and citizenship. For information about scholarships, contact Mark Pearlstein.

■ Harry Heller
4065 Lake Cook Rd., Northbrook 60062

An authority on the history of sports and athletics in the Jewish community of Chicago. He also writes a weekly column on Jews in sports for the *Sentinel*. (The *Sentinel* shares Heller's interest in sports and sponsors an annual Chicago Area High School Football Team.)

Support and Self-Help Groups

Self Help Institute
Center for Urban Affairs, Northwestern University
2040 Sheridan Rd., Evanston 60201; 492-3395
Dr. Leonard Borman

A resource for new self-help groups as well as a clearinghouse for those already in existence. Has published a *Directory of Self Help Groups for Serious and Chronic Illnesses and Bereavement* with Project Hope of Northeastern Illinois University.

Anita M. Stone Jewish Community Center
18600 Governors Highway, Flossmoor 60422; 799-7650

Groups for widows. Groups for women that deal with various emotional concerns.

Bernard Horwich Jewish Community Center
3003 W. Touhy, 60645; 761-9100

Groups in preparing for childbirth, preparing for baby, parenting. Groups for parents of preschoolers deal with concerns of separation, sibling rivalry, setting limits, etc. Support group, for young widows age 45 and younger, cosponsored by Piser Funeral Directors; it explores the process of grieving and encourages the widow to seek support from others. Group for separated or divorced women, called Solo, meets 3 to 5 P.M. Sundays for informal discussion of common concerns.

B'nai Jehoshua Beth Elohim Congregation
901 Milwaukee, Glenview 60025; 729-7575

Group on grieving and bereavement.

Board of Jewish Education Department of Family Education
72 E. 11th St., 60605; 427-5570

Moshe Samber, Director

The Board of Jewish Education assists the United Synagogue of America in implementing the Parent Education Programs (PEP) in the Chicago area:

PEP I—a joint parent-child study program.
PEP II—for parents of Jewish adolescents.

Dysautonomia Foundation Chicago Chapter
550 Frontage Rd., Suite 2085, Northfield 60093; 441-5653

A support group offering information and referrals concerning this Jewish disease.

Hyde Park Jewish Community Center
1100 E. Hyde Park Blvd., 60615; 268-4600

Group for single-parent mothers, open to new participants. Group for losing weight—Weight No Longer.

Jewish Family and Community Service
1 S. Franklin, 60606; 346-6700

Family Life Educators in each JFCS district set up support groups when there is a need or interest. Support group topics have been divorce and separation, the single-parent family, fathering, middle-life concerns, coping with loss, adolescent depression and suicide, adolescent drugs.

Rabbi Robert Marx
433-3555 (Solel Congregation)
Rabbi Marx's own support group for parents who have lost a child through death is open to anyone in need of such help. A second group for young people, 12 to 22, who have experienced the death of a brother or sister is led by a social worker. Rabbi Marx is consultant to the latter group.

Mayer Kaplan Jewish Community Center
5050 Church, Skokie 60077; 675-2200
Minna Davis coordinates all support groups throughout the JCCs for children of Holocaust survivors. These are set up whenever and wherever there is demand.

Group for widows over 40 to deal with grieving process. Group for single men and women to discuss common problems of concern.

Michael Reese Hospital and Medical Center
29th St. and Ellis Ave., 60616; 791-2000
Suicide Help Line: call 791-2050. Also sponsors self-help groups for its own heart, cancer, and diabetic patients.

Piser Memorial Chapels
679-4740
Piser sponsors widow support groups, including those at the Jewish Community Centers.

Temple Sholom
3480 N. Lake Shore Dr., 60657; 525-4707
A continuing group of divorced and separated parents of school-age children.

Virginia Frank Child Development Center
3033 W. Touhy, 60645; 761-4550
Divorced and separated fathers and their children under age 9 meet on Sunday mornings. A parent-child stress-prevention program is co-sponsored with the Board of Jewish Education.

Women's Business and Professional Organizations

B'nai B'rith Women
7701 N. Lincoln, Skokie 60077; 679-6077
The Connection Center, a network of special-interest groups.

B'nai Zion Congregation
6759 N. Greenview Ave., 60626; 465-2161
Business and Professional Women's Organization.

Hadassah-Chicago
111 N. Wabash Ave., 60602; 263-7473
Aviva Hadassah, for women ages 25 to 45. Downtown Business and Professional Women's Group. Simcha—Young Working Women's Chapter.

Hadassah–North Shore
1710 First St., Highland Park 60035; 433-6350
Business and Professional Women's Chapter.

HIAS (Hebrew Immigrant Aid Society)
1 S. Franklin, 60606; 263-6880
Business Women's Auxiliary.

Jewish United Fund
1 S. Franklin St., 60606; 346-6700
Young Leadership Division Professional Women.

Temple Sholom
3480 N. Lake Shore Dr., 60657; 525-4707
Business and Professional Women's Organization.

For information on Women's Concerns, see Chapter 10, "Social and Political Concerns."

Youth

Call the Response Center, 338-2292, for problems regarding adolescents. A recording device will take messages when the office is closed.

BBYO (B'nai B'rith Youth Organization)
4432 W. Oakton, Skokie 60076; 675-9260
Edward Silverman, Director of Illinois Region
BBYO, encompassing the AZA for boys and B'nai B'rith Girls (BBG), is an international organization offering Jewish-oriented programs designed to expand the mental, physical, and spiritual horizons of youth. Both the Illinois and the Chicago councils operate out of this office, and together they are the umbrella for many chapters, some of which have both boys and girls. BBYO is for 14- to 18-year-olds. Activities include social events, athletics, community service, and cultural and religious programming. BBYO is the world's largest Jewish youth organization, with 40,000 high school youths in over 1,500 local chapters throughout the free world. Summer programs include the BBYO International Leadership Kallah and the International Leader-

ship Training Conference, which provide intensive experiences in Judaism, leadership training, and creative arts. AZA, which stands for Ahovoh (brotherly love), TZadakah (benevolence), and Achdoos (harmony), was founded in Omaha by a group that included Philip Klutznick and Sam Beber, both of whom later moved to Chicago. Beber Camp in Wisconsin is the B'nai B'rith camp for this region.

B'nei Akiva, the Religious Zionist Youth Movement
6500 N. California, 60645; 338-6569 (after 7:30 P.M.)
B'nei Akiva is a modern Orthodox organization for boys and girls who join together to study Torah, celebrate Judaism, and work for Israel, with eventual immigration (aliyah). B'nei Akiva includes grammar school, high school, and college divisions. Since 1979, there has been a North Shore branch. The B'nei Akiva camp is Camp Moshava. The organization also sponsors a travel program to Israel with stops en route to see historic Jewish sites in Europe, an annual Independence Day celebration, Simchat Torah II, and other annual events.

B'nos Chabad
Lubavitch Chabad of Greater Chicago
2014 Orrington, Evanston 60201; 869-8060
The girls' organization within the network of Lubavitch Chabad groups. Many functions are held in association with the Lubavitch women's organization, Neshei Chabad.

CFTY (Chicago Federation of Temple Youth)
100 W. Monroe, 60603; 782-1477
Gerard (Jerry) Kaye, Director, Camping and Youth Activities
The local region of the National Federation of Temple Youth is affiliated with the youth groups of Reform congregations throughout the area. CFTY's goal is to build a Reform Jewish youth corps with a strong sense of Jewish identity and commitment to the Jewish community and synagogue life. CFTY provides citywide programs and assistance to member groups in areas of Jewish study, worship, social action, and recreation. CFTY's camp is the Olin-Sang-Ruby Union Institute in Wisconsin.

■ **Jerry Kaye, CFTY Director**
782-1477
Kaye is also available as a resource and lecturer on various topics related to youth and to psychotherapy (in which he has an advanced degree). Titles for some of his talks on youth are Show Down at General Gulch, concerning the generation gap; Baseball and Jewish Education, regarding informal Jewish education; Fourfathers Abraham, Isaac, Jacob, and Freud; and My Travels Around the Country

Where I Met 47 Psychologists and Stayed Jewish. Jerry even tells Chassidic tales—perhaps a carry-over from the campfire at Olin-Sang

- **Janet Moss**
2341 Meadow Lane S., Wilmette 60091; 251-2676
A counselor trainer (and curriculum consultant) who has worked closely through the years with Olin-Sang.

Chicago Jewish Youth Council
3003 W. Touhy, 60645; 761-9100
Beverly Fox, CJYC Worker

CJYC is the umbrella organization, under the Jewish Federation, that coordinates the many youth programs and projects in Chicago, including the Walk for Israel, leadership training, and the Chicago Community Israel Project, which is cosponsored by the Associated Talmud Torahs and the Board of Jewish Education. CJYC provides information to graduating high school seniors on the Jewish resources of local colleges and universities.

Habonim
4155 Main, Skokie 60076; 679-4061

The youth movement of Labor Zionism. There are chapters for all age groups, with educational programs on Israel and Zionism. The high school group has a fine Israeli dance troupe. Summer activities are at Camp Habonim in Michigan.

Hashachar
4155 Main, Skokie 60076; 676-9790

Sponsored by Hadassah, the Women's Zionist Organization, Hashachar is the oldest and largest of the Zionist youth movements in the United States; for youth between the ages of 8 and 18. Groups meet throughout the metropolitan area, in some cases at Jewish Community Centers. The Hashachar camp in the area is Camp Young Judaea, which perpetuates the historic name of the organization.

Hashomer Hatzair
c/o Israel Aliyah Center
205 W. Wacker Dr., Rm. 516, 60606; 332-2709

The pioneering youth movement that is socialist-Zionist in ideology and is allied with the Americans for Progressive Israel in the United States and Kibbutz Artzi and the Mapam party in Israel. There is a wide variety in local programming, with several age groups spanning ages 10 to 22. The camp for Hashomer Hatzair is in Canada.

Jewish Community Centers
1 S. Franklin, 60606; 346-6700

All the JCCs have programming for youth, although North Suburban and Lincoln Park–Lakeview JCCs emphasize activities for young children. The other JCCs also have groups for junior high and/or high school youth. At the Rogers Park JCC, the Coach House Crowd for 7th through 12th graders includes a variety of activities that center around the Coach House and the main JCC building. Hart JCC has a drop-in center for 6th through 8th graders. The Odyssey program for 14- to 18-year-olds at the Mayer Kaplan JCC offers a broad range of activities.

Masada
6328 N. California, 60659; 262-5949

Masada is the national youth group of the Zionist Organization of America and, locally, of the Zionist Organization of Chicago. Masada stands for Jewish identity, Zionist education and action, and eventual aliyah, immigration to Israel. Masada's summer programs in the United States and Israel are available to 13- to 22-year-olds. One summer option is Camp Yehudah in Michigan.

NCSY-TSY (National Conference of Synagogue Youth–Traditional Synagogue Youth)
Chicago Region
6716 N. Whipple St., 60645; 761-2188
Rabbi Shmuel Spiegel, Director

The umbrella organization for local congregations having NCSY-TSY groups (currently about ten Orthodox and Traditional congregations). Although most programming locally is for high school aged youths, nationally the organization includes preteen, teen, and college levels. The orientation is modern Orthodox, with special concern for the American Jewish community. The program includes religious, educational, athletic, and social activities. In Chicago NCSY-TSY is sponsored by the Council of Traditional/Orthodox Synagogues.

Pirchei Agudath Israel (for boys)
B'nos Agudath Israel (for girls)
3540 W. Peterson, 60659; 588-5078

The boys' and girls' movements of Agudath Israel, completely separate from each other, are organized on all age levels. Emphasis is on study, observances, and close identity with the most traditional group within the broader Orthodox community. Although there are activities planned throughout the week, special emphasis is placed on Sabbath observances. Overall youth activities are cultural, educational, and religious.

USY (United Synagogue Youth)
72 E. 11th St., 60605; 939-2353
Richard Moline, Director

USY is the international organization for Jewish high school students associated with the Conservative Movement. An affiliated Kadimah program serves junior high school youth. USY administers citywide programs and acts as a central resource for affiliated synagogue youth groups. A unique Tzadaka (charity) program sends 30 percent of the money raised back to Chicago for summer-program scholarships. USY aims to develop in youth a strong and lasting attachment to the Jewish people and the land of Israel with the greatest loyalty to the synagogue as the central institution in Jewish life. Service to others and religious observance are also stressed.

A Miscellany of Organizations

AFTA (Association for Torah Advancement)
2852-D W. Touhy, 60645; 338-2575
Rabbi Jacob Zimmerman, Director

Dedicated to the highest ideals of traditional Judaism. In addition to the establishment of the Ark (a community outreach agency) and the Jewish Sacred Society, AFTA's credits include programs for visiting the sick, religious services on college campuses, and shaatnes testing (to determine whether linen and wool have been mixed in the same garment, which is contrary to Jewish law). AFTA also subsidizes kosher food service at the Hillel Foundation–University of Chicago, provides short-term free loans, and presents annual awards to day-school students for excellence in Torah studies. Cooperates with COLPA, a national program that fights employment discrimination against Orthodox Jewish practices. Hotline for questions about kosher observance, 338-3764.

Aid-All
Helen Marx, President
288-5131

A 53-year-old organization of no more than 40 women, all from the South Side, which meets monthly and raises money to support good works. Began as a layette organization but now supports such agencies as the Ark, JUF, and Drexel Home. The quota of 40 members is currently filled.

American Council for Judaism
Louis M. Goldman, Jr., Vice-President
477-5053

Although less vocal in recent years, the ACJ still exists as a "national organization dedicated to the preservation of Judaism as a religion of universal values, consonant with the democratic society of America." ACJ remains adamantly opposed to the assumption that the State of Israel is central to all Jews. "We regard the State of Israel as the homeland only of its own citizens and nationals. We affirm that no individual or group of Jews can speak for all Jews."

The Ark
3509 W. Lawrence Ave., 60625; 463-4545
Arden Geldman, Executive Director

Founded in 1971 by members of AFTA, the Ark has become a national model as a community outreach agency. It is the only neighborhood-based, multi-service center that is partially funded by private support that supplies free services to disadvantaged Jews. Non-Jews are served on an emergency basis.

The Ark provides kosher meals-on-wheels, home visiting, short-term free loans, crisis intervention, referral to appropriate agencies, individual counseling, and medical, dental, and legal services. There are a medical lab and pharmacy on the premises. Other resources are an emergency food pantry, Shabbat food baskets, shopping and driving services, social drop-in activities, and Jewish holiday celebrations. Volunteers are needed to carry out all programs. Funded through the Federation, contributions, a resale shop, and an annual benefit.

B'nai B'rith Council of Greater Chicago
8 S. Michigan, Rm. 2301, 60603; 346-8555
Gerald M. Dicker, Executive Director

Chicago's first B'nai B'rith Lodge, Ramah, was founded in 1857. No organization exerted greater influence on the early development of the Chicago Jewish community than did B'nai B'rith. Among its many contributions were the founding of the United Hebrew Relief Association in 1859, the creation of the program that was to become the Jewish Vocational Service, the adoption of the Anti-Defamation League in 1913, and the creation of the first Hillel Foundation, an organization that has continued under the wing of B'nai B'rith.

Within the Council of Greater Chicago are *lodges*, for men only, or *units*, for men and women, jointly sponsored with B'nai B'rith Women. (New units for young couples seem to be the trend for the 1980s.) Some special-interest lodges and units are the following:

Adlai E. Stevenson II Lodge, for accountants and men in finance
Chicago Justice Lodge, for judges, lawyers, and policemen
Sports Lodge, for sports enthusiasts and sportsmen
Dr. Janusz Korczak Unit, made up of Holocaust survivors

Educator's Lodge, for professional educators
Electrical Industrial Lodge
Jacob M. Arvey Lodge, for public-service employees
Opportunities Unlimited, for singles from 35 to 60
Mazel Couples Unit, the first to pioneer the young couples unit

B'nai B'rith operates on the premise that where there is a need, it will try to fill it. B'nai B'rith is concerned with youth, Israel, intergroup relations, athletics and recreation, visiting nursing homes, and veterans' hospitals. B'nai B'rith is a member of the Public Affairs Committee of the JUF.

B'nai B'rith Hillel Foundations Jewish Federation
College Age Youth Services
1 S. Franklin, 60606; 346-6700
Rabbi Yehiel Poupko, Director

This is the agency of the Jewish Federation administering Chicago-area Jewish college programs. In 1974, a step-by-step process began to combine the separate efforts of the B'nai B'rith Hillel Foundations with the programs sponsored by College Age Youth Services. The consolidation now complete, the Hillel units are served by this office, as are other Jewish college-student organizations. Also, this agency provides counseling services to college students, a summer intern program placing college students in agencies and offices, and a broad-based community volunteer service, the Jewish Action Corps. The agency also sponsors athletic, social, and other recreational programs, often in cooperation with the JCCs, and oversees the annual JUF/UJA campaign on campuses throughout Illinois.

B'nai B'rith Women Land of Lakes Region
7701 N. Lincoln, Skokie 60077; 679-6077
Susan Bernstein, Director

Supports a wide variety of youth and adult programs here and throughout the world, including a children's home in Israel for emotionally disturbed boys, an Arab-Jewish human-relations program (assisted by the B'nai B'rith Hillel of Hebrew University), the B'nai B'rith Youth Organization, ERA, and Women's Plea for Soviet Jewry.

BBW cooperates with the Anti-Defamation League in fighting anti-Semitism and initiates social action within the community.

Locally, the innovative Connection Center is a networking system recently started by BBW that offers opportunities for women to pursue common interests with others—such as community-service projects, book discussion or theater groups, or work on the ERA Action Team. All in all, BBW is an independent international service organization dedicated to improving the quality of life and ensuring the continuation of the Jewish heritage. BBW is a member of the Public Affairs Committee of JUF.

Dolls for Democracy is a program developed by BBW that tells the story of great men and women of all nationalities through the use of beautiful dolls. The "cast" includes such personalities as Albert Einstein, Anne Frank, Golda Meir, and Chaim Weizman.

Brandeis University Development Office for the Midwest Region
22 W. Monroe, 60603; 368-8635
Gertrude Schwartz, Midwest Director

Primarily concerned with fund-raising in behalf of Brandeis University, Waltham, MA.

Brandeis University National Women's Committee
372-3510
Greater Chicago Chapter
North Suburban Chapter
Northwest Suburban Chapter, chartered in 1980

The primary purpose of these chapters is to raise funds to support the Brandeis University Library. Chief project of the North Suburban Chapter is the used-book sale, the largest such sale in the world. Always held the week beginning with the Memorial Day weekend. Members of the National Women's Committee may participate in a series of educational/recreational class options offered at minimal charge; the University on Wheels, a day of dialogue in spring with Brandeis faculty members; and international chartered travel.

Chicago Woman's Aid
30 S. Michigan Ave., 60603; 236-9656

One of Chicago's oldest Jewish women's organizations, founded in 1882, CWA supports a large number of Jewish and nonsectarian causes. It has donated eye-exam equipment to the Ark, two minibuses to the Council for Jewish Elderly, and aid to the Response Center study on adolescent grieving. CWA provides members with cultural and educational programs.

Conference of Jewish Women's Organizations
6724 N. Karlov, Lincolnwood 60646; 679-1361

Founded in 1910, CJWO serves the programming needs of women's organizations throughout the Chicago metropolitan area. CJWO holds four public auditions each year at which member-organization program chairmen preview a wide variety of entertainment and educational programs. Workshops and assistance with publicity are also provided. The annual directory contains lists of endorsed programs and of public-service organizations providing programs at little or no charge. CJWO is a good way for qualified entertainers, performers, and lecturers to become known in the community.

Deborah Women's Club
30 W. Washington, Rm. 500, 60602; 726-8891
Elsie Epstein, Contact, 527-3058

Deborah Women, organized in Chicago in 1872 and incorporated in 1897, became part of the Young Men's Jewish Council in the twentieth century. Board meetings are still held once a month in the offices of YMJC. All efforts go to supporting YMJC programs; current projects include the Build-A-Boy Fund and Phantom Dance (the annual ball that never takes place!) for a Deborah Women's Building at Camp Henry Horner. Originally DWC sponsored the Deborah Home on South Grand Boulevard (now King Drive) for boys from the Cleveland Jewish Orphanage. Later efforts turned to boys' clubs, which were eventually taken over by the YMJC. Mrs. Epstein, whose association with DWC began when she was a young girl shortly after 1900, estimates that there are still several hundred members at large.

Emma Lazarus Jewish Women's Club
1673 W. Pratt, 60626

Completely reorganized in 1950, the ELJWC of Chicago includes five chapters united in their common concern for social and political justice. They are pro–civil rights, anti-nuclear, pro-consumer, pro-peace, and pro-Israel. Many members have a Yiddish cultural background. They have circulated petitions and otherwise provided visible support for the study of the Holocaust in Chicago public schools, deportation of Nazis, and senior-citizen rights. They have participated in the COJO-ERA coalition. They especially want new members from the young-adult age bracket.

Free Sons of Israel Hakoah Lodge
6335 N. California, 60659; 338-9810

Founded nationally in 1849, this fraternal order provides members with life-insurance benefits, supports causes within the Jewish community such as Israel and JUF, and awards scholarships. Rooms in the Hakoah Lodge building are available to other organizations.

HIAS (Hebrew Immigrant Aid Society)
1 S. Franklin, 60606; 263-6880

Founded in Chicago in 1911, national HIAS began operations in the early 1880s to assist the Russian Jewish immigrant. Although HIAS's main emphasis has been on the Jewish immigrant, its work has helped all groups of newcomers to America. HIAS has participated nationally and locally in developing policy and procedures for the assistance of Indo-Chinese, Cuban, and Haitian refugees. There are six aspects to HIAS's work: helping immigrants or potential immigrants find lost relatives in the United States; issuing the official "Vysov" (invitation) required by the USSR government for Soviet refugees; assisting citizenship applicants with filling out papers; counseling on all aspects of immigration, including national efforts to relocate non-Jewish refugee groups identified above; searching for proof of age, so that immigrants, even those who came many years ago, can comply with Social Security and other requirements; and protecting people against deportation. HIAS is assisted by six local auxiliaries.

Impala Club
Sonya Abrahamson
432-8353

An informal social club that welcomes all new and recent immigrants to Chicago from South Africa. Although all religions and races are welcomed into membership, the overwhelming majority of members are Jews. For that reason, the club is a good resource on Jewish life in South Africa and on the history of the Jewish community there. IC holds four meetings a year and exchanges professional services among its members. Most of these immigrants are professionally trained. The Jews among them share a strong Jewish identity.

Jewish Big Sisters
2451 N. Sacramento Blvd., 60647; 235-3939
Louise Franks, Additional Contact, 835-2628

A 65-year-old outreach organization within the Jewish community. Since its founding in 1916, JBS has served over 4,000 deprived Jewish girls of the Chicago metropolitan area. JBS continues to assist girls from 10 to 18 years of age who are either fully Jewish or have one Jewish parent. The girls are economically, socially, or emotionally deprived. Services include recreational opportunities, medical care, camp scholarships, and referral to a social-service worker who visits the girls in their homes for counseling.

Membership is open, and more volunteers are needed. Sources of support are membership dues, direct fund-raising efforts, the sale of Happy Day and Memorial cards, and income earned on stocks that were purchased or donated in past years.

Jewish Children's Bureau
1 S. Franklin, 60606; 346-6700
Donna C. Pressma, Executive Director

The JCB, an agency of the Jewish Federation, provides comprehensive child-care services for dependent and emotionally disturbed children and adolescents. Its network of services gives critical help to children and families; and assists parents and children learning to live together, children without families, parents and children learning to live apart, and young people and their relatives who are coping with problem pregnancies, decisions on abortion, sexuality, and child and drug abuse. JCB also deals with children and families who need intensive therapy and with educators, teachers, and administrators who seek consultation on emotionally disturbed children and problem areas within their fields of professional responsibility.

Placement options include adoption, foster care, group homes with therapeutic and transitional residential services, and temporary shelter. Assistance to older adolescents requiring independent living arrangements is also provided. Eight affiliated support groups—seven auxiliaries and the Jewish Children's Bureau Foster Parents Association—are associated with JCB.

JCB still operates under the charter of the Chicago Home for Jewish Orphans, which dates from 1893. JCB itself dates from 1937 with the merger of the Home for Jewish Orphans, the Home for Jewish Friendless and Working Girls, and the Jewish Home Finding Society.

For a fine history, see Mitchell Alan Horwich, *Conflict and Child Care Policy in the Chicago Jewish Community 1893-1942,* published in 1977 and available from the JCB.

Jewish Civil Service Employees of Chicago
Herman R. Fiarman, Contact
7075 N. Paulina St., 60626; 973-6125

Founded in 1937 as the Federal Fellowship Club of Jewish Postal Workers, this organization is mainly concerned today with identifying and combating job discrimination at all levels of government. JCSE will protect the rights of Jewish employees regardless of status—that is, whether they are covered by civil service or not—public-service workers, social workers, teachers, wherever federal funding is involved. Fiarman, a former president of JCSE, is currently president of the related National Jewish Civil Service Employees and National Council of Jewish Government Employees—both headquartered in New York. The latter organization has a membership of 200,000 throughout the country and has within its network the JCSE and one other Chicago organization: Shomrim, the fraternal organization of Jewish police officers.

Jewish Community Centers
1 S. Franklin, 60606; 346-6700
Jerry Witkovsky, Director

The JCCs have been serving the recreational, educational, and social needs of Chicago Jews for over 75 years. The original Chicago Hebrew Institute (acronym still used in Camp Chi) was founded in 1903. It was the first "American" institution developed for and by West Side Jewish immigrants. Today the JCCs have eight community centers serving a wide variety of purposes, ages, and programs. The JCCs provide a sense of Jewish community within the neighborhoods they serve. Membership is required for some, though not all, programs. The Women's Auxiliary provides both money and volunteers. Following is a list of Chicago-area JCCs.

Anita M. Stone JCC
18600 Governors Highway, Flossmoor 60422; 799-7650
Formerly known as the South Suburban JCC, the Anita M. Stone JCC took its name in 1980 upon acquisition of its building, the former Etz Chaim Synagogue. All ages are served at this center, with special programs for singles, seniors, nursery-school children, tweens, and teens.

Bernard Horwich JCC
3003 W. Touhy Ave., 60645; 761-9100
Serves as a community center in the broadest sense for Jews of West Rogers Park and, in many of its programs, for the entire Chicago Jewish community. Full range of activities: sports, athletics, recreation, fine arts, performing arts, preschool, senior center. Also support groups, community events, and annual invitational art fair and auction. There is a year-round gift shop and a pool and health club.

Henry N. Hart JCC
2961 W. Peterson Ave., 60659; 275-8445
A full-program JCC, serving all ages from preschoolers through senior adults. Has a performing arts group, the Henry Street Players. An annual rummage sale is held each spring.

Hyde Park JCC
1100 E. Hyde Park Blvd., 60615; 268-4600
Serves all ages. There are day camps, women's programs, an Adult Yiddish Mobile Theater group that presents play readings in English from Yiddish writings, and a new community theater. An exchange program with Michael Reese Hospital has been organized. HPJCC uses the Reese pool and gym, and hospital personnel are able in turn to join JCC programs. HPJCC runs a preschool program for Reese families and sponsors a summer concert series that performs on the grass behind the interns' quarters at 29th and Ellis.

Lincoln Park–Lakeview JCC
524 W. Melrose, 60657; 871-6780

The newest of the JCCs. Headquarters are adjacent to Anshe Sholom B'nai Israel congregation. Programming is targeted for three population groups: singles, young marrieds, and young children.

Mayer Kaplan JCC
5050 Church St., Skokie 60077; 675-2200

A full-service JCC, with programs for all age groups, preschoolers through senior adults. Pool and health club on premises. Performing arts, singles, support groups, women's programming.

North Suburban JCC
601 Skokie Blvd., Northbrook 60062; 272-2267

Program especially geared to young marrieds and their preschool and school-age children. Full range of moms-and-tots and dads-and-tots programs, early-childhood social and Jewish celebrations. Has a unique program that provides enrichment for intellectually curious children.

Rogers Park JCC
7101 N. Greenview, 60626; 274-0920

The oldest JCC in Chicago has programs for all ages. A great deal of programming is directed to Soviet Jews in Chicago, many of whom live in the Rogers Park community. Has programs for singles, teens, and tweens, as well as a day-care program for young children.

All JCCs have programs concerning Israel and Jewish festivals.
Mayer Kaplan offers JET—Jewish Effectiveness Training.
Judaica classes are taught at most JCCs, and Hebrew is taught at Bernard Horwich, Mayer Kaplan, and Rogers Park. Yiddish is offered at Bernard Horwich, Mayer Kaplan, and North Suburban.
Children Welcoming the Sabbath—Kaballat Shabbat—classes are held at most JCCs.

Jewish Family and Community Service
1 S. Franklin St., 60606; 346-6700
Martin E. Langer, Executive Director

An agency of the Jewish Federation devoted to strengthening the quality of family life through professional family, marital, and individual counseling; family-life education; and homemaker services. Help is given to individuals of all ages and to their families. Specialized services include legal, homemaker, and financial services, home-economist consultations, and restitution advice to assist Holocaust victims in processing claims. Counseling is provided to individuals, couples, families, and groups. Social-service workers are prepared to deal with crisis intervention and crisis prevention.

In each of the six JFCS district offices, there is a Family Life Educator who will lead small group discussions and workshops and will participate in community efforts to deal with family-life issues. Ongoing discussion groups deal with topics related to marriage, parenting, preschoolers, relations with adolescents, marriage, mid-life expectations, relations with elderly parents, etc. Speakers and programs are available to congregations and parent-teacher groups, as well as other organizations.

The JFCS operates six district offices and the Virginia Frank Child Development Center:

Central District, 1 S. Franklin St., 60606; 346-6700

Niles Township District, 5050 Church, Skokie 60077; 675-2200

North Suburban District, 210 Skokie Valley Rd., Highland Park 60035; 831-4225

Northern District, 2710 W. Devon, 60659; 274-1324

Northwest Suburban, 120 W. Eastman, Arlington Heights 60004; 255-4410

South Suburban, 18250 Harwood, Homewood 60430; 799-1869

Virginia Frank Child Development Center
3033 W. Touhy, 60645; 761-4550

The VFCDC provides diagnostic, counseling, and treatment services to families and single-parent families with children under age 6 who are suffering from emotional traumas or developmental difficulties: family counseling, therapy groups for parents and children, outreach services, a therapeutic nursery school, and a therapeutic summer program. The VFCDC has a drop-in program for single parents and workshops that focus on single fathers with children under 9. A basic objective of the agency is to prepare client children to enter public school by the time they reach age 6. As part of the Jewish Family and Community Service, the VFCDC offers a large network of consultative services to which clients may be referred.

Jewish Federation of Metropolitan Chicago
1 S. Franklin St., 60606; 346-6700
Dr. Steven B. Nasatir, Executive Director

Founded as the Associated Jewish Charities in 1900 to centralize and coordinate the social-welfare services of the Jewish community. Prior agencies, dating from the United Hebrew Relief Association of 1859, only partially addressed the problems of coordinating and avoiding duplication in offering professional services and developing programs of aid and assistance. Federation's stated purpose is to plan, coordinate, study, develop, and implement principles, standards, and programs of social service, medical care, Jewish education, community relations, and other charitable and philanthropic activities directed primarily to the Jewish community but available, where practical and necessary, to people of all faiths, races, and national backgrounds in the Chicago area. Federation agencies include the Jewish Children's Bureau, Jewish Community Centers, Jewish Family and Community Service, Jewish Vocational Service, and Council for Jewish Elderly. Also under the Federation are the Chicago Jewish Youth Council, B'nai B'rith Hillel Foundations Jewish Federation College Age Youth Services, Response Center, and Michael Reese and Mount Sinai hospitals and medical centers. The Jewish Federation's primary source for funding is the Jewish United Fund of Metropolitan Chicago.

Most Federation agencies are headquartered at 1 S. Franklin St. in the Loop. Four suburban locations house a combination of agency offices:

In Skokie, in the Mayer Kaplan Jewish Community Center building, 5050 Church St.: the Jewish Children's Bureau, Jewish Family and Community Service, and Jewish Vocational Service.

In Highland Park, at 210 Skokie Valley Rd.: the Jewish Children's Bureau and Jewish Family and Community Service, serving Lake County.

In Arlington Heights, at 120 W. Eastman: the Jewish Family and Community Service, Jewish Vocational Service, and Jewish Children's Bureau.

In Flossmoor, at the Anita M. Stone Jewish Community Center, 18600 Governors Highway: offices of the Jewish Vocational Service and Jewish Children's Bureau.

Jewish Shelter House of Chicago, Inc. (Hachnasat Orchim)
5050 N. Kimball, 60625; 539-6956

Provides temporary shelter, limited to a stay of three or four days, and usually limited to travelers with insufficient means to pay for accommodations. Strictly kosher. Write or call in advance for information and reservations. Resident contact is Rev. Yochanan Nathan.

A historic aside: According to the 1920–21 *American Jewish Year Book*, the National Union of Jewish Sheltering Societies was founded in 1911 "to help worthy wayfarers, put a check on habitual wanderers, and prevent wife-deserters from using the Hachnoses Orchim as a means of escape from family responsibilities."

Jewish United Fund of Metropolitan Chicago
1 S. Franklin St., 60606; 346-6700
Dr. Steven B. Nasatir, Executive Director

The major fund-raising arm of the Chicago Jewish community, JUF, through its communitywide network of divisions, committees, and groups, raises funds for the Jewish Federation and its agencies, beneficiaries, and grant recipients. JUF also raises money for worldwide agencies serving Jewish communities in 30 countries outside the United States, particularly Israel. Besides direct fund raising, the JUF sponsors programs of leadership development, community relations, and the Public Affairs Committee. Fund raising is carried out by an army of volunteers with divisions broken down by various categories: Women's Division; Young Leadership; Congregations; College Campaign; and Trades, Industries, and Professions.

JUF also publishes the monthly *JUF News* with worldwide coverage of Jewish news. The special JUF $1-a-Year Corps is a group of crack salesmen ranging in age from about 75 to 100 who are full-time fund raisers at 1 S. Franklin.

Women's Division of the Jewish United Fund
1 S. Franklin, 60606; 346-6700

One of two JUF divisions represented on the Public Affairs Committee (the other being the Young Leadership Division). The Young Women's Board of the Women's Division holds a large children's fashion show each summer, La Petite Fashionplate. Anyone interested in having her child or grandchild appear in the next Fashionplate should call the Women's Division.

Jewish Vocational Service
1 S. Franklin St., 60606; 346-6700

A Federation agency actually founded in 1936 but with antecedents in the Chicago Jewish community as far back as 1884, when the Employment Bureau was established. JVS provides a wide-reaching program for the training and employment in gainful occupations of all people, including the disadvantaged and handicapped: immigrants, students requiring educational counseling, persons needing training and placement, and the disabled. Services are offered at the following locations:

Central Office, 1 S. Franklin, 60606; 346-6700
Sampson-Katz Center, 2020 W. Devon, 60659; 761-9000
Angel Guardian Center, 2001 W. Devon, 60659; 973-3800
Vocational Adjustment Center, 320 N. Dearborn, 60610; 828-9700
Self-Actualization Center, 325 W. Huron St., 60610; 440-1107

Mayer Kaplan JCC, 5050 Church St., Skokie 60077; 675-2200
South Suburban, 18600 Governors Highway, Flossmoor 60422; 799-6555
Northwest Suburban, 120 W. Eastman Dr., Arlington Heights 60004; 255-4410
Project TEAM (Training and Employment of Auto Mechanics), 5650 N. Western Ave., 60659; 769-1233.

The JVS program includes the following:
Family and individual services in vocational guidance as well as testing
Professional, managerial, and technical placement program
Project with Industry—on-the-job training for the handicapped
Indochinese Placement Program for newly arrived Indo-Chinese refugees in the Chicago area
Russian Resettlement Program to help Soviet refugees, supported by the Jewish Family and Community Service, adjust to and find employment in Chicago
Clerical training—for both handicapped and nonhandicapped
"Hi Risk" Placement Program to increase the employability and job placement possibilities of mentally ill applicants
Reploy, a program of part-time work and vocational rehabilitation for senior adults
Research Utilization Laboratory, to develop, test, disseminate, and assist in the application of research knowledge to rehabilitation practice
Self-Actualization Center, to increase the employability of mentally ill persons who have difficulties in a work situation

National Council of Jewish Women
Central District Office
53 W. Jackson, Suite 724, 60604; 663-9400
Hazel Blumenthal, National District Representative

Founded in 1893 in Chicago. Now, nearly 90 years later, the NCJW maintains the role of advocate for improving the human condition in five specific areas: Jewish life in America, Israel, women's issues, aging, and children and youth. The organization in the greater Chicago area is divided into eight sections: Chicago (the only one to maintain a separate office: 53 W. Jackson, Suite 1511, 987-1927); Evanston-Niles; Lincolnway (Park Forest area); North Shore; Northwest Suburban; South Cook; West Valley (Lincolnwood to Glenview); and Aurora. Together the sections support employment services for youth and seniors, Tay-Sachs screening, performing arts for seniors and handicapped.

NCJW packs "Ship-a-Box" boxes with new toys and articles of

clothing made by senior adults for Israel's children. It participates in coalitions for day care, ERA (member of COJO-ERA), and WICS (Women in Community Service) founded by NCJW along with non-Jewish women's organizations. It monitors juvenile court foster-care placement records. NCJW is concerned with consumer protection, economic policy, energy and the environment, foreign policy, health and human services, and much more. NCJW is represented on the Public Affairs Committee of JUF.

ORT (Organization for Rehabilitation through Training)

ORT was founded in Russia in 1880. Its original purpose was to provide training for displaced Jews who were forced to learn new skills in order to survive in their new environment. Today ORT maintains over 600 schools in 22 countries and teaches over 70 trades. ORT schools have over 90,000 students, two-thirds in Israel. ORT also plays a significant role in working with Soviet Jews who have left the USSR. The American ORT Federation—the overall umbrella organization for all ORT-related groups in this country—was founded in 1924.

Chicago Men's ORT Midwest Region

Devon Bank Bldg., 6445 N. Western Ave., 60645; 764-9745

Founded in 1957, this is one of 45 men's ORT chapters in the United States. It supports ORT's international program and has established a scholarship for the ORT School of Engineering at the Hebrew University in Jerusalem.

Women's American ORT Midwest District VIII

111 N. Wabash Ave., 60602; 726-6466

Elaine Bachman-Levin, Executive Director

Locally, there are five regions of the Women's American ORT: Chicago, Lake County, Northern Illinois, West Suburban, and South Suburban Chapter-at-Large. Each region is made up of many chapters, and because each chapter engages in its own programming, the organization's efforts are seen and felt throughout the Jewish community in the area.

WAO serves on the Public Affairs Committee of JUF and participates in COJO-ERA. An international concern for Soviet immigrants has carried over into helping these newcomers in Chicago. Scholarships for vocational education are awarded each year by WAO regions to graduating high school students.

The many chapters throughout the area generate almost an equal number of annual fund-raising events. The annual Design House of the Lake County Region receives what may be the widest publicity.

Members of the American Society of Interior Designers redesign a selected estate and open it to visitors for a charge. WAO has a library of films and slide programs available to interested organizations. Most spectacular is *L'Chaim—to Life!*, featuring Eli Wallach and winner of first prize in the 1974 American Film Festival. This 80-minute, black-and-white and color montage of stills and film clips documents more than a century of Jewish life, in Russia through World War I to the Holocaust, the Warsaw Ghetto, the DP Camps, and the establishment of Israel. Call for information.

The Response Center
7457 N. Western Ave., 60645; 338-2292
Martha Chernov, Director

The Jewish community's major facility for providing assistance to adolescents 12 to 20, the Response Center is a consortium of four agencies and one hospital, all under the umbrella of the Jewish Federation. Participating agencies are the Jewish Community Centers, Jewish Children's Bureau, Jewish Vocational Service, Jewish Family and Community Service, and Mount Sinai Hospital. Counseling is provided on an individual, group, or family basis. Medical assistance, rape counseling, and abortion counseling are available. Emphasis is given to problems of cults, grieving, depression, alienation, drug abuse, teen pregnancies, and family and sex education. There is an outreach counseling program at Mather High School.

Hours are 10 A.M. to 10 P.M. Mondays through Thursdays; 10 A.M. to 6 P.M. Fridays. Medical services are provided 7 to 10 P.M. Tuesdays and Thursdays. When the center is closed, a recording device on the telephone will take crisis messages. Posters dramatizing adolescent problems are available. The center also distributes a special booklet for girls that describes female health care and common misconceptions about menstruation.

Shomrim Society of Illinois
P.O. Box 59258, 60659
Harold (Sonny) Lukatsky, Historian and Past President

Shomrim is a religious fraternal Jewish police organization founded in the late 1950s that is affiliated with the National Shomrim Society headquartered in New York. In the 1970s the local Shomrim became affiliated with the National Council of Jewish Government Employees. (The only other affiliated Chicago-based organization is the Jewish Civil Service Employees.) Shomrim provides its members and member families with death benefits and supports various charities. Illinois membership totals about 300. Monthly meetings are held in Chicago.

UOTS (United Order True Sisters)

UOTS is the pioneer Jewish women's fraternal organization in the United States; it was founded in 1846. Chicago has two lodges, one of the oldest and one of the newest in UOTS:

Johanna, Lodge #9
Mrs. Noah Levin, President
222 Valley View Rd., Wilmette 60091

Assists the blind and other handicapped groups. Johanna (originally spelled "Jochannah") was founded in 1874. It played a significant role in Chicago's history. Johanna started Chicago's first free kindergarten and first penny lunchroom and introduced the first "moving picture machine" into Chicago public schools. Johanna provided free loans to the poor, after-school classes in congested neighborhoods, and scholarships for Jewish children.

Through the years, Johanna has absorbed other UOTS Lodges, including the Sarah Greenebaum Lodge, which established Resthaven on South Grand Blvd. (now Martin Luther King Dr.) and which is now located on the West Side under the name of Schwab Rehabilitation Hospital. (Sarah Greenebaum was the mother of Hannah Greenebaum Solomon, founder of the National Council of Jewish Women.)

As years passed, Johanna's work for the blind became increasingly important. Today, besides supporting the Johanna Bureau for the Blind and Visually Handicapped, Johanna contributes to Michael Reese, Mount Sinai, and Highland Park hospitals for cancer care and research, and to Bene Shalom Congregation of the Deaf. Current membership is about 650 women in the Chicago area.

Lake Cook Chapter, Lodge #67
Maxine Szmulewitz
537-6767

Chartered in November 1977, this lodge is seeking members and is devoting its efforts to hospitals and health, particularly in the field of cancer support. Lake Cook Chapter is nonsectarian, and not all members are Jewish.

Yiddish Sons of Erin
Larry Yaseen
798-0660

This organization is *not* what it appears to be. It is not an organization of Irish-born Jews. Rather it is the smallest marching unit in Chicago's annual St. Patrick's Day Parade! Larry Yaseen's late father, Harry, a South Holland Jewish jeweler, was a lifelong admirer of the Irish people. He grew up in Chicago Heights when the community was largely Irish. Around 1960 the elder Yaseen organized the Yiddish Sons of Erin with his friend Pat Conran. Larry Yaseen is continuing the association—and maintains his membership in the Irish Fellowship Club. The Yiddish Sons of Erin would welcome additional marchers to join them next March 17.

Young Men's Jewish Council
30 W. Washington St., 60602; 726-8891
9301 Gross Point Rd., Skokie 60076; 679-8490 (Center for
 Enriched Living)

A nonsectarian, nonprofit social-service agency founded in 1907 to benefit children and youth. Though YMJC originally sponsored boys' clubs in Chicago and a camp for underprivileged children, it has grown to serve all segments of the population—boys and girls.

After-school and holiday programs throughout the year; five summer day camps for children 5 through 11; tween camps for 11- to 14-year-olds; Parent and Child Care Centers for preschoolers; Camp Henry Horner, an overnight camp with various programs operating throughout the year; and the Center for Enriched Living, a unique social center for children and young adults who are mildly and moderately retarded.

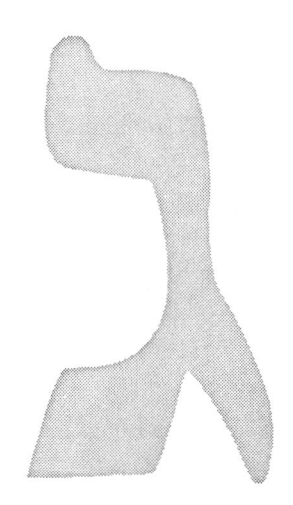

3
Religious Life

Chicago Board of Rabbis
72 E. 11th St., 60605; 427-5863
Rabbi Mordecai Simon, Executive Director
The central organization in Chicago representing rabbis from all Jewish movements. Also maintains the Chaplaincy Commission, which coordinates all nonmilitary chaplains and related programs in the area. The Broadcasting Commission of the CBR produces television programs. A clearinghouse for all matters related to counseling, crisis intervention, and other situations where referral to specific rabbis may be desired. Newcomers to Chicago may contact the CBR for information regarding congregations. A member of the Public Affairs Committee of JUF.

Conservative Judaism

Rabbinical Assembly of Chicago
Rabbi Harold I. Stern, President, 674-9292
Local chapter of the national association of Conservative rabbis. A member of the Public Affairs Committee of JUF.

United Synagogue of America, Midwest Region
72 E. 11th St., 60605; 939-2351
Chana Rosen, Regional Director
The central organization of Conservative congregations. A member of the Public Affairs Committee of JUF.

Jewish Educators' Assembly
Dr. Irving Skolnick, National President
Board of Jewish Education, 72 E. 11th St., 60605

Jewish Theological Seminary of America
72 E. 11th St., 60605

National Federation of Jewish Men's Clubs Midwest Region
72 E. 11th St., 60605
Phillip Rothenberg, President, 470-0018

United Synagogue Youth
72 E. 11th St., 60605; 939-2353
Richard Moline, Director

Women's League for Conservative Judaism Central Branch
72 E. 11th St., 60605; 939-2351

Orthodox Judaism

Chicago Rabbinical Council
2735 W. Devon Ave., 60659; 764-0259
Rabbi Nathan I. Weiss, Executive Director

One of two central agencies of the Orthodox rabbinate in Chicago; members tend to be American-trained rabbis. Office includes the Beth Din Zedek, the Jewish Ecclesiastical Court. Supervises kashrut (kosher certification) for most categories of concern (cRc is the trademark). Also publishes booklets on Jewish observances for the layman. A central clearinghouse to which requests for rabbinical referrals can be addressed. Membership includes pastoral counselors. A member of the Public Affairs Committee of the JUF.

Merkaz Harabonim—Chicago Orthodox Rabbinate
6500 N. California Ave., 60645; 761-3800
Rabbi Yehudah D. Goldman, Executive Director

One of two associations representing Orthodox rabbis in Chicago; membership tends to be European trained. Members supervise the laws of kashrut (koshering) at Chicago meat-packing houses and meat markets. Assists in many ways with the religious education in the congregations of its affiliated rabbis.

Council of Traditional/Orthodox Synagogues
6716 N. Whipple St., 60645; 973-2522
Rabbi Shmuel Spiegel, Director

Represents two dozen congregations in the Chicago area. Also represents the Union of Orthodox Jewish Congregations. Provides a regional youth director to oversee and coordinate youth programming of member congregations. Sponsors educational programs from time to time.

Rabbinical Council of America
c/o Rabbi Benzion Kaganoff
Ezras Israel Congregation, 7001 N. California, 60645; 764-8320
An association of Orthodox rabbis.

AFTA (Association for Torah Advancement)
2852-D W. Touhy, 60645; 338-2575

Agudath Israel
3540 W. Peterson, 60659; 588-5078 (Center)
5621 N. St. Louis, 60659 (Office)
Rabbi Yitzchok Bider

Agudath Israel's focus is on worship, study, and strict adherence to Jewish law. The local branch of this national organization provides religious and educational opportunities for all ages, with special emphasis on the young. Also provides assistance and information to the Orthodox traveler. Sponsors the Pirchei Agudath program for boys and the B'nos Agudath for girls. Established a children's lending library in 1980. Rabbi Shmuel Fuerst will answer questions pertaining to Jewish law from 7 to 9 P.M. at 539-4241. During the Passover season, he will take calls from 7 to 10 P.M. Publishes a calendar including a list of Orthodox religious services throughout the Chicago area.

Brisk Rabbinical College
9000 Forest View, Skokie 60203; 674-4652

Hebrew Theological College
7135 N. Carpenter Rd., Skokie 60077; 674-7750

National Conference of Synagogue Youth
6716 N. Whipple St., 60645; 761-2188

Telshe Yeshiva
3535 W. Foster, 60625; 463-7738

Lubavitch Chabad of Greater Chicago
2014 Orrington, Evanston 60201; 869-8060
Rabbi Daniel Moscowitz, Director

The Chabad House is located near the campus of Northwestern University, but its outreach program is designed for the entire state of Illinois. Chabad provides a network of outreach programs to encourage non-Orthodox Jews and Jews with a limited Judaic background to learn about and begin to practice the traditions embraced by the Chassidic movement. Specifically, Chabad provides study groups for college students and adults. A women's class meets weekly in a home in West Rogers Park. Cultural events include an annual benefit devoted to Chassidic song and music. Chabad sponsors a radio program, The Jewish Sound, 9:30 to 11 A.M. Sundays, on Highland Park-based WEEF-AM (1430). At community celebrations, hospitals, and public places like the Daley Center, members of this movement distribute Sabbath kits and literature about traditional Jewish observance. The women's organization is Neshei Chabad.

- Baila Grinker
2014 Orrington, Evanston 60201; 869-8060
Answers questions about the Neshei Chabad women's organization.

- Rabbi and Mrs. Yosef Shanowitz
433-3842 or 869-8060
Highland Park representatives of Lubavitch Chabad.

The Reconstructionist Movement

Federation of Reconstructionist Congregations and Havurot
c/o Jewish Reconstructionist Congregation, 328-7678 *or*
    Niles Township Jewish Congregation, 583-2191 or 675-4141
A member of the Public Affairs Committee of JUF.

Niles Township Jewish Congregation
4500 Dempster, Skokie 60076; 583-2191 or 675-4141
Rabbi Neil Brief

Jewish Reconstructionist Congregation
2525 Hartrey, Evanston 60201; 328-7678
Rabbi Arnold Rachlis

Reform Judaism

Union of American Hebrew Congregations, Chicago Federation, Great Lakes Council
100 W. Monroe, Rm. 312, 60603; 782-1477
Rabbi Alan Bregman, Executive Director
The central organization of Reform congregations. A member of the Public Affairs Committee of JUF.

ARZA (Association of Reform Zionists of America) Chicago Chapter
100 W. Monroe, Rm. 312, 60603; 782-1477
Jerry Kaye, Contact
Affiliated with the World Zionist Organization, the Chicago chapter of ARZA has two purposes: membership recruitment and programming on Israel, particularly on Reform and liberal Judaism in Israel.

CATA (Chicago Association of Temple Administrators)
100 W. Monroe, Rm. 312, 60603; 782-1477

CATE (Chicago Association of Temple Educators)
Barbara (Cookie) Gross, President
c/o Temple Sholom religious school, 525-4707

CFTY (Chicago Federation of Temple Youth)
100 W. Monroe, Rm. 312, 60603; 782-1477
Jerry Kaye, Director of Camping and Youth Activities

Chicago Association of Reform Rabbis
100 W. Monroe, Rm. 312, 60603; 782-1477

Midwest Federation of Temple Sisterhoods
100 W. Monroe, Rm. 312, 60603; 782-1477

National Federation of Temple Brotherhoods
100 W. Monroe, Rm. 312, 60603; 782-1477

For information about Reform Jewish practices, see *A Guide for Reform Jews* by Rabbis Frederic A. Doppelt and David Polish, published in 1957. Also see the new Gates prayer books, for the Sabbath, High Holidays, and home use, published in the 1970s by the UAHC.

Congregations

Congregations are identified as follows:
- C = Conservative
- I = Independent
- O = Orthodox
- Rec = Reconstructionist
- R = Reform
- T = Traditional (Orthodox)

Congregational affiliation is indicated as follows:
- CTOS = Council of Traditional/Orthodox Synagogues
- FRCH = Federation of Reconstructionist Congregations and Havurot
- UAHC = Union of American Hebrew Congregations (Reform)
- US = United Synagogue of America (Conservative)

Most Orthodox and Traditional and some Conservative and Reform congregations have daily services (daily minyan) in the early morning and/or late afternoon. *Some* of these are noted below. All services, whether weekday or Shabbat, are subject to time variation and cancellation. Interested persons should call ahead for specific schedules.

(When an Orthodox congregation in the Chicago area is designated "Traditional," this usually means that men and women are permitted to sit together.)

A. G. Beth Israel (T) (CTOS)
3635 W. Devon, 60659; 539-9060
Rabbi Moses Eichenstein

A. G. stands for Austro-Galician, the national origin of founding members. Sisterhood, men's club, gift shop, religious school (A. G. Beth Torah), and daily services. Current membership is around 400 families.

Achay Bais Itzchok (O)
4645 N. Drake, 60625; 478-6416

Also known as the Drake Shul and Beth Itzchok of Albany Park. This congregation, without a rabbi for some years, has fallen on hard times. The congregation was founded in Albany Park in 1919. Daily services.

Adas B'nai Israel (O)
6200 N. Kimball, 60659; 583-8141
Rabbi Jacob Nayman
Daily services.

Adas Shalom (T) (CTOS)
6945 Dempster, Morton Grove 60053; 965-1880
Rabbi Israel Porush

Adas Yeschurun (O) (CTOS)
2949 W. Touhy, 60645; 465-2288
Rabbi Hershel Berger

Undergoing a major remodeling program. Sisterhood, daily services.

Adat Yisrael Congregation (C) (US)
2550 N. Arlington Heights Rd., Arlington Heights 60004; 885-1569
Rabbi Norman Kleinman

Founded in 1978 with a dozen families, this congregation now has about 100 from Arlington Heights, Buffalo Grove, Palatine, and Wheeling. Weekly Friday night services at Rand Junior High School, Arlington Heights; religious school at the Poe School. USY Youth group and Kadimah junior high school group.

Agudas Achim North Shore (T) (CTOS)
5029 N. Kenmore, 60640; 561-0435
Rabbi Oscar M. Lifshutz

Pioneer congregation in Uptown community since the 1920s. Many original members had Hungarian roots. Sisterhood. Nonmembers welcome at High Holiday services; daily services.

Agudas Anshei Lubavitch (O)
7424 N. Paulina, 60626; 274-0623

Agudath Achim-Bikur Cholim (0)
8927 S. Houston, 60617; 768-7685
Millie Miller, Contact, 493-8880

Bikur Cholim has used this synagogue since 1902. It's the oldest synagogue in continuous use in the greater Chicago area. Agudath Achim South Shore merged with Bikur Cholim in the 1970s.

Agudath Jacob (T)
633 W. Howard, Evanston 60202; 475-9317
Rabbi Nachman Rosenthal

Founded in the 1950s in Chicago and at this site since 1963, the congregation acquired the name and property of old Agudath Jacob, formerly in Lawndale at 13th and Keeler. Sisterhood.

Am Chai Congregation (C)
c/o Mr. and Mrs. Jerome Taitel, 359-3559

New Conservative congregation serving the Schaumburg-Hoffman Estates area and surrounding communities. Services currently held biweekly at a Schaumburg location.

Am Echad (C) (US)
160 Westwood Dr., Park Forest 60466; 747-9513
Rabbi Roy D. Tanenbaum

Formed by merger in 1977 of Etz Chaim, Flossmoor, and South Suburban Beth Israel, Park Forest. Using the former Beth Israel synagogue. (The former Etz Chaim synagogue is the newly purchased and renamed Anita M. Stone Jewish Community Center.) Religious school takes nonmember children. Daily services. Sisterhood, couples club, youth group, library, gift shop. Sells seats to nonmembers for the High Holidays. New independent day school meets here.

Am Echod (C)
1500 Sunset Ave., Waukegan 60085; 336-9110
Rabbi William Fertiz

Founded in the 1890s, AE is the pioneer congregation of Waukegan. Among seventeen founders was Mayer Kubelsky, who served as an early congregation president. Kubelsky, partner in the 1890s of Kubelsky Brothers Clothing and Gents Furnishing Goods Store, was the father of comedian Jack Benny. Waukegan Federation of Jewish Women includes the Am Echod Sisterhood, Hadassah, and B'nai B'rith Women. Gift shop, BBYO youth group. Current membership at about 200 families.

■ **Rose J. Lidschin**
926 N. Sheridan Rd., Waukegan 60085; 623-5565

Author and historian of the Jewish community of Waukegan in general and Am Echod congregation in particular.

Am Shalom (R)
614 Sheridan Rd., Glencoe 60022; 835-4800
Rabbi Harold Kudan

Located in the Congregation Home, a large rambling mansion that Am Shalom has occupied since its founding in 1972. Religious-school classes are at the Glencoe Central School; 8 P.M. Friday services, at the Women's Library Club of Glencoe. During the summer, services are held in the Congregation Home. Couples club and two singles groups. Youth groups. Current membership, at 350 families, fills the allowable quota. There's a waiting list for membership.

Am Yisrael (C)
4 Happ Rd., Northfield 60093; 446-7215
Rabbi William Frankel

Calls itself "Independent Conservative"; current membership, over 400 families. Three youth groups, funeral plan for members, library.

Anshe Emet (C) (US)
3760 N. Pine Grove, 60613; 281-1423
Rabbi Seymour J. Cohen

Chicago's oldest Conservative congregation, founded in 1872. Nonmember children may attend the congregation's day school and religious school. Sisterhood, men's club, senior adult club. Biweekly Friday night alternative minyan for young adults. Library, extensive adult education, rotating art exhibits, gift shop, daily services. Special student seats available for the High Holidays.

Anshe Mizrach (O)
627 W. Patterson, 60613; 525-4034
Rabbi Solomon Rockove

Anshe Mizrach was founded about 1928 when the congregation moved into a synagogue vacated by Anshe Emet. (That's when Anshe Emet moved into Temple Sholom's synagogue and Temple Sholom moved into a new building on Lake Shore Drive.) Daily services.

Anshe Motele (O) (CTOS)
6520 N. California, 60645; 743-9452
Rabbi Menahim M. Goodman

Anshe Motele celebrated its Diamond Jubilee in 1978. Founded in the Maxwell Street area in 1903 by men from Motele, White Russia, which was the birthplace of Chaim Weizmann. Nearly all Chicago Motelers claim a relationship to the first president of Israel. Sisterhood, men's club. The Rabbi L. Kaplan Hebrew Education Center, 6525 N. California, contains Rabbi Kaplan's library. A second morning minyan is held daily in his memory. It is also the location of the Bais Yaacov Parochial School for Boys.

Temple Anshe Sholom a Beth Torah (R) (UAHC)
20820 Western Ave., Olympia Fields 60461; 748-6010
Rabbi Donald N. Gluckman

Beth Torah, formerly at 92d and Vanderpoel, merged with Anshe Sholom in 1974. Sisterhood holds annual antiques and crafts show. Two youth groups are TASTY—*T*emple *A*nshe *S*holom *T*een *Y*outh— and TASSEL—*T*emple *A*nshe *S*holom *S*eventh and *E*ighth (grade) *L*eague. Also men's club, couples club, chavurot, singles, seniors, large Judaica library, gift shop, nursery school, and the Rabbi Frank F. Rosenthal Memorial Museum. Current membership is 650.

Anshe Sholom B'nai Israel (O) (CTOS)
540 W. Melrose, 60657; 248-9200
Rabbi Joseph Deitcher

The Anshe Sholom part of this congregation dates from 1870 with the establishment of Ohave Sholom Mariampoler, formed in a legendary break from Beth Hamedrash Hagodol. (BHH was founded in the 1860s as Chicago's first Eastern-European Jewish congregation. BHH survived until the 1950s. Anshe Sholom B'nai Israel is probably the city's oldest remaining Orthodox congregation.) The legend is that on a hot summer day in 1870, Mr. Bernard Ginsburg, native of Mariampol, Lithuania, went to Beth Hamedrash Hagodol to say Kaddish (mourning prayers) for his son. Ginsburg had the audacity to wear a straw hat instead of the customary head covering. He was turned away, and so without delay started his own congregation with other Mariampolers.

Ohave Sholom Mariampoler was called the Straw Hat Shul by some. In 1916, Anshe Kalvaria merged with Ohave Sholom; the name became Anshe Sholom. The current location on Melrose, established in the 1940s, was at first a branch of AS, then on Independence Blvd.

Archives, including pinkasim (handwritten record books) of OSM, are in the Rabbi Saul Silber Memorial Library of the Hebrew Theological College.

Sisterhood, adult education, some young-adult programming, daily services.

Ateres Yehoshua Congregation (O)
2819 W. Touhy, 60645
Rabbi Eichenstein

Bene Shalom of the Deaf (UAHC)
4435 Oakton, Skokie 60076; 677-3330
Rabbi Douglas H. Goldhamer

This unique congregation serves the deaf and their families from all branches of Judaism. Also open to those without hearing problems. Rabbi provides simultaneous sign language for services, religious school, and all activities. Sisterhood, men's club, adult education. Special funeral plan for members. Some sign-language instruction offered from time to time.

Beth Am (I)
c/o 2005 Kiowa Lane, Mt. Prospect 60056; 827-7599 or 541-3255

Combines features of both Reform and Conservative worship. Based on the principle of chavurah, a friendship circle involving a variety of activities. Members from Wheeling, Mt. Prospect, Arlington Heights, Buffalo Grove, Northbrook, Glenview. Services at Kingswood Methodist Church, Buffalo Grove; school at Eugene Field Elementary School, Wheeling. Founded in 1978; current membership around 50 families. Congregation possesses the wooden Ark from the former Albany Park Hebrew Congregation.

Temple Beth-El Chicago (R) (UAHC)
3050 W. Touhy, 60645; 274-0341
Rabbi Victor H. Weissberg

Pioneer congregation of the northwest side, founded in 1871 during the Chicago Fire. Original name, Rodef Sholom, abandoned in early years when the small synagogue was blown away in a cyclone. Sisterhood, men's club, gift shop, young adult club, several youth groups, well-established chavurah program, library, adult education. Weekday Hebrew school option at Northbrook branch school, Pfingsten and Dundee. Daily services (6 P.M. weekdays). Windows designed for Beth-El by Chicago artist Sidney Rafilson. Membership nearly 1,000.

Beth Emet The Free Synagogue (R) (UAHC)
1224 Dempster, Evanston 60202; 869-4230
Rabbi Peter S. Knobel

Founded in 1950 by Rabbi David Polish, Beth Emet was the first Jewish congregation in Evanston. Men's club, senior and junior youth groups, library, museum, preschool. Has a chug program offering congregants an option of about a dozen special-interest groups, from adult theater to Yiddishkeit. Alternative lay-led minyan at 9:30 A.M. Saturdays. Membership about 650 families.

Beth Hamedrosh Hagodol Kesser Maariv Anshe Luknik (O)
6418 N. Greenview, 60626; 764-5370
Rabbi Zev W. Wein

Also known as Kesser Maariv or, simply, Beth Hamedrosh Hagodol, the name of the city's pioneer Orthodox congregation, though the current congregation is not really its descendant. There's a women's council. Only services are a morning minyan. The synagogue is used by FREE, a program for Soviet Jews in Chicago.

Beth Hillel (C) (US)
3220 Big Tree Lane, Wilmette 60091; 256-1213
Rabbi David H. Lincoln

Sisterhood, men's club, couples club, youth group, library, gift shop. United Synagogue funeral plan optional for members. Daily services. Membership, 600 families.

Beth Israel (R) (UAHC)
4850 N. Bernard St., 60625; 588-0915
Rabbi Ernst M. Lorge

The pioneer congregation in Albany Park, founded in 1917. About 500 families are members. Sisterhood, men's club, youth group, seniors, gift shop, library. Two religious schools: at 3939 W. Howard, Skokie (jointly with Temple Menorah) nonmember children are accepted; at Deerfield High School (without Menorah) membership is required. Lay-led Saturday morning services at Skokie branch school. Monthly services and adult education in Deerfield.

Beth Itzchok of West Rogers Park (O) (CTOC)
6716 N. Whipple, 60645; 973-2522
Rabbi Aaron M. Rine

Sisterhood, daily services.

Beth Judea (C) (US)
P.O. Box 763, Buffalo Grove 60090; 634-0777
Sanctuary: Route 83, ½ mile south of Route 22, Long Grove 60047
Rabbi Mordecai Rosen

Founded by 4 families in 1968 and chartered by 40 the following year, Beth Judea now has 300 families, primarily from Arlington

Heights, Barrington, Buffalo Grove, Hoffman Estates, Lake Zurich, Libertyville, Lincolnshire, Long Grove, Palatine, Rolling Meadows, and Wheeling. Sisterhood, men's club, three youth groups, gift shop, optional United Synagogue funeral plan. Inside the synagogue are two stained-glass windows by Nota Koslowsky, late Chicago artist, donated by the David Goldbogen family.

Beth Or (Humanistic)
2075 Deerfield Rd., Deerfield 60015; 945-0477
Rabbi Daniel Friedman

Beth Or, founded in 1962, is affiliated with the Society for Humanistic Judaism. The liturgy has been re-created for those who do not believe in a personal God—or in any at all; all reference to the deity has been removed. Independent religious school, no auxiliaries, funeral plan in progress. Library open to the community. Courtyard setting for summer services. Membership, 185 families.

Beth Shalom (C) (US)
3433 Walters, Northbrook 60062; 498-4100
Rabbi Carl Wolkin

Founded in Northbrook in 1967, now numbering over 500 families; new building addition includes sanctuary, recently completed. Sisterhood, men's club, very active youth group, gift shop. United Synagogue funeral plan, daily services.

Beth Shalom of Naperville
P.O. Box 516, Naperville 60540; 963-1818
Rabbi Morris Fishman

Founded as religious school in the middle 1970s, this congregation serves Naperville's growing Jewish population. There are about 100 families in Beth Shalom, with nearly 150 children in the religious school. A new sisterhood was formed in 1980. High Holiday seats are available to nonmembers. Most functions are held in the basement of the Weslyan United Methodist Church; however, the congregation owns land for a future synagogue.

Beth Sholom (R) (UAHC)
1 Dogwood, Park Forest 60466; 747-3040
Rabbi Minard Klein

Sisterhood, men's club, couples club, youth group, chavurot, gift shop, library, funeral package, about 200 families.

Beth Sholom Ahavas Achim (O)
5665 N. Jersey, 60659; 267-9055
Rabbi Victor Amster

Congregation traces its history back to Lawndale (15th and Drake), and even earlier to the "East Side," a term that refers to the neighborhood of the earlier Jewish settlement encompassing Maxwell Street. At present address since late 1950s. Sisterhood, men's club, daily services. The synagogue is used by other groups, especially as the main location for Yeshiva Migdal Torah.

Beth Sholom of Rogers Park (T) (CTOC)
1233 W. Pratt, 60626; 743-4160
Rabbi Haskell Wachsmann

Founded in 1938. Both religious school and High Holiday seats are open to nonmembers. Daily services, sisterhood, men's club. Senior adults from the Council for Jewish Elderly use building. Welcomes nonmember bar/bat mitzvah. Separate seating for men and women during High Holidays only. Membership is about 200.

Beth Tikvah (R) (UAHC)
300 Hillcrest Blvd., Hoffman Estates 60195; 885-4545
Rabbi Hillel Gamoran

Founded in 1957, Beth Tikvah is the pioneer congregation in the far northwest suburbs. Sisterhood, men's club, couples club, two singles groups, two youth groups (for teens and tweens), gift shop, funeral plan. Location of an Early Childhood Center (preschool) run by the Board of Jewish Education. Membership, 330 families.

B'nai Chai (R)
c/o Ruth Factor, 272-7260
Rabbi Robert Goodman

Founded in 1977, this unique congregation has reached its membership quota of 25 families, and there's a waiting list! BC meets in homes and provides services, adult education including Hebrew instruction, and an adult bar mitzvah class. Focus is entirely on adults. None of the members have young children, but teenage and older children are welcome to attend services. Members are from north and northwest suburbs.

B'nai David Shaare Zedek (C) (US)
2626 W. Foster, 60625; 561-9895
Cantor Moses Rontal

In 1977, when its synagogue was sold and demolished, Logan Square Shaare Zedek joined B'nai David on Foster. LSSZ was the first (ca. 1917) and last Jewish congregation in the Logan Square area. B'nai David's history is even longer, going back to the turn of the century when several Hungarian and Russian groups on the old Northwest

Side joined together. Later B'nai David Ohave Zedek synagogue was known as the Humboldt Boulevard Temple. Sisterhood, men's club, gift shop.

B'nai Emunah (C) (US)
9131 Niles Center Rd., Skokie 60076; 674-9292 or 267-5685
Rabbi Harold I. Stern

The striking mosaic on the synagogue facade is by I. Avret of Safed. Founded in 1954, there are now about 800 families in the congregation. Sisterhood, men's club, youth group, seniors, gift shop, daily services. Religious school is open to nonmembers. Has an alternative minyan in lower social hall—more traditional, but maintains mixed seating.

B'nai Israel (I)
601 Skokie Blvd., Northbrook 60062; 480-0092
Rabbi Gerry J. Rosenberg

Services are held weekly in the Sager Solomon Schechter School.

Temple B'nai Israel (C)
400 N. Edgelawn Dr., Aurora 60506; 892-2450
Rabbi Hyman Agress

Aurora's only synagogue is also the center of Jewish life in that city. The Women's Federation includes a sisterhood, Hadassah, and National Council of Jewish Women. The Aurora B'nai B'rith Lodge sponsors a BBYO group there for high school age youths. Younger children in the congregation are members of Hashachar, sponsored by Hadassah. Synagogue windows were designed by Todros Geller. On the bimah is a beautiful wooden *tik*—a Sephardic-style mounted Torah case and stand. The congregation was originally founded in 1904 as the YMHA Temple. Today there are about 150 member families.

B'nai Israel of Proviso (T)
10216 Kitchener St., Westchester 60153; 343-0288
Rabbi Louis H. Lieberworth

B'nai Israel of Proviso was founded about 1910 in Maywood, an outpost of the Jewish community at that time. For over 50 years the synagogue served its congregation on 13th Avenue in that suburb. In 1962, BIP moved to Westchester. The school closed in 1980. Sixty active families in the congregation receive support from others who have moved away. Very active sisterhood, gift shop, library, adult education. High Holiday seats are available to nonmembers.

B'nai Jacob of West Rogers Park (C)
6200 N. Artesian, 60659; 274-1586
Rabbi Elliot J. Einhorn

Founded in 1944. Auxiliaries, gift shop, daily services. No religious school. The few children are placed in other schools. Nonmembers may purchase High Holiday seats. Membership, 230 families.

B'nai Jehoshua Beth Elohim (R) (UAHC)
901 Milwaukee Ave., Glenview 60025; 729-7575
Rabbi Mark S. Shapiro

B'nai Jehoshua was founded in 1893 by Bohemian Jews in a largely Bohemian neighborhood. For 70 years, BJ remained at 20th and South Ashland, with ties to both Chicago's Jewish and Bohemian communities. In the middle 1960s, BJ joined newly formed Beth Elohim of Morton Grove. Together they moved to Glenview to become that community's first Jewish congregation. A chandelier and a piece of stained-glass window from the old synagogue hang in the present building. The sisterhood was 85 years old in 1980. BJBE also has youth groups, a men's club, chavurot, a gift shop, an optional funeral plan, and a bereavement support group. High Holiday seats are sold to nonmembers. Membership totals 700 families. A quota for families with school-age children may be in effect.

B'nai Shalom Traditional (T) (CTOC)
P.O. Box 173, Wheeling 60090; 541-1460

Founded in 1977, BST now has over 100 families, primarily from Wheeling, Arlington Heights, Palatine, Des Plaines, Northbrook. The congregation holds services at the Alcott School in Buffalo Grove. School-age children attend the Buffalo Grove Community Hebrew School of the Associated Talmud Torahs. There are a sisterhood, men's club, and youth group. All of this, plus High Holiday tickets for members only, comes with membership, perhaps at the lowest cost available in the metropolitan area—$150 per family.

B'nai Tikvah (C) (US)
795 Wilmot Rd., Deerfield 60015; 945-0470
Rabbi Reuven Frankel

Founded in 1976, BT now has about 275 families. In 1980, a new library was dedicated and the first annual book fair was held. The Tallis and Tefillin Club is for fathers and their sons age 12 and older. The hanging appliqué of Jerusalem is by Abby Block. Sisterhood, youth group, gift shop, United Synagogue funeral plan. Nursery school on premises is an Early Childhood Center of the Board of Jewish Education.

B'nai Torah (R)
2789 Oak St., Highland Park 60035; 433-7100
Rabbi Sholom A. Singer

This modern lakefront synagogue was built in the 1960s. Sisterhood, men's club, youth group, museum, gift shop, and an autonomous nursery school, the Abe and Sadie Becker Nursery School of B'nai Torah Temple. Noteworthy funeral plan offers members free funerals in the synagogue, paid for by the congregation. Founded in 1954, the congregation has reached its maximum quota of 650 members. There is a waiting list.

Temple B'nai Yehuda (R) (UAHC)
1424 W. 183d St., Homewood 60430; 799-4110
Rabbi Leo R. Wolkow

B'nai Yehuda was founded in 1944 by German Jews who had escaped Hitler. Originally the congregation was in Hyde Park, as the Hyde Park Liberal Congregation; later, in South Shore at 82d and Jeffery. By 1970, with only 30 families remaining in the area, BY decided to relocate in Homewood. Today, there are about 200 members. Sisterhood (founded in 1944), gift shop, youth group. An annual bazaar is sponsored by the sisterhood.

B'nai Zion (C) (US)
6759 N. Greenview, 60626; 465-2161
Rabbi Haim Kemelman

BZ officially dates its origin to 1919 and Rabbi Abraham Lassen. But records and a former neighbor's recollection indicate that the congregation may have been founded between 1916 and 1918 by Rabbi David Almond. Sisterhood, business and professional women's club, men's club, library, gift shop, daily services, no religious school. Programming for Soviet Jews, including English lessons, sponsored by the JCC. High Holiday seats available to nonmembers; tickets given to Soviet Jews. Much Yiddish-oriented programming. Synagogue is used by Minyan Sheni for alternative services each Saturday.

B'nei Ruven (O)
6350 N. Whipple, 60659; 743-5434
Rabbi Harold Shusterman

Part of the Lubavitch Chassidic Movement, BR celebrates its 85th anniversary in 1981. Daily services, sisterhood, men's club, youth group, singles. Young People's Minyan, formed in 1979, brings 150 to

200 each Shabbat. Rabbi may accept nonmembers for bar mitzvah. High Holiday seats available to nonmembers. Second minyan on High Holidays focuses on youth.

Central Synagogue of South Side Hebrew Congregation (C) (US)
30 E. Cedar, 60611; 787-0450
Rabbi Irving A. Weingart

Founded before the turn of the century, SSHC's last South Side synagogue was at 74th and Chappel in South Shore. Today the congregation occupies a charming and elegant Gold Coast townhouse. Sisterhood, men's club, discussion group, gift shop.

Temple Chai (R) (UAHC)
Rt. 1, Box 271, Long Grove 60047; 537-1771
Synagogue location: Checker Road west of Arlington Heights Road, Long Grove
Rabbi Floyd Herman

New synagogue structure. Outstanding learning-disabilities program in religious school. Sisterhood, men's club in formation, youth group, new chavurah program. Membership close to 300 families. Choir open to new members.

Chesed L'Avrohom Nachlas David (O)
3135 W. Devon, 60659; 743-2156
Rabbi Yehoshua H. Eichenstein

Rabbi lives near this small synagogue. Behind the synagogue is a mikvah for men only. Daily services.

Chevro Kadisho Machzikai Hadas (O)
2040 W. Devon Ave., 60659; 764-8760
Rabbi Yehuda D. Goldman

Rabbi Goldman is director of the Merkaz Harabonim—the Chicago Orthodox Rabbinate. Daily services.

Chicago Loop Synagogue (O) (CTOS)
16 S. Clark, 60603; 346-7370
Rabbi Stanley E. Kroll

Founded in the 1920s to serve the needs of transients in the Loop, this synagogue originally held services in the old Hotel Morrison. The building is an art and architectural treasure worth a visit. Daily morning, afternoon, and late afternoon services and a 12:30 P.M. Bible class. Saturday services are at 9 A.M., 4:30 and 5:30 P.M.; Sunday, at 9:30 A.M., 4:30 and 4:45 P.M. Holds various other classes and special scheduled events. For group tours, write in advance for permission to visit. Individuals are welcome at all times. CLS sells seats for the High Holidays.

Chicago Sinai Congregation (R) (UAHC)
5350 S. South Shore Dr., 60615; 288-1600

Founded in 1861 as Chicago's first Reform congregation, Sinai has remained true to the principles of classical Reform Judaism. Sisterhood, men's club, couples club, youth group, singles, nursery school, library, congregational archives on display, gift shop. Services held Fridays, Saturdays, and Sundays. Congregational staff includes a program coordinator for adult education. Many lectures, programs, and meetings are held in the congregational suite in McClurg Court Center, 600 McClurg Court. Membership is nearly 900 families.

Emanuel Congregation (R) (UAHC)
5959 N. Sheridan Rd., 60660; 561-5173
Rabbi Herman Schaalman

Founded in 1880 as a German-speaking Orthodox congregation, Emanuel quickly adopted liberal practices. Moved to its Edgewater lakefront location in the middle 1950s. The sisterhood, known originally as Gemeinde Frauen Verein, was founded in 1897; changed its name to "Sisterhood" in 1910. Men's club, youth group, single-parents group, seniors program. Library, active social-action committee, significant windows and sculpture. Membership over 900 families.

Etz Chaim (R) (UAHC)
1710 S. Highland, Lombard 60148; 627-3912
Rabbi Bernard J. Robinson

Founded in 1960; currently has 225 families. Sisterhood, men's club, junior and senior youth group, two singles groups in association with Oak Park Temple. Library, gift shop. High Holiday seats for sale to nonmembers.

Ezra-Habonim (C) (US)
2620 W. Touhy, 60645; 743-0154
Rabbi Shlomo D. Levine

Both Ezra and Habonim were congregations founded by refugees from Hitler's Germany. Merger took place in 1973. Ezra-Habonim was the first congregation to write a mandatory observance of Crystal Night into its bylaws. Sisterhood, men's club, gift shop. Artifacts on display, including a parochet from Bad Kissingen dated 1745, were salvaged from the Holocaust. EH Hyde Park branch provides South Side members with convenient Friday evening services in Hyde Park;

but this group is growing smaller each year, and its future is questionable. EH congregation in Northbrook, which was originally sponsored by the parent congregation, now operates autonomously.

Ezra Habonim of Northbrook (C) (US)
2095 Landwehr Rd., Northbrook 60062; 480-1690
Rabbi Shlomo D. Levine

Synagogue dedicated on June 1, 1980. Congregation is incorporated separately from Ezra Habonim of Chicago. Some founding members have family associations with the older congregation. The Northbrook EH was founded in 1977.

Ezras Israel (T) (CTOC)
7001 N. California, 60645; 764-8320
Rabbi Benzion C. Kaganoff

Ezras Israel was founded in the 1890s on the Northwest Side. It has been called the largest Traditional synagogue in the Midwest. Congregation publishes annual Memorial book for Yom Kippur that is really an anthology of original essays, inspirational and reminiscent. Impressive mural by Nota Koslowsky. Daily services, sisterhood, gift shop, couples club, youth group, singles.

Garfield Ridge Hebrew Congregation (T)
6524 W. Archer, 60638; 586-7108

Independent Temple (O)
355 Bellaire Dr., Des Plaines 60016; 296-5641
Rabbi Dov Schwarcz

Iran Hebrew Congregation (O) (CTOC)
3820 Main, Skokie 60076; 674-5444
Rabbi Nathan I. Weiss

One of two Sephardic congregations in the area. Founded in 1910 by Jews from Iran. Today, membership totals about 100 families and is no longer restricted to members of Sephardic background. Current synagogue was built in 1960. Rabbi Weiss is also executive director of the Chicago Rabbinical Council. Sisterhood, men's club.

Temple Jeremiah (R) (UAHC)
937 Happ Rd., Northfield 60093; 441-5760
Rabbi Robert D. Schreibman

Founded in 1959 as a classical Reform congregation. In the past few years the congregation has more than doubled in size, topping 500 member families. A large proportion of new members are young parents of preschool and school-age children. Increasing religious and cultural options are available to the growing membership while maintaining a definite commitment to Reform Judaism. Women's association, youth group, chavurot, library, biennial tours to Israel. Twentieth anniversary tapestry on sanctuary north wall was designed by Russell Blanchard and sewn by members.

Jewish Reconstructionist Congregation (Rec) (FRCH)
2525 Hartrey, Evanston 60201; 328-7678
Rabbi Arnold Rachlis

Founded in late 1960s, now has 175 members. Creative services are offered most Friday nights, but members attend a home-held Shabbat dinner observance bimonthly. More traditional services are offered Saturday mornings. Some summer services are held at the beach. Congregation intends no separate men's or women's auxiliaries. The Chevra Committee provides one-to-one contact with each member of the congregation throughout the year. High Holiday tickets are available to nonmembers.

Joliet Jewish Congregation (C)
250 N. Midland, Joliet 60435; (815) 725-7078
Rabbi Morris Hershman

Congregation is served by the Board of Jewish Education but is outside the jurisdiction of most other Chicago metropolitan agencies. Joliet Jewish Congregation is the center of Jewish activities, including fund raising, in that community.

Temple Judea-Mizpah (R) (UAHC)
8610 Niles Center Rd., Skokie 60077; 676-1566
Rabbi Marc Berkson

In 1977, Temple Mizpah left the synagogue it had occupied for nearly 55 years on Morse Avenue in Rogers Park and joined Judea, which had been in Skokie since the 1950s. Judea, founded by the late Rabbi Karl Weiner, has no historic linkage with the congregation of the same name that once was Lawndale's only liberal Jewish congregation. Sisterhood, men's club, youth group, gift shop, library.

KAM-Isaiah Israel (R) (UAHC)
1100 E. Hyde Park Blvd., 60615; 924-1234
Rabbi Arnold J. Wolf

This congregation has so much history, it's hard to know where to begin, without having to begin again. KAM-Isaiah Israel is the amalgamation of the two oldest congregations—KAM, founded in 1847, and Isaiah Israel, founded as B'nai Sholom in 1851. Congregation archivist is Herbert Levy. Building has been designated an official landmark. Architecture, museum, archives, and rich history make this a place to visit. Men's club, sisterhood, chavurot, young-adult group, youth group, library, gift shop. The Hyde Park Chamber Orchestra performs there. Location for the Hyde Park JCC.

KINS of West Rogers Park (T) (CTOC)
2800 W. North Shore, 60645; 761-4000
Rabbi Moses Mesheloff

Initials stand for *K*neses *I*srael *N*usach *S*fard, the latter two words indicating the use of a liturgy that incorporates some of the Eastern Sephardic ritual into the Ashkenazic service. This Nusach Sfard rite is used for the weekday minyan. Traditional Ashkenazic service is provided on Shabbat. Congregation was founded in 1921 through consolidation of three smaller congregations. The former synagogue still stands on Independence Blvd. in Lawndale.

Sisterhood, men's club, youth group, singles, library, nursery school, gift shop. Sponsor of neighborhood annual Purim Parade. Location for an alternative minyan. High Holiday services and religious school open to nonmembers. Free school for 5- and 6-year-olds.

Kehilat Jeshurun (C)
3707 W. Ainslie, 60625; 539-7776 or 539-7777
Rabbi Ephraim H. Prombaum

The only Conservative congregation remaining in Albany Park, Kehilat Jeshurun was founded in 1939 as Orthodox but became Conservative in 1948. Sisterhood. Daily services.

Kehilath Jacob Beth Samuel (O) (CTOC)
3701 W. Devon, 60659; 539-7779
Rabbi Jack D. Frank

This congregation bears the name of the great Drohitchin synagogue Kehilath Jacob, which stood at Hamlin and Douglas on the West Side. Auxiliaries and a teen minyan meet regularly. Daily minyan.

Kneseth Israel (C)
330 Division, Elgin 60120; 741-5656
Rabbi Arthur Gould

This is the historic congregation of Elgin. The religious school is affiliated with the Board of Jewish Education. Sisterhood and gift shop.

Kol Ami-The Near North Temple (R) (UAHC)
233 E. Erie, 60611; 644-6900
Rabbi Arnold G. Kaiman

Services are held at the Water Tower Hyatt House. The congregation is an outgrowth of South Shore Temple. The congregation still uses the Ark from 7215 S. Jeffery, designed by Milton Horn. Auxiliaries.

Kol Emeth (C) (US)
5130 W. Touhy, Skokie 60077; 673-3370
Rabbi Bernard A. Mussman

Sisterhood, men's club, gift shop, annual auction. Founded in 1967.

Lake Shore Drive Synagogue (T)
70 E. Elm, 60611; 337-6811

Lakeside Congregation for Reform Judaism (R) (UAHC)
1221 County Line Rd., Highland Park 60035; 432-7950
Rabbi Harold S. Jaye

Founded in 1955 in an attempt to maintain and perpetuate classical Reform Judaism. In the early days, the congregation was identified closely with the American Council for Judaism. Women's association, social club. The congregation has an award-winning modern synagogue structure.

Lawn Manor–Beth Jacob (C) (US)
6601 S. Kedzie, 60629; 476-2924
Rabbi Abraham Garamaize

In 1974, Beth Jacob of Scottsdale congregation merged with Lawn Manor Hebrew Congregation to become the last full-service congregation on the southwest side within the city limits. Sisterhood and gift shop.

Lev Someach (O)
5555 N. Bernard, 60625; 267-4390
Rabbi Eshia H. Twersky

Daily minyan. Sisterhood. Has sponsored tours to Israel.

Lincolnwood Jewish Congregation (O) (CTOC)
7117 N. Crawford, Lincolnwood 60646; 676-0491
Rabbi Joel Lehrfield

Founded in 1958 as the first congregation in Lincolnwood. Daily services, sisterhood, men's club, youth group, library, gift shop.

Maine Township Jewish Congregation (C) (US)
8800 Ballard Rd., Des Plaines 60016; 297-2006 or 694-4477
Rabbi Jay Karzen

Founded in 1963 with ten families, MTJC was the first Jewish congregation in Des Plaines. Sisterhood, men's club, youth group and lounge, gift shop, daily services, preschool. Membership is currently 575 families.

McHenry County Jewish Congregation (US)
c/o Mr. and Mrs. Harvey Schneider, (815) 338-1278

This congregation, founded in 1979, is based in Woodstock, where services are held at the Congregational Universalist Church. Members, however, come from other communities in the county as well. Although the synagogue is affiliated with the Conservative movement, the religious school is run by the Associated Talmud Torahs. Weekly Friday night services. Student rabbis have assisted for the High Holidays.

Temple Menorah Congregation (R) (UAHC)
2800 W. Sherwin, 60645; 761-5700
Rabbi Joseph M. Strauss

Founded in 1946 as the first Reform congregation to be formed in Chicago in 25 years. Utilized portions of a World War II army chapel in the construction of the sanctuary. Children attend the Beth Israel Menorah School, 3939 W. Howard, Skokie, administered by Beth Israel congregation. Sisterhood, men's club, couples club, library, gift shop. High Holiday seats available to nonmembers. About 300 families in the congregation.

Mikdosh El Hagro Hebrew Center (C) (US)
303 Dodge, Evanston 60202; 328-9677
Rabbi Mayer Gruber

Both the religious school and High Holiday seats are available to nonmembers. Auxiliaries, gift shop, daily services.

Mikro Kodesh Anshe Tikton Ravenswood Budlong Congregation (O) (CTOC)
2832 W. Foster, 60625; 784-1010
Rabbi Irving Miller

Daily services, sisterhood, gift shop.

Mishne Ugmoro (O)
6045 N. California, 60659; 465-1433
Rabbi Israel Karno

Founded in 1890 in the Maxwell Street area. Fifty years ago, this congregation had the reputation of being the most strictly Orthodox in the entire country. Daily services.

Moriah (C) (US)
200 Hyacinth Lane, Deerfield 60015; 948-5340
Rabbi Samuel Dresner

A young congregation, founded in 1977, with great emphasis on adult and family education. Occupies a former public elementary school where the gym has been miraculously transformed into a beautiful sanctuary. Chavurot program; sponsors Saturday evening cultural events. Also has sponsored several visits by Elie Weisel in cooperation with Loyola University Institute of Pastoral Studies.

Mount Sinai (O)
4710 N. Kedzie, 60625; 478-8545
Evening minyan.

Ner Tamid Congregation of North Town (C) (US)
2754 W. Rosemont, 60659; 465-6090
Rabbi Samuel Klein

Sisterhood, men's club, gift shop, project for visually handicapped, library. Organized volunteer corps assists elderly through programs of the Council for Jewish Elderly. Daily services. The location of the Egalitarian Minyan.

Niles Township Jewish Congregation (Rec) (US) (FRCH)
4500 Dempster, Skokie 60076; 675-4141
Rabbi Neil Brief

Congregation and youth group are members of Conservative United Synagogue; the congregation also is a member of the Reconstructionist movement; and the ritual followed is Reconstructionist. Sisterhood, men's club, youth groups, chavurot, library, museum, daily services, gift shop, nursery school. Membership is at 700. Founded in 1952 with 40 families, NTJC was the first Jewish congregation in Skokie.

North Sheridan Hebrew Congregation Adath Israel
6301 N. Sheridan Rd., 60660; 262-0330
Rabbi Morris Gutstein

Although located in the Shoreline Towers Condominium, this congregation holds High Holiday services and major events at the Sovereign Hotel.

North Shore Congregation Israel (R) (UAHC)
1185 Sheridan Rd., Glencoe 60022; 835-0724
Rabbi Herbert Bronstein

Founded in 1920 as the North Shore branch of Chicago Sinai Congregation, this was the pioneer congregation on the North Shore and the only Jewish congregation between Chicago and Waukegan until the 1940s. Sisterhood, men's club, youth group, senior adults, library, rotating art exhibits, gift shop. During the summer months, late afternoon Kabbalah Shabbat services to welcome the Sabbath are held on a terrace in a parklike setting. Membership, about 1,400 families.

North Suburban Synagogue Beth El (C) (US)
1175 Sheridan Rd., Highland Park 60035; 432-8900
Rabbi William H. Lebeau

Founded in the late 1940s to serve the needs of Conservative Jews on the North Shore. Synagogue, designed by Percival Goodman, incorporates the original mansion on its lakefront site. Sisterhood, men's club, couples club, youth group, daily services, gift shop, preschool. Nonmember children may attend religious school. Kol Ami Museum features rotating exhibits of Jewish interest.

Northwest Suburban Jewish Congregation (C) (US)
7800 Lyons, Morton Grove 60053; 965-0900
Rabbi Lawrence H. Charney

Sisterhood, men's club, singles, youth activities, seniors, gift shop, preschool, daily services.

Nusach Arie of Albany Park (O)
4706 N. Monticello, 60625; 588-9520

One of the remaining Albany Park congregations, Nusach Arie has a mikvah for men only. Daily services.

Oak Park Temple (R) (UAHC)
1235 N. Harlem, Oak Park 60302; 386-3937
Rabbi Gary S. Gerson

Oak Park Temple—really B'nai Abraham Zion—traces its origins back to Temple Zion, founded in 1864 as the first West Side congregation, the classical Reform congregation of Rabbi Bernhard Felsenthal, and B'nai Abraham, a Bohemian congregation founded about 1870, the first to be founded in the Maxwell Street area. Following their merger in 1919, their synagogue became known as the Washington Blvd. Temple. Moved to Oak Park in the 1950s. Sisterhood, men's club, youth group, singles groups, gift shop.

Oir-Israel (O)
4610 N. Kedzie Ave., 60625; 463-9325
Rabbi Joshua Goodman

Daily services.

Or Chadash
656 W. Barry, 60657; 248-9456

This is Chicago's congregation of and for gay and lesbian Jews. Services are held every second and fourth Friday at 8:30 P.M. at the Second Unitarian Church. The congregation offers services and/or parties on all Jewish holidays, full High Holiday services, a Passover seder, and adult education.

Or Chadash Traditional Congregation (T) (CTOC)
664 S. Roselle Rd., Schaumburg 60172; 529-6390
Rabbi Michael Myers

Closely allied with the Woodfield Community Hebrew School of the Associated Talmud Torahs. Founded in 1975 as a supportive, affiliated congregation, Or Chadash shares the site with the Hebrew school. Active youth group, gift shop.

Or Shalom (R) (UAHC)
P.O. Box 773, Libertyville 60048; 680-9696
Rabbi David Spitz

Founded in 1978, this new congregation currently meets at the First Presbyterian Church of Libertyville, Maple and Douglas avenues. The central focus of the congregation is the religious school. High Holiday services are held at Legion Hall, Grayslake Park District, and tickets are available to nonmembers. Membership—now numbering about 100 families—is primarily drawn from Libertyville, Mundelein, and Vernon Hills.

Or Torah (O) (CTOC)
3738 Dempster, Skokie 60076; 679-9333
Rabbi Irwin R. Pollock

A remarkable congregation of young adults with young children operating in a "storefront" synagogue that bulges at the seams. Founded in 1970, in a break from an older, established traditional congregation, Or Torah effuses with its youth and its fervent individual commitment to traditional Judaism. Weekly crowds are estimated at between 100 and 200 congregants who come to celebrate Shabbat together. Daily services.

Park Synagogue Shaare Shalom (O)
505 N. Michigan, 60611; 467-5928
Rabbi Alvin I. Kleinerman

The hotel name has changed at least twice—now it's the Radisson Chicago. In 1964 when the sanctuary was installed on the 16th floor, it was the Sheraton-Chicago Hotel. The sanctuary, designed by Bernheim and Kahn, was called the Synagogue in the Sky, and Richard Tucker sang for the dedication. Sisterhood, gift shop.

Poalie Zedek (O)
2801 W. Albion, 60645; 764-5680
Rabbi Michael Small

Daily services.

Rodfei Zedek (C) (US)
5200 S. Hyde Park Blvd., 60615; 752-2770
Rabbi Ralph Simon

On April 27, 1975, RZ held its 100th annual meeting. An excellent history of the congregation, *Rodfei Zedek, the First Hundred Years*, written in honor of the occasion by Carole Krucoff, is available from RZ ($7.50 hardcover; $4.50 soft cover; plus 50¢ mailing). Sisterhood, men's club, youth group, gift shop, library, active chavurah program. Daily services. Site of Akiba-Schechter Jewish Day School. Special program for the blind.

Sephardic Congregation (O)
1819 W. Howard, Evanston 60202; 475-9287
Rabbi Michael Azose

Officially named the Israelite Portuguese Fraternity, this is one of two Sephardic congregations in Chicago. Both follow the Eastern Sephardic rite. Membership here is limited to Sephardic Jews or their spouses. The congregation has members from many North African countries as well as from other nations. Many different languages are spoken by congregants. The ten-year-old synagogue was designed by Aaron Daniel, brother of the current president.

Shaare Tikvah (C) (US)
5800 N. Kimball, 60659; 539-2202
Rabbi Howard A. Addison

During 1980, this congregation absorbed the Albany Park Hebrew Congregation when the latter's synagogue was sold to a Korean church group. Sisterhood, men's club, gift shop.

Shaarei Torah Anshei Maariv (O)
2756 W. Morse, 60645; 262-0430
Rabbi Benzion Rosenthal

Daily services.

Temple Sholom (R) (UAHC)
3480 N. Lake Shore Dr., 60657; 525-4707
Rabbi Frederick C. Schwartz

Originally the North Chicago Hebrew Congregation, founded in 1867, this was the pioneer congregation on the North Side. Today Sholom is the largest congregation in the Chicago area, with close to 2,000 families. Absorbed Beth Am of South Shore in 1970s. Sisterhood; men's club; also groups for youths, senior adults, single parents, singles, business and professional women; drop-in center for Soviet Jews; gift shop. Weekday services at 5:45 P.M.

Sinai of Rogers Park (O)
6905 N. Sheridan Rd., 60626; 764-0042
Rabbi E. M. Romirowsky

Founded in the early 1940s, when this congregation bought the house it occupies: a small single-family home on the east side of Sheridan Road dwarfed by the surrounding high-rise apartment buildings. Daily services.

Skokie Central Traditional Congregation (T) (CTOC)
4040 Main, Skokie 60076; 674-4117
Rabbi Lawrence Montrose

Sisterhood, men's club, youth group, gift shop, daily services.

Skokie Valley Traditional Synagogue (T) (CTOC)
8825 E. Prairie Rd., Skokie 60076; 574-3473
Rabbi Milton Kanter

Sisterhood, men's club, youth group, gift shop, daily services.

Solel (R) (UAHC)
1301 Clavey Rd., Highland Park 60035; 433-3555
Rabbi Robert J. Marx

Founded in 1957, this congregation had roots in a Jewish study group and ties to KAM Congregation on Chicago's South Side. Lay participation has always been strong in this congregation. A lay-run Saturday afternoon Torah school, for family members of all ages, is open to nonmembers. Strong interest in social action. Library, funeral plan. Choir open to nonmembers. Membership quota is filled. There are membership waiting lists.

Tifereth Moshe (O)
6308 N. Francisco, 60659; 764-5322
Rabbi Chaim Goldzweig

Small synagogue on premises of Rabbi Goldzweig's home.

Warsaw Bickur Cholim (O)
3541 W. Peterson, 60659; 588-0021

One of the Lubavitch Chassidic congregations of Chicago.

West Suburban Temple Har Zion (C) (US)
1040 N. Harlem, River Forest 60305; 366-9000
Rabbi Joseph Tabachnik

One of several congregations built in the west suburbs in the 1950s in anticipation of a large movement of Jews to those communities—a movement that never fully occurred. Only about 1 percent of River Forest's population is Jewish. An impressive synagogue designed by

Richard Bennett, spectacular stained-glass windows by William Gropper, exterior and interior sculpture by Milton Horn—this is a place to visit. Sisterhood, library, and preschool.

Yehuda Moshe (O) (CTOC)
4721 W. Touhy, Lincolnwood 60646; 673-5870
Rabbi Oscar Z. Fasman
Daily services. Sisterhood has its own mikvah.

Young Israel of Chicago (O)
4931 N. Kimball, 60625; 463-5298
Rabbi David Farkas

Chicago's only local branch of the Young Israel Movement, which recently celebrated its 50th anniversary. This synagogue has been used for some programs of the Hamasmid Institute. Shabbat and High Holiday services only.

Northwest Indiana

This area is often regarded, especially by those living there, as a part of the Chicago community. Actually, some of the organizations that serve the Chicago metropolitan area, like the Board of Jewish Education, also serve Northwest Indiana. Following are congregations that form the base of the Jewish community of Northwest Indiana:

Beth-El (Reform)
6947 Hohman Ave., Hammond 46324; (219) 932-3754

Beth Israel (Conservative)
7105 Hohman, Hammond 46324; (219) 931-1312

B'nai Judah
1545 Davis, Whiting 46394; (219) 659-1304

B'nai Shalom (Conservative)
4508 Baring, East Chicago 46312; (219) 397-3106

Israel (Reform)
601 N. Montgomery, Gary 46403; (219) 938-5232

Israel (Reform)
22 N. Washington St., Valparaiso 46383

Sinai (Reform)
2800 S. Franklin St., Michigan City 46360; (219) 874-4477

Additional Religious Services

Regular religious services are held at the Hillels of Northwestern University, Evanston, and the University of Chicago during the school year. The Agudath Israel Center holds Shabbat services. A daily minyan is held at the three Orthodox rabbinical seminaries, Sundays through Fridays, and at the Arie Crown Hebrew Day School in Skokie. A daily minyan is held Mondays through Fridays at the Ida Crown Jewish Academy.

The Chavurah and the Alternative Minyan

In their search for meaning and personal involvement, some Jews, particularly young adults, are forming chavurot (plural) and alternative minyanim. The chavurah (singular) is a friendship circle usually involving a variety of Jewish activities that may include religious worship. The alternative minyan is organized primarily for worship.

Am Chai
P.O. Box 60142, 60660

Part of the Am Chai–Chutzpah network, involved in shared Shabbat dinners/worship as well as Israeli folk dancing, Yiddish play reading, and singing.

Beth Am Congregation
c/o 2005 Kiowa Lane, Mt. Prospect 60056; 827-7599 or 541-3255

New congregation with about 50 members, based on the concept of chavurah. Most activities of the congregation function through three chavurot.

Chavurah Chai
c/o Young Leadership Division of JUF
1 S. Franklin, 60606; 346-6700

A chavurah that was the outgrowth of a mission sponsored by JUF and the product of many months of learning together in preparation.

Rogers Park JCC
7101 N. Greenview, 60626; 274-0920

Two chavurot have come from this JCC: one from a Jewish philosophy class that evolved into a continuing chavurah; and the other, a Russian-American chavurah with about equal numbers of Soviet newcomers and residents of Chicago and the North Shore.

Many congregations have chavurot; among others are Temple Beth El, Temple Chai, Temple Jeremiah, Moriah, and Rodfei Zedek congregations. The bimonthly Shabbat observance in members' homes sponsored by the Jewish Reconstructionist Congregation also achieves a sense of chavurah.

Upstairs Minyan
Hillel–University of Chicago
5715 S. Woodlawn Ave., 60637; 752-1127

This has been called the first of its kind in the country. Still continuing after a decade, the Upstairs Minyan is an egalitarian community of students, faculty, children, and nonuniversity neighbors who meet every Saturday morning for worship and discussion. The UM also holds large High Holiday services on campus. The UM has been a model for and an influence on the formation of similar minyanim in Chicago and elsewhere.

The following alternative minyanim are listed by the name of the synagogue where they meet. Usually no more than a few of the members, if any at all, are members of the host congregation. Whatever the format of the worship, whether Orthodox or egalitarian, traditional or experimental, they all give participants a sense of personal involvement. They are all lay led. (Some congregations provide their own members with opportunities for alternatives in worship. Several Traditional congregations, for example, though they have mixed seating for men and women, offer members an optional service elsewhere in the synagogue that separates the sexes.)

Anshe Emet
3760 N. Pine Grove Ave., 60613; 281-1423

Single and married young adults meet biweekly on Friday evenings for a traditional Conservative minyan.

Beth Emet The Free Synagogue
1224 Dempster, Evanston 60202; 869-4230

Meets downstairs, 9:30 A.M. Saturdays.

Beth Israel
3939 W. Howard, Skokie 60076; 588-0915

A lay-led, Saturday morning service is held at the Beth Israel–Menorah branch school.

B'nai Emunah
9131 Niles Center Rd., Skokie 60076; 674-9292

A nonmember minyan, more traditional than the regular services in this Conservative congregation, takes place in the lower social hall.

B'nai Zion
6759 N. Greenview, 60626; 465-2161

Minyan Sheni is a group of young adults who meet at 10 A.M. Saturdays in the school building of B'nai Zion at 1447 W. Pratt. Their own flyer says, "We are open to all our traditions—to Hasidism and also secular Yiddishism, Jewish political activism along with historical and textual scholarship. We encourage everyone to participate, whether by leading services, guiding a Torah discussion, or hosting a meal. . . . Children and new ideas are welcome." For information call 761-6839 or 743-7945.

B'nei Ruven
6350 N. Whipple, 60659; 743-5434

The Young People's Minyan, formed in 1979, involves 150 to 200 each Shabbat, usually starting at 9:15 A.M.

KINS of West Rogers Park
2800 W. North Shore, 60645; 761-4000

Young-adult minyan in the chapel follows Orthodox separation of sexes.

Ner Tamid Congregation of North Town
2754 W. Rosemont, 60659; 465-6090

The Egalitarian Minyan meets at 9:30 A.M. Saturdays and has a shared Friday night dinner on occasion. Newcomers are welcome.

Chaplaincy Services

Chaplaincy Commission
Chicago Board of Rabbis
72 E. 11th St., 60605; 427-5863

Rabbi Ephraim Prombaum, Senior Chaplain

Founded in 1938 by Rabbi Irving Melamed, the Chaplaincy Commission of the Chicago Board of Rabbis is the central agency providing chaplains and chaplaincy services to civilian institutions. (Although some of the chaplains serving military bases are civilians, they are under the aegis of the military or the Veterans Administration and are listed in the section on the Armed Forces in Chapter 10, "Social and Political Concerns.") Regular rabbinical chaplaincy service is provided at the following Chicago-area institutions:

Billings Hospital, University of Chicago
Chicago-Read Mental Health Center
   Rabbi Morris Fishman, Chaplain
   Rabbi Harry Shapiro, Jewish Chaplain
Columbus Hospital
Cook County Jail and the Metropolitan Correction Center

Drexel Home
Loyola Medical Center
Lutheran General Hospital
   Rabbi Norman Berlat, Chaplain
Michael Reese Hospital and Medical Center
Mount Sinai Hospital Medical Center
Park View Home
Rush-Presbyterian St. Lukes Hospital
Stateville-Joliet prisons

The Chaplaincy Commission is on call for many other institutions as well, including, for example, Northwestern University hospitals and Cook County Hospital.

Conversion

Persons who are interested in exploring conversion to Judaism but do not know a rabbi may call the Chicago Board of Rabbis, 427-5863. Persons wanting an Orthodox conversion may contact the Chicago Rabbinical Council, 764-0259. A series of conversion classes, cosponsored by the Conservative and Reform movements, is held at Spertus College of Judaica for persons who have already undertaken the process of conversion with a rabbi.

Halacha (Jewish Religious Law)

Orthodox and Conservative branches of Judaism abide by Jewish Law. The following resources regarding Halacha and its specific applications are available to anyone.

Agudath Israel
539-4241 (between 7 and 9 P.M.)
Rabbi Shmuel Fuerst

Rabbi Fuerst will answer questions on Halacha throughout the year during the evening hours designated. Prior to and during Passover, calls will be received between 7 and 10 P.M.

Bet Din of the Chicago Region of the Rabbinical Assembly
Dr. David Graubart, Presiding Rabbi
5718 N. Drake, 60659

This is the court of arbitration for the Conservative movement in Chicago.

Beth Din Zedek, Jewish Ecclesiastical Court of the Orthodox Rabbinate
Chicago Rabbinical Council
2735 W. Devon, 60659; 764-0259

The Orthodox rabbinical court of arbitration, once housed in the Sherman Hotel.

Jewish Information Service
Hebrew Theological College
7135 N. Carpenter Rd., Skokie 60077; 677-9220

Answers either walk-in or telephone questions concerning Halacha and Jewish observance. Walk-in hours are 6 to 8:30 P.M. Sundays through Thursdays; 1 to 3:30 P.M. Wednesdays. Call the telephone number at any hour.

For information on kosher laws, call the Kashrut Hotline, 338-3764, a service of AFTA.

Holidays

High Holidays

The alphabetical listing of congregations above indicates those that sell seats for the High Holidays to nonmembers. Some additional opportunities for High Holiday observance:

Chicago Jewish Experience

Especially designed for young adults who do not as yet have the financial means to become affiliated with a synagogue. For information, call the United Synagogue of America, 939-2351; Union of American Hebrew Congregations, 782-1477; or the Jewish Federation of Metropolitan Chicago, 346-6700.

Sons of Joshua Congregation
Cantor Dale Lind
272-0252

Though not a congregation in the customary sense, Sons of Joshua, founded in 1971 in memory of Cantor Joshua Lind, holds annual High Holiday services at the Orrington Hotel, Evanston. Services are conducted primarily by Cantor Dale Lind, with a 23-voice choir under the direction of Dale's son Cary. In all, eight Lind family members participate. The services follow the Conservative prayer book.

Labor Zionist Alliance
973-3924

Holds annual High Holiday services.

Chicago Board of Rabbis
72 E. 11th St., 60605; 427-5863

Will assist newcomers in finding seats for the High Holidays.

■ **Michael Katz**
325 Prospect, Highland Park 60035; 432-3844
Will demonstrate and instruct persons in the art of shofar blowing.

Tashlich is the symbolic ceremony observed by traditional Jews in which one's sins are thrown off into a river or stream on Rosh Hashannah. Groups and individuals walk from services on the afternoon of the first day of Rosh Hashannah (unless that is on a Saturday, in which case Tashlich is observed on the afternoon of the second day) to the designated water. The ceremony takes place around 5 P.M. east of McCormick Blvd. near Dempster, Main, and Touhy. For more details, call the Chicago Rabbinical Council, 764-0259.

In Highland Park in the ravines on Woodpath Rd., at the end of Yom Kippur each year, a group of neighbors assembles to hear the blowing of a shofar. This custom began in 1974.

Chanukah

B'nai B'rith Hillel Foundation–University of Chicago
5715 S. Woodlawn, 60637; 752-1127
The Chanukah festival is annually ushered in with the erudite but delectable Latke vs. Hamentash Symposium, an interdisciplinary debate held since 1946 to argue the relative merits of the Chanukah potato pancake (Latke) versus the Purim triangular fruit-filled pastry (Hamentash). A similar mind-blowing dialogue is sponsored by the Hillel Foundation of Northwestern University at a different time of the year.

Young Leadership Division of Jewish United Fund
1 S. Franklin, 60606; 346-6700
An annual Hanukafest was introduced in 1980, filled with Yiddish folk music, Israeli dancing, multimedia presentations, and a traditional candlelighting ceremony. Festivities took place at Beth Hillel Congregation, Wilmette.

Zionist Organization of Chicago
6328 N. California Ave., 60659; 973-3232
ZOC's highlight of the year is the annual Chanukah festival featuring the Masada Pageant, gala dinner, and entertainment. The 44th annual festival will take place in 1981. Masada, the youth movement of the ZOC, sponsors a Chanukah torch relay with Jewish youth groups citywide. The torch, lit at the tomb of the Maccabees in Israel and

flown to the U.S. by El Al Airlines, is carried through various city and suburban communities.

Passover

Questions pertaining to Passover observance, particularly those concerned with dietary requirements or restrictions, can be referred to Rabbi Shmuel Fuerst, Agudath Israel; call 539-4241, between 7 and 10 P.M.

The kosher food stores, restaurants, and caterers listed in this book adhere to the requirements of Passover. Special food services are indicated. The largest food chains—Dominick's, Jewel, and Kohl's—carry Passover food products in areas where there are a number of Jewish customers. Some also give away Haggadahs and program Passover food demonstrations given by sisterhoods and other women's organizations.

Hillel Foundations are a good general resource for Passover. At the University of Chicago and Northwestern University, arrangements can be made for food service during Passover and for seder attendance. University of Illinois–Chicago Circle has a Pesach coffeehouse during the holiday. Limited amounts of matzo, shemurah matzo, and wine may be available.

Shemurah matzo is prepared by hand according to ritual recipe and procedure. Shemurah matzo is also available at some Chicago Jewish bookstores and by order from the Kosher Wine Corporation, 4751 N. St. Louis, 60625; 478-6869.

American Mizrachi Women
3018 W. Devon, 60659; 973-0688
Offers a kit for Beur Chometz—brushing away the chometz, or leavening crumbs. The kit includes instructions, a prayer, a feather for sweeping the chometz, and a candle. The envelope used to mail the kit becomes the receptacle for the ashes of the burned chometz. The kit is free; a donation is appreciated.

Chicago Action for Soviet Jewry
474 Central Ave., Highland Park 60035; 433-0144
Members receive a Haggadah Supplement, *Let My People Go*, for use in the family seder, which is dedicated to all Refuseniks and prisoners of conscience.

Chicago Rabbinical Council
2735 W. Devon Ave., 60659; 764-0259

Passover in the Jewish Home: Your Guide to a Meaningful and Enriching Passover Observance is published annually by the CRC. It is available through the CRC office or through local synagogues.

Jewish Community Centers
Many of the JCCs sponsor Passover workshops. The workshop at the Rogers Park JCC is planned for Soviet Jews and serves many as a first-time introduction to Passover observance.

Lubavitch Chabad of Greater Chicago
2014 Orrington, Evanston 60201; 869-8060

Publishes and distributes a booklet on the observances of the holiday. Also will assist persons in obtaining shemurah matzo.

Moes Chitim Committee of Greater Chicago
55 E. Washington St., Suite 1505, 60602; 463-4545

A direct-help organization with no agency subsidy. The address indicated here is simply the mailing address for inquiries and donations. Each year, Moes Chitim sets up a storefront operation (in 1980 a rented store in West Rogers Park), where basic provisions for a traditional Passover observance are packed for distribution in different neighborhoods to low-income Jewish households. In 1980, 1,400 households received food boxes containing matzoth, wine, fish, and chicken. Moes Chitim also provides supplemental food to Hillel houses in the area and sponsors seder dinners for newly arrived Soviet immigrants. Needy families may call the Ark (463-4545) to find out how to register for a food box.

Yeshivah Migdal Torah
583-9535

Has conducted spring holiday seminars on Passover and Purim observance. Call for information.

The Passover Seder

FREE (Friends of Refugees of Eastern Europe)
6418 N. Greenview, 60626; 274-5123

Has sponsored a seder on the first and second nights of Passover for newcomers from the Soviet Union. Held at the Associated Talmud Torahs building, 2828 W. Pratt.

Jewish Community Centers
Mayer Kaplan JCC and Bernard Horwich JCC have sponsored a community seder for members only.

Maine Township Jewish Congregation
8800 Ballard Rd., Des Plaines 60016; 297-2006

Although many congregations sponsor a seder on the second night of Passover, Maine Township Jewish Congregation holds a first-night seder, open to the public, catered by the Mayer Stiebel Organization.

Or Chadash Congregation
656 W. Barry, 60657; 248-9456

This congregation of Chicago's gay and lesbian Jewish community has sponsored an annual seder.

Super Singles Seder
c/o Sholom Singles
525-4707

An annual seder cosponsored by Sholom Singles and Menorah Pioneer Women—for singles.

Senior Adult Department Jewish Community Centers
3003 W. Touhy, 60645; 761-9100

Sponsors second-seder observances held in conjunction with the Council for Jewish Elderly, Union of American Hebrew Congregations, and United Synagogue of America. In 1980 they were held at two synagogues—Ner Tamid and B'nai Zion—but were conducted separately from the congregations' own second-night observances. Nonmember senior adults are also welcome at many congregations for seder dinner. Transportation from suburban areas can often be arranged.

Seder Placements

The Ark
3509 W. Lawrence, 60625; 463-4545

Refers area residents to a family or a communal seder within walking distance from home.

Henry N. Hart JCC
2961 W. Peterson, 60659; 275-8445

Arranges placement in a home seder for people age 60 and older who are alone.

Jewish Family and Community Service
1 S. Franklin, 60606; 346-6700

Places needy families in homes for the seder or gives them financial assistance for their own. Many served are Soviet immigrants.

Families wishing to invite persons to their home for a seder should contact the Ark, Henry Hart JCC, or the Jewish Family and Community Service.

Other Observances

Senior Adult Department Jewish Community Centers
3003 W. Touhy, 60645; 761-9100
Senior Adult clubs sponsor a third seder during the week of Passover at various senior adult centers.

Labor Zionist Alliance
6122 N. California, 60659; 973-3924
2600 W. Peterson, 60659 (during construction)
In 1982 the LZA will observe its 36th annual third seder. An original Haggadah, often prepared around a specific theme, is used each year. This moving observance, filled with music and kosher-for-Passover refreshments, draws 200 to 300 people. Newcomers are welcome.

B'nai B'rith, Anti-Defamation League of B'nai B'rith, and the Center for Religious Education sponsor an interfaith seder held at Mundelein College.

B'nai B'rith Women present seder symbols at two geriatric centers in the Highland Park community—Abbott House and the Pavillion.

Drexel Home has a seder for residents and their families.

Niles Township Jewish Congregation, in its outreach program Adopt-a-Nursing-Home, observes a special seder in a nursing home.

Northeast Council of Interfaith Ministry, of which Temple Beth Israel is a member, has an interfaith seder.

Northside Chaplaincy Committee presents a seder at Chicago-Read Mental Health Center.

Park View Home has a seder for residents and their families.

Purim

American Mizrachi Women, Hannah Senesh Chapter
3018 W. Devon, 60659; 973-0688
Sells gift packages for Purim in keeping with the tradition of bestowing a gift of food on a friend. Gift packages include wine, hamentashen, fruit, nuts, and candy—all kosher.

Bernard Sachs Community School
KINS of West Rogers Park Congregation
2800 W. North Shore Ave., 60645; 761-4000
Conducts an annual Purim parade and carnival, open to the public.

Lubavitch Chabad of Greater Chicago
2014 Orrington, Evanston 60201; 869-8060
Distributes thousands of Purim kits to college campuses, Hebrew schools, hospitals, homes for the aged, and prisons. Each kit contains some food edibles and two coins, as well as a brochure explaining the Jewish traditions of giving a gift of food to a friend and money to the poor.

- **Prof. Perry Gethner**
  Department of Romance Languages
  University of Chicago
  753-2693 (or leave message in the Romance Language Department, 753-3884)

Prof. Gethner discovered a 1622 Purim Play in French while he was working at the Bibliotèque Nationale in Paris. The *New Tragedy of the Perfidy of Haman*, a farce more-or-less that Prof. Gethner has translated into English, lends itself beautifully to being used as a Purim Spiel.

- **Shelley Kaplan**
  5206 S. Dorchester, 60615; 493-2767

Kaplan, also known as Shellebelle the Clown, has organized a production of Prof. Gethner's Purim Spiel for congregations, schools, and organizations. Contact her for information and bookings.

Simchat Torah

In the year 5632 by the Jewish calendar, and 1871 by the secular calendar, Simchat Torah shared a date with Chicago history. The ordinarily joyous celebration was interrupted when Chicago started burning. Chicago's Great Fire began on that Simchat Torah.

Currently, Simchat Torah is observed by the Chicago Jewish community on the streets and in the synagogues of West Rogers Park. Although not an official community celebration, perhaps thousands go to the vicinity of Whipple and Devon on the evening of Simchat Torah for processions, prayer, song, and dancing. The following evening, B'nei Akiva sponsors a continuation of the celebration with Simchat Torah II. Everyone is welcome.

Sukkot

B'nei Akiva
6500 N. California, 60645; 338-6569
B'nei Akiva, the Religious Zionist Youth Organization, sells prefabricated sukkot (booths) and s'chach (the greens used to decorate the top of the sukkah) as an annual fund-raising project.

Craftwood Lumber Company
1590 Old Deerfield Rd., Highland Park 60035; 831-2800
The Craftwood Sukkah Assembly Kit contains only wood materials, including wooden nuts and bolts, plus easy-to-follow instructions. The $8 \times 12 \times 7$ sukkah may be expanded through the purchase of additional kits.

Lubavitch Chabad of Greater Chicago
2014 Orrington, Evanston 60201; 869-8060
Sponsors a mobile sukkah on a flat truck that visits college campuses and public places, including Daley Center, to inform people, especially Jews, about observances in connection with this holiday.

These Chicago Jewish bookstores sell etrogim and lulavim, the fruits of Sukkot, imported from Israel:
Chicago Hebrew Book Store, 2942 W. Devon, 60659; 973-6636
Hamakor-Judaica, Inc., 6112 N. Lincoln, 60659; 463-6186
Schwartz-Rosenblum Hebrew Bookstore, 2906 W. Devon, 60659; 262-1700

Mezuzah

Questions pertaining to the traditionally correct location and placement of mezuzot as well as their authenticity can be referred to Rabbi Shmuel Fuerst, Agudath Israel; call 539-4241, from 7 to 9 P.M.

Lubavitch Chabad of Greater Chicago
2014 Orrington, Evanston 60201; 869-8060
Offers printed information on the use of the mezuzah and will answer questions.

Every mezuzah has two parts: the outer case, which may be of great artistic value and which can be executed in metal, ceramic, or other materials; and the inner parchment, which, according to traditional Judaism, must be written and prepared by an authorized scribe. Artists who create the outer case are listed in Chapter 8, "The Arts."

Chicago's resident scribe is listed in Chapter 13, "Goods and Services." Many gift shops and bookstores sell mezuzot that meet religious requirements; some of these are from Israel.

Mikvah

Chicago's earliest recorded mikvah was located at KAM Congregation, in its second permanent location (1853 to 1868) on the northeast corner of Wells and Adams.

Modern Ritualarium-Mikvah
3110 W. Touhy Ave., 60645; 274-7425

The mikvah for the Chicago community, designed by Edmond N. Zisook & Associates, opened in 1976. Actually three in one—there are a mikvah for women, a mikvah for men, and a kalim mikvah for the cleansing and purification of dishes and cookware.

Women's hours: In summer, the mikvah opens 45 minutes after candlelighting and closes at 10:30 P.M.; in winter, hours are from 7 to 9:30 P.M. Those who must use the mikvah late should call the attendants in advance. Fees: $6.50 per visit; 50¢ for optional linen; $2 for late fee.

Men's hours: Times not designated for women. There is a daily, monthly, or yearly fee schedule. Call in advance for information.

Kalim mikvah: Times not designated for women. Call ahead for information. A donation is requested.

A small convenience satellite mikvah is in the W. Peterson area.

Chicago Mikvah Association Inc.
3110 W. Touhy, 60645

This is the organization that owns the mikvah and sustains it.

Daughters of Israel
3110 W. Touhy, 60645; 274-7425
Cyndee Meystel, President, 973-6955

This is the organization that helps to maintain the mikvah, arranges for assistance and volunteers, and provides speakers on the use of the mikvah. A Bride's Kit, prepared by Daughters of Israel, includes publications pertaining to the mikvah and the Jewish Laws of Purity. Brides' classes and tours of the facility are also offered.

Edmond N. Zisook & Associates
176 W. Adams St., 60603

Available as architects and consultants on the design of the mikvah. Photographs of the Chicago Mikvah and of the firm's other mikvah commission, Vaad Hoeir of St. Louis, are available.

Pastoral Counseling

Chicago Board of Rabbis
427-5863
Makes referrals to a rabbinic pastoral counselor.

Chicago Rabbinical Council
764-0259
Makes referrals to an Orthodox rabbinic pastoral counselor.

Hebrew Theological College
267-9800 or 674-7750
Has a graduate degree program in pastoral counseling that leads to state licensing.

Rabbinic Counseling Service
3050 W. Touhy Ave., 60645; 973-2500
Rabbi Victor Weissberg, Director
Rabbis certified as pastoral counselors and psychotherapists have organized this service to meet the psychotherapeutic needs of the Jewish community in areas such as marriage, education, and individual growth. The RCS offers family, individual, and group counseling; special programs for synagogues; and consultations with rabbinic colleagues who are functioning as pastoral counselors. The service will also set up programs to deal with specific family and personal stresses, including grief, aging parents, single-parenting, and alternative lifestyles. Although they do not attempt the deprogramming of cult members, they do attempt to deal with the religious and psychological needs of individual cult members and their families.

Jewish Philosophy and Theology

Brisk Rabbinical College
9000 Forest View Rd., Skokie 60203; 674-4652
Call for referral.

■ **Rabbi Yechiel Eckstein**
222 W. Adams, Rm. 1449, 60606; 782-5080
Rabbi Eckstein's areas of expertise include the Bible, Judaism, and other religions. He lectures and gives classroom presentations. He did graduate work at Columbia University in Modern Jewish Philosophy.

■ **Dr. Manfred Harris**
Professor of Jewish Texts and Institutions
Spertus College of Judaica
618 S. Michigan Ave., 60605; 922-9012
Among his many subject areas are the Philosophic Texts, Maimonides, and Buber.

Hebrew Theological College
7135 N. Carpenter Rd., Skokie 60077; 674-7750
Call for referral.

■ **Rabbi Daniel Leifer**
B'nai B'rith Hillel Foundation
University of Chicago
5715 S. Woodlawn, 60637; 752-1127
Speaks on the subject of Jewish mysticism.

■ **Dr. Abba Lessing**
Professor, Department of Philosophy
Lake Forest College
683 Cherry Ave., Lake Forest 60045; 234-3649
Lecturer and adult-education leader on Jewish Philosophy in Literature, Existentialism and Zionism, the Holocaust, Martin Buber's Philosophy, and Recent Jewish Philosophy.

■ **Dr. Paul Raccah**
Chairman, Physics Department
University of Illinois–Chicago Circle
7521 N. Albany, 60645 (home)
Lectures include Foundations of Science and Religious Ideology and Challenge to Jewish Identity.

■ **Rabbi Robert Schreibman**
Temple Jeremiah
937 Happ Rd., Northfield 60093; 441-5760
Speaks on various topics, including Can We Believe in God Today? and Is Reform Judaism Authentic?

■ **Dr. Byron L. Sherwin**
David C. Verson Professor of Jewish Religious Thought
Spertus College of Judaica
618 S. Michigan Ave., 60605; 922-9012
Lectures on Mysticism, Chassidism, How to Teach the Holocaust, and God Encounter: An Examination of Jewish Prayer.

Telshe Yeshiva
3535 W. Foster Ave., 60625; 463-7738
Call for referral.

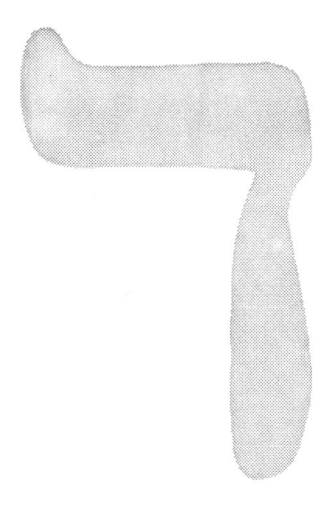

4
Cultural Judaism

Am Chai–Chutzpah Network

Am Chai, the Alternative Chavurah
P.O. Box 60142, 60660

Originally a pioneer chavurah in the early 1970s, Am Chai today is at the center of a network of Jewish consciousness groups, including the more political Chutzpah. As a chavurah, members (from young children to young forties) share monthly Shabbats and participate both separately and collectively in SADIE (Stimulating *a*nd *D*elightfully *I*nteresting *E*xperiences), which currently includes workshops in Jewish crafts and Israeli folk dance. The Am Chai Players, a theater troupe, specializes in Yiddish play reading, acting, and music. Interested persons may write for a membership packet.

Chutzpah
P.O. Box 60142, 60660

Chutzpah shares with Am Chai the center of this young-adult, socialist, Jewish-cultural network. The best introduction to this organization is probably through its wonderful collection *Chutzpah: A Jewish Liberation Anthology* (San Francisco: New Glide Publications, 1977), which is available for $5.95 plus 50¢ postage from the post office box number. Members may be at-large or active members of a work group. Work groups include one that publishes *Chutzpah* (see below); a second is involved with Yiddish; a third, on the Mideast, explores Israel's survival with peace; and a fourth has undertaken to study and deal with growing anti-Jewish attitudes in places where Jews live. Chutzpah is also interested in the women's movement and in Jewish feminism and has lent support to the gay-rights movement. Chutzpah has confronted other leftist groups that have been indifferent or hostile to Israel. Some members of Chutzpah and its sister organization, Am Chai, own two six-flats, which they operate as condos. Residents share work in building maintenance and child care. Anyone interested in membership should write for a statement of principles and membership information.

Chutzpah
Radical Jewish Journal
P.O. Box 60142, 60660

National publication of Chutzpah, tabloid in format, issued irregularly but usually twice a year. Has some local coverage but this is not its primary purpose. New members of Chutzpah may join the work group that publishes the *Chutzpah* newspaper.

Tsadaka Collective
P.O. Box 60142, 60660

The Tsadaka Collective is associated with Am Chai. The collective collects and disburses its own funds. Semiannual meetings consider worthy causes seeking money. Any agency or project wishing to petition the Tsadaka Collective may write to the address shown.

Folk Groups

Founded by Eastern European Jews who arrived in Chicago between the 1880s and 1930s, the folk groups, or landsmanshaften organizations, were usually based on village or city of origin. They formed a significant bridge for Jewish immigrants from Eastern Europe who were adjusting to the new country. The verein, as they were called, were the basis for mutual aid, funeral protection (including cemetery ownership), and religious worship. They performed both a social and an economic function. (In 1916, Chicago's combined landsmanshaften collected $1 million for Jewish relief in Europe.) Many had distinct customs, even varying pronunciation of Yiddish. Of the six or seven hundred folk groups that once existed in Chicago, only a handful remain.

American Sokolover Verein
Mrs. Solomon Behr, Contact
6547 N. California Ave., 60645; 262-8706

Meets at the Anshe Motele Synagogue, 6520 N. California, at noon on the third Sunday of the month.

Antipoler Aid Society
Mrs. Jack Wolansky, President
6313 N. Washtenaw Ave., 60659; 743-1785

Meets at 7 P.M., the second Sunday of the month, at the Workmen's Circle, 6506 N. California.

Bialistoker Ladies Auxiliary
Rose Zukerman, President
5700 N. Sheridan Rd., 60660; 878-1736
Meets at noon, the first and third Mondays of the month, at the Workmen's Circle, 6506 N. California. Founded in 1925. The predecessor (men's) Bialistoker Social Club was founded in 1922.

Dr. Herzl UKU Verein
Meets at 2 P.M., the second Sunday of the month, at the Free Sons of Israel, 6335 N. California. Although historically a men's club, a women's group also meets with the men. This verein is of Hungarian origin.

Hungarian Ladies Charities
Julia Marks, Secretary
761-1954
Meets at 2 P.M., the third Sunday of the month, at the Free Sons of Israel, 6335 N. California.

Independent Breziner
Meets on the third Sunday of the month at the What's Cooking Restaurant.

Lagower Ladies Aid Society
Annie Klein, Contact
5924 S. Kostner, 60629; 767-1992
Founded in 1935. Meets at 6:30 P.M., the first Sunday of the month, at the Workmen's Circle. Originally called the Lagower Aid Society.

Mariampol Aid Society
Janice Finelsen, Secretary
2611 W. Lunt, 60645; 761-2760
Meets monthly, except in winter, at a member's house. Mariampolers were in Chicago in 1870 and perhaps earlier. The society was incorporated in 1907. In 1929 women were invited into membership.

Plonsk Mutual Benefit Aid Society
Morris Blatt, Treasurer
2727 W. Jarvis, 60645; 973-2097
Founded in 1920, this group meets irregularly. In 1980 there were about 70 remaining members. Plonsk, Poland, was the birthplace of David Ben Gurion.

SSRS Association (Sudilkov Shepetovker Relief Society)
Harvey Fleishman, Chairman
274-3316

Children of original members meet four times a year for two purposes: sociability and care of the cemetery.

United Chicago Jews of Hungarian Descent
Julia Marks, Financial Secretary and Bulletin Editor
761-1954

Meets at 2 P.M., the third Sunday of the month, at the Free Sons of Israel. Issues a newsletter. Has the largest membership of the three remaining Hungarian Jewish organizations—about 200 individuals. Raises about $10,000 a year, half of which goes to JUF. Other recipients include Jewish National Fund and a yeshiva in Israel.

Other Folk Group Resources

Samuel Shkolnik
111 W. Washington, 60602; 782-9156

An attorney who is a resource person for the Drohitchin Verein in Chicago and its former great synagogue on Douglas Blvd. in Lawndale, Kehilath Jacob.

■ **Sidney Sorkin**
8343 S. Kenwood, 60619; 221-4096

Sorkin, a board member of the Chicago Jewish Historical Society, has been studying and researching Chicago's verein for many years. He has compiled what is probably the closest thing to a complete list. He is continually contacting and meeting with persons associated with past and present organizations.

The American Irish Jewish Club, whose Irish-born members are one or two generations removed from Eastern Europe but whose ties to the "old country" were to Ireland, has not met for a few years. The members keep in contact with one another and maintain a section in Westlawn Cemetery.

In 1977 Congregation KINS of West Rogers Park accepted the responsibility for the maintenance and service of the cemetery section in Waldheim that had been owned by former landsmanshaften congregation Anshe Korostishev.

Other folk groups may still exist—perhaps the Umaners, the Ekaterinoslavers, and others. The following sources may be leads to tracking them down:

Jewish Labor Committee, 127 N. Dearborn, 60602
Israel Histadrut Campaign, 220 S. State St., 60604
JUF Folks Division, 1 S. Franklin, 60606
The Jewish funeral directors
The four organizations that rent space to many groups: Free Sons of Israel, Labor Zionist Alliance, Workmen's Circle, and the Zionist Organization of Chicago

Organizations That Once Were Folk Groups

Aids to Motor Handicapped Children began with a nucleus of daughters from the Motele community.

B. Friendly Ladies' Aid Society, which until 1980 supported many worthy causes, started in 1912 as a Berditchover society.

The Midwest Chenstochower Society, now a Holocaust survivors' organization, was founded in 1927 by a group of immigrants who came to Chicago after World War I.

Jewish Cultural Clubs
1740 W. Greenleaf, 60626; 338-9283

Although the name is plural, the organization is singular. JCC offers cultural activities, programs, and lectures to members.

Jewish Cultural Discussion Group
Elaine Kessler, Contact
1755 Sherwood, Highland Park 60035

This group has met bimonthly for many years for discussions about Jewish cultural topics. A nucleus of the membership comes from the Yiddish cultural movement.

Jewish Humor

- **Dr. Ted Cohen**
  5716 S. Dorchester, 60637; 288-2434

Dr. Cohen is associate professor of philosophy in the Committee on Arts and Design at the University of Chicago. His interest in Jewish humor is an avocation. He lectures to Jewish audiences on Jewish Jokes: Reflections on Intimacy.

John Heimovics
P.O. Box 524, Highland Park 60035

Information on the *Hasidonder* legend provided upon request.

Jewish Literature

- **Dr. Irving Abrahamson**
  888 Bobolink Rd., Highland Park 60035

Lecturer, book reviewer, expert on Elie Wiesel and Philip Roth. On leave from Kennedy-King College in order to assemble the uncollected works of Elie Wiesel. Abrahamson's book reviews on literature of the Holocaust have appeared in the *Chicago Tribune* Book World. He has also conducted study groups and adult-education classes.

- **Joan Bernick**
  795 Vernon Ave., Glencoe 60022

Gives dramatic readings in English of Jewish literature originally written in Yiddish and Hebrew, such as Sholom Aleichem and Agnon. Most of these readings are from her own translations. Her translations have been published in a number of national magazines.

- **Prof. Ellen S. Cannon**
  468 W. Melrose, Apt. 455, 60657

Lectures include Yiddish Literature and Jewish Politics. Member of the Department of Political Science, Northeastern Illinois University.

- **Benjamin Fain**
  Jewish Book Mart, 782-5199

Bibliophile lectures on great literature of the Jewish tradition.

- **Jacob Gordon**
  100 N. LaSalle St., 60602; 236-2155 or 835-2646 (evenings)

A lecturer on Yiddish literature, Jewish history, and American-Jewish literature. Topics have included Bellow, Malamud, Philip Roth, Henry Roth, Singer, and Wiesel.

- **Dr. Babette Inglehart**
  5000 S. Cornell, 60615; 241-5416

As part of a larger study of Chicago as a literary center, Dr. Inglehart has researched Jewish writers in Chicago for a book and documentary film. Lecture subjects include Chicago Jewish Writers, Bellow, Malamud, and Immigrant Jewish Literature. Dr. Inglehart is on the faculty of the Department of English, Chicago State University.

Judaica Literary Group
Paul Levinson, Founder, 328-8041
Estelle Miller, Contact, 878-8693

Founded in 1980. Meets in homes every four to five weeks to discuss a work of Jewish interest, either fiction or nonfiction. New members are welcome.

■ **Dr. Abba Lessing**
683 Cherry Ave., Lake Forest 60045; 234-3649
Lecturer and class leader on Jewish Philosophy in Literature and on many other topics. Member of the Department of Philosophy, Lake Forest College.

■ **Marvin Mirsky**
Assistant Dean, University Extension
Assistant Professor of Humanities (the College)
University of Chicago
753-2763 or 643-0462 (home)
Lecturer and study-group leader on the Bible as Literature and on Jewish Literature. Topics also include Jewish Short Fiction; Modern Jewish-American Writers; Jewish Sensibility in Recent American Literature; Isaac Bashevis Singer: Considerably Lower Than the Angels; Selected Works of Franz Kafka, Isaac Bashevis Singer, Saul Bellow, Bernard Malamud, and Elie Wiesel; and Biblical Themes in Modern Literature.

■ **Irene Nathan**
743-8421
A book reviewer as well as dramatist, humorist, and speaker for all occasions. Gives dramatizations of the short stories of S. Y. Agnon, followed by a discussion of each selection. Also lectures on other Jewish literary subjects and on Jewish authors. Works with senior adults through the Adult Continuing Education Department at Truman College.

■ **Holly Rozner**
766 LaCrosse, Wilmette 60091; 251-7395
Speaker and study-group leader on topics related to Jewish-American women in literature, existentialism, and psychoanalysis in Jewish literature.

■ **Ruth Rubin**
6304 N. Central Park Ave., 60659; 539-0374
Book reviewer and dramatist whose subjects include Golda Meir, Louis Brandeis, *Evergreen* by Belva Plain, the Jewish Woman in America, and *Sophie's Choice* by William Styron.

■ **Joyce S. Schrager**
475-8093
Teaches and lectures on topics relating to American Jewish literature.

- **Allen Schwartz**
  9032 Kenneth, Skokie 60076; 679-4123

  Discussion leader and lecturer on topics relating to Jewish-American literature and writers; Yiddish humor, poetry, and literature (in original and in translation); Hebrew and Israeli literature (in translation). Also instructor of creative writing, field-trip and travel-study escort, and expert in the history and art of Yiddish and Israeli films and drama.

- **Janet B. Stern**
  765 Walden Rd., Winnetka 60093; 446-1501

  Lecturer, teacher, and study-group leader. Uses the following Jewish materials in translation: nineteenth- and twentieth-century Yiddish and Russian literature (Sholem Aleichem, Mendele, Peretz, Babel, etc.); twentieth-century Hebrew literature (Amos, Oz, Agnon, Yehoshua, Brenner, Hazaz, Shamir, etc.); and twentieth-century Jewish-American writers (Bellow, Roth, Malamud, Arthur Cohen, Cynthia Ozick, Hugh Nissenson, etc.). Stern has led a women's afternoon cultural group at the Horwich JCC for the past fifteen years—her emphasis is on twentieth-century literature.

- **Beverly Yusim**
  1620 Robin Hood Lane, Highland Park 60035; 831-4671

  Book reviewer, study-group leader, lecturer, and writer; all for adult audiences on topics of modern Jewish literature, writers, the Holocaust, and other subjects of Jewish interest.

Secular Judaism

Secular Judaism affirms the cultural aspects of Judaism while denying the religious. Often connected with the Yiddish culture movement and often committed to Zionism, Secular Jews do not support synagogues or engage in formal worship. Holiday observances stress the history of the Jewish people.

Conference of Secular Jewish Organizations
Gerry Revzin, Newsletter Editor
1130 S. Michigan Ave., Apt. 2101, 60605

Founded in 1970, the CSJO now has membership (individuals and organizations) from all over the United States and Canada, especially in the cities of Chicago, Los Angeles, San Francisco, Cleveland, Detroit, Philadelphia, and Columbus. Many, but not all, of the affiliated organizations are Yiddish cultural groups. Three Chicago organizations affiliated with the CSJO are the following:

North Shore School of Jewish Studies
5050 Church, Skokie 60077

South Side Jewish Study Group
Gerry Revzin, Contact
1130 S. Michigan Ave., Apt. 2101, 60605
Meets monthly in homes to discuss topics of Jewish interest. Members are middle-aged men and women. This group helped start the Jewish Adult Mobile Theater of the Hyde Park JCC.

South Side School of Jewish Studies
5715 S. Woodlawn Ave., 60637; 752-5655
The school curriculum is no longer limited to the secular viewpoint.

Sephardic Resources

- **Rabbi Michael Azose**
  Contact through Sephardic Congregation, 475-9287; Crown Academy, 973-1450; or KINS, 761-4000
  Rabbi Azose is himself a Sephardic Jew. His congregation is one of two Sephardic congregations in Chicago, and among its membership there are many resources on Sephardic Jewry.

- **Board of Jewish Education**
  72 E. 11th St., 60605; 427-5570
  Contact Dr. Robert Goodman and/or Dr. Irving Skolnick regarding curriculum units prepared by the BJE that deal with the history and culture of Sephardic Jewry.

- **Dr. Isaac Daniel**
  6708 N. Francisco, 60645; 761-1571
  Although especially concerned with Sephardic Jewry of Greece, Dr. Daniel is also a resource for the Judaeo-Spanish language, Ladino.

- **Dr. Maxine Ribstein Kanter**
  741 Green Bay Rd., Highland Park 60035; 433-2853
  Lecturer and educator on the History and Culture of Sephardic Jewry. Received her doctorate, on the subject of Sephardic High Holy Day liturgical music, at Northwestern University in 1978. Dr. Kanter did field work in the Sephardic communities of Amsterdam, London, New York, Montreal, and Philadelphia.

- **Dr. Paul Raccah**
  7521 N. Albany, 60645
  Speaks on topics pertaining to the contrast between the customs of Sephardic and Ashkenazic Jews. Dr. Raccah also speaks on The Challenge to Jewish Identity and other topics.

■ **Rabbi Nathan I. Weiss**
Chicago Rabbinical Council
2735 W. Devon, 60659; 764-0259

Rabbi Weiss is spiritual leader of Iran Hebrew Congregation, which has among its membership a wide range of resources on Sephardic Jewry. Iran Hebrew Congregation is one of two Sephardic congregations in Chicago.

Judaeo-Arabic

Judaeo-Arabic is the spoken Arabic language as used today by Jews of North Africa. Judaeo-Arabic also refers to the Arabic literature of Jews of the Middle Ages and to the body of studies concerning Jews who have lived in predominantly Arab and Arabic-speaking lands.

■ **Dr. Norman Golb**
5813 S. Blackstone Ave., 60637; 324-7858

A specialist in Hebrew and Judaeo-Arabic studies at the University of Chicago.

■ **Dr. Paul Raccah**
7521 N. Albany, 60645

A resource on the Judaeo-Arabic dialect.

■ **Dr. Yaacov Selhub**
363-0321

A resource on Judaeo-Arabic.

Ladino

Ladino is the language spoken by descendants of Jews who left Spain at the time of the Expulsion in 1492 and who carried the language or dialect with them to what is today Greece, Turkey, and the Balkans.

■ **Dr. Isaac Daniel**
6708 N. Francisco, 60645; 761-1571

Dr. Daniel, a native of Greece, is proficient in Ladino. His father, who also lives in Chicago, sings Ladino songs.

Targum

Targum, a spoken language of Kurdish Jews from a region of Iran, is a modern form of Aramaic. Some Iranian Jews in Chicago speak Targum. They may be contacted through the Iran Hebrew Congregation of Skokie, which is a possible source for other Judaeo-dialects from Iran.

Workmen's Circle
6506 N. California, 60645; 274-5400
Harry J. Goldfarb, Contact

Founded nationally in 1900, the Arbeiter Ring, the Workmen's Circle, continues to be a fraternal insurance organization with close ties to the labor movement, the Yiddish secular community, and the remaining folk groups. The Workmen's Circle has aimed at preserving Yiddish culture, at promoting the humanities, and at fostering Yiddish education. At one time it sponsored Yiddish theater and Yiddish schools in Chicago. About seven branches remain, each of which sponsors its own activities. Some branch meetings are conducted in Yiddish; however, one active branch, the Cordoza, is not a Yiddish-centered group. Rooms in the Workmen's Circle building may be rented by groups.

Yiddish

Am Chai Players
P.O. Box 60142, 60660

A performing group from Am Chai that puts on Yiddish and English translations of Yiddish stories with music and singing.

American Jewish Congress
Commission on Jewish Life and Culture
22 W. Monroe St., Suite 2102, 60603; 332-7355

Very supportive of Yiddish cultural programs in Chicago. Initiates some programs of its own and has sponsored Yiddish films. This commission is represented on the Chicago Council for Yiddish and Yiddish Culture.

B. Good Yiddish Poetry Reading Group
Sonia Rockler, Reader
262-9655

This group meets at 1 P.M., the first Friday of the month, at Bank Hapoalim, 174 N. Michigan Ave. Sonia Rockler gives readings in Yiddish preceded by a short synopsis in English. She reads a variety of poetry and stories. The group is named after founding member Bertha Good. Anyone is welcome to attend.

Beth Emet The Free Synagogue
1224 Dempster, Evanston 60202; 869-4230

At least two of the chugim sponsored by this congregation are concerned with Yiddish content.

Chicago Council for Yiddish and Yiddish Culture
Sonia Rockler, Recording Secretary
262-9655

Founded in the summer of 1980, the CCYYC will support and sponsor Yiddish cultural-literary programs conducted only in Yiddish. The executive committee includes representatives from the Chicago Committee for YIVO, American Jewish Congress, Labor Zionist Alliance, and Workmen's Circle.

Chutzpah
P.O. Box 60142, 60660

Chutzpah has a Yiddish work group in its organization.

Der Driter Dor
Adar Rossman, Contact
1323 W. Albion, 60626

Small Yiddish performing troupe.

Hyde Park JCC Jewish Adult Mobile Theater
1100 E. Hyde Park Blvd., 60615; 268-4600

Jewish Adult Mobile Theater is a traveling troupe that performs, in English, material dramatized from Yiddish sources.

Jewish People's Choral Society
Philip Fox, 673-8748
Sonia Matz, 262-4863

Originally the Freiheit Gsang Verein, this group now rehearses and annually performs at the Bernard Horwich JCC. New members are welcome.

Labor Zionist Alliance
6122 N. California, 60659; 973-3924
2600 W. Peterson, 60659 (during construction)

Of the various branches of the LZA today, three are Yiddish centered. They are the Dr. Hurwitz Branch, Bialik-Boganskoy Branch, and Gordon Dolnick Branch. The latter branch brings Chaim Grade to Chicago regularly for a Yiddish reading. Most of the proceedings of these branches continue to be in Yiddish.

Yiddish Literary Club
Avrom Gurwitz
8324 Christiana Ave., Skokie 60076; 676-4693

Meets at noon on the third Monday of each month at Bank Hapoalim, 174 N. Michigan Ave., for a program of Yiddish content.

YIVO Institute for Jewish Research, Chicago Committee
Ezra Perkal, Chairman
72 E. 11th St., 60605; 427-5570
Usually sponsors one big Yiddish program a year on behalf of YIVO.

Yugntruf Youth for Yiddish
Adar Rossman
1323 W. Albion, 60626
The local representative for Yugntruf, the worldwide organization that promotes Yiddish among high school and college students.

Resource People

- **Claire Aronson**
4300 Marine Dr., 60613
Although primarily active in Hebrew education, Claire Aronson has a great interest in the Yiddish language and promotes it through Yiddish theater and presentations.

- **Joan Bernick**
795 Vernon Ave., Glencoe 60022
Singer, storyteller, and translator of Yiddish.

- **Prof. Ellen S. Cannon**
468 W. Melrose, Apt. 455, 60657
A member of the faculty of Northeastern Illinois University, Prof. Cannon lectures on a variety of topics. One of her most intriguing titles is Yiddish Literature and Jewish Politics.

- **Jacob Gordon**
100 N. LaSalle St., 60602; 236-2155 or 835-2646 (evenings)
Lectures on Yiddish, Yiddish writers, and Yiddish literature.

- **Clare Chaike Greenberg**
725-7330
Yiddish translator and resource on all matters pertaining to Yiddish programming in Chicago. She grew up in Chicago's Yiddish community, where her father was a prominent Yiddish teacher.

- **Avrom Gurwitz**
8324 Christiana Ave., Skokie 60076; 676-4693
A Yiddish teacher and general resource on Yiddish culture in Chicago. He teaches Yiddish at the Mayer Kaplan JCC. Gurwitz is available to lecture in or on Yiddish to organizations.

■ **Dina Halpern**
c/o Danny Newman
Lyric Opera of Chicago
20 N. Wacker Dr., 60606; 346-6111 or 327-2914 (home)

A star of the international Yiddish Theater, Dina Halpern presents Yiddish readings. She is a resource on Yiddish theater and has prepared a lecture on the history of Yiddish theater in the United States and Poland.

■ **Pearl Kahan**
Spertus College of Judaica
618 S. Michigan Ave., 60605; 922-9012

Teaches the only Yiddish courses for college credit offered regularly in Chicago.

■ **Dr. Saul Kasman**
432-7404

Translates Yiddish into English.

■ **Aviva May**
864-8733

Teaches Yiddish and has written on Yiddish as a second language.

■ **Adar Rossman**
1323 W. Albion, 60626

Offers Yiddish-language classes at beginner and intermediate levels. Private lessons also given. After an eight-week program students may join the Reading Circle, which reads authors such as Sholem Aleichem and Isaac Bashevis Singer in the original. Rossman also participates in Yiddish performing groups. She spends her summers teaching Yiddish and Jewish culture at Camp Kinderring, New York. She is an excellent resource for Yiddish culture programming for all ages but particularly for children and young adults.

■ **Allen Schwartz**
9032 Kenneth, Skokie 60076; 679-4123

Discussion leader and lecturer. Presents programs and classes on Yiddish humor, poetry, and literature, both in Yiddish and in English translation.

Other Resources

Yiddish classes are offered by Bernard Horwich JCC, Mayer Kaplan JCC, North Suburban JCC, Hillel Foundation at Northwestern University, Hillel Foundation at University of Chicago, Spertus College of Judaica, and by Adar Rossman.

Yiddish books are on the shelves of the Albany Park, Northtown, and Rogers Park branches of the Chicago Public Library; and also at the public libraries of the suburbs of Skokie, Park Forest, and Highland Park.

Chicago's greatest living Yiddish poet is Selwyn Shlomo Schwartz, who has published ten books of poetry, half of which are in English. The latest of his many honors is as representative of the Yiddish language in the International P.E.N. *International Portland Review,* 1980, an anthology of poetry and prose in 51 languages.

The University of Chicago Press published a significant translation in 1979: Max Weinreich's *History of the Yiddish Language,* translated by Shlomo Noble with the assistance of Joshua A. Fishman. The hardcover edition costs $35 and may be ordered from the University of Chicago Press, 5801 S. Ellis; 753-3331.

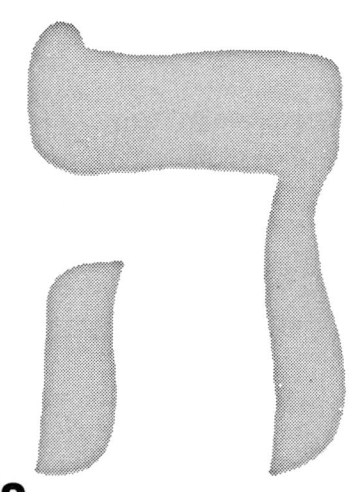

5
Life-Cycle Events

Chicago Rabbinical Council
2735 W. Devon, 60659; 764-0259
Rabbi Nathan I. Weiss, Executive Secretary
The CRC publishes a series of ten booklets, *From Birth to Death*, covering many aspects of the various life-cycle events and observances. Total package is $3.50.

Birth

Prenatal Care

Jewish Community Centers
1 S. Franklin, 60606; 346-6700
Prenatal care classes are offered at the JCCs.

B'nai B'rith Women
7701 N. Lincoln, Skokie 60077; 679-6077
Operation Stork—cosponsored with the National Foundation–March of Dimes—teaches women the importance of prenatal care.

Infant–New Mother's Aid

Shifrah and Puah Project
Neshei Chabad, 869-8060
Provides clothing, food, nursing, and other assistance to newborn babies and their mothers. Will also teach parents how to make a brit milah for a boy baby and a Shabbat ceremony for naming a girl baby.

Neonatology Support

Infants' Aid
821-23 Dempster, Evanston 60201; 475-9182

This nondenominational organization, founded in 1915, has endowed nurseries for premature infants at Mount Sinai and Michael Reese hospitals and has provided research fellowships in neonatology and prenatal medicine. Begun originally at the urging of Dr. Julius Hays Hess of Michael Reese. Funds are raised through a resale shop.

Mothers' Aid of Chicago Lying-in Hospital
667 Vernon, Glencoe 60022; 835-2555

This nondenominational organization benefits maternity research at Chicago Lying-in Hospital. Founded in 1904 by six Jewish women, including Ida DeLee Neuman, to assist the work of her brother, Dr. Joseph Bolivar DeLee. Began as a layette organization, sewing clothing for indigent Jewish mothers and their infants. Today funds are raised by a Glencoe boutique and by sale of the now classic *Our Baby's First Seven Years*.

Circumcision (Brit Milah)

Chicago Rabbinical Council
2735 W. Devon, 60659; 764-0259

The CRC has prepared a prayer booklet with the traditional brit milah service along with English readings. This office will also answer questions regarding circumcision.

The four Chicago mohelim who are certified to perform circumcision are the following:
Rev. Benjamin Perlstein, 478-5704
Rabbi Haskel Wachsmann, 743-4160
Rabbi Ben Zion Well, 262-9845
Rev. Noah Wolff, 338-5599

Highland Park Hospital
718 Glenview Ave., Highland Park 60035; 432-8000

A special family room is made available to Jewish families for celebrating a brit milah. (Highland Park Hospital has also dedicated an ecumenical chapel, including an Ark with a Torah. A small meditation room, designed for pastoral counseling, adjoins the sanctuary.)

Naming Ceremony for Baby Girls

Rabbi Daniel Leifer
B'nai B'rith Hillel Foundation
5715 S. Woodlawn Ave., 60637; 752-1127

Rabbi Leifer's beautiful naming ceremony, created on the occasion of his own daughter's birth, has been published at least twice, in *The Jewish Woman* by Elizabeth Koltun and in *The Second Jewish Catalog* by Sharon Strassfeld and Michael Strassfeld. Included in the three-part ceremony is a Pidyon ha-Bat for redemption of the firstborn—in this case, a daughter.

Bar and Bat Mitzvah

Travel agents who specialize in Israel bookings will assist in making bar and bat mitzvah arrangements in Israel.

Beth Sholom of Rogers Park
1233 W. Pratt, 60626; 743-4160
This Traditional congregation will accept the children of nonmembers for bar or bat mitzvah. Other congregations that welcome nonmember children into religious school are so indicated in the listing of congregations in Chapter 3, "Religious Life."

Sons of Joshua Congregation
Cantor Dale Lind
272-0252
Although Sons of Joshua Congregation is not really a congregation in the traditional sense, Cantor Lind and members of the Lind family will perform a bar mitzvah ceremony when special arrangements are made.

IBM (Israeli Bar Mitzvah) Service
c/o Sue Mednick
936 Rollingwood Rd., Highland Park 60035; 433-0962
Mednick refers interested parties to former Chicagoans, Dr. and Mrs. Michael Roskin of Jerusalem. The Roskins have developed a minimum-cost plan that includes all necessary arrangements for an Israeli bar or bat mitzvah—including securing the services of a Reform, Conservative, or Orthodox rabbi. Arrangements can include luncheon or dinner, flowers, photographer, even limousine to and from Masada, as well as personal introduction to Israeli families. The Roskins' current charge for making all arrangements is $35. Price list for specifics is available.

Bank Leumi Le-Israel B.M.
100 N. LaSalle St., 60602; 781-1800
Will assist with bar or bat mitzvah arrangements in Israel.

Weddings

Chicago Board of Rabbis
72 E. 11th St., 60605; 427-5863

Couples who want a Jewish wedding but are not members of a congregation and do not know a rabbi may call for referral.

Daughters of Israel
3110 W. Touhy Ave., 60645; 274-7425
Cyndee Meystel, President, 973-6955

Although the main purpose of this organization is running the mikvah, Daughters of Israel also provides two special services to brides and brides-to-be:

Bride's Classes
Hadassah Goodman
6641 N. Maplewood Ave., 60645; 764-1482

Mrs. Goodman conducts year-round classes for brides-to-be. At least six class series are held throughout the year, with four sessions in each series, including a visit to the mikvah. Classes are held in Mrs. Goodman's home and there is no charge. (In addition, married women who are interested in a class or in a review of the Laws of Taharat Hamishpocho, the laws of family purity, may also call.)

Bridal Fair
Baila Grinker
869-8060

Daughters of Israel conducts an annual bridal fair, usually in fall. Exhibits by florists, photographers, bridal consultants, ketubot makers, and so forth are displayed. There are films and presentations, all in keeping with the dignity of a religious wedding observance. Daughters of Israel also has a kit for brides containing literature pertaining to the mikvah and Jewish traditions in the home.

Rabbi Shmuel Fuerst
Agudath Israel
539-4241

Rabbi Fuerst conducts classes for grooms, in a group or individually, covering the laws of purity from the groom's standpoint. Classes are held about three times a year.

Jewish Family and Community Service
1 S. Franklin, 60606; 346-6700

Family Life Educators conduct workshops on preparing for marriage. Call for information.

Intermarriage and Mixed Marriage

American Jewish Committee
55 E. Jackson, Rm. 1870, 60604; 663-5500

Has conducted a major study on intermarriage and on mixed marriage (in which neither party converts to the other's religion) among American Jews. As an outgrowth of this study, AJC, in cooperation with the Union of American Hebrew Congregations and Temple Jeremiah, sponsored a series of programs designed for partners in intermarriages and mixed marriages.

■ Dr. Louis A. Berman
928 Asbury, Evanston 60202; 475-3148

Psychologist, writer, lecturer, and author of *Jews and Intermarriage: A Study in Personality and Culture* (Cranberry, N.J.: Thomas Yoseloff, 1968), Dr. Berman is a member of the Student Counseling Service, University of Illinois–Chicago Circle, Box 4348, 60680.

Chicago Board of Rabbis
72 E. 11th St., 60605; 427-5863
Rabbi Mordecai Simon, Executive Director

For questions about intermarriage—direct assistance or referral—consult the CBR.

Death and Dying

Jewish Funeral Directors

Furth & Companies
9200 Skokie Blvd., Skokie 60077; 677-4300
5206 N. Broadway, 60640; 784-4300
6130 N. California, 60659; 338-2300

Founded in 1864. Today, associated with Piser.

Gratch-Mandel
Associated with Piser. For information, call Piser.

Hartman-Miller
463-5500
Associated with Piser.

Original Weinstein and Sons, Inc.
3019 W. Peterson Ave., 60659; 561-1890

This funeral home has been serving Chicago Jews since 1890. Robert Weinstein is a resource for the deaf and hearing impaired and conducts seminars on the traditional Jewish funeral. The telecommunication number (TTY) for the hearing impaired is TTY 561-0655.

Palmer-Lauer
Associated with Weinstein Brothers. For information, call Weinstein Brothers.

Piser Memorial Chapels
6130 N. California, 60659; 338-2300
5206 N. Broadway, 60640; 561-4740
9200 N. Skokie Blvd., Skokie 60077; 679-4740

Among many other contributions to the Jewish community, Piser Memorial Chapels sponsors widow support groups at the Jewish Community Centers. The toll-free number from the South Side and the southern suburbs is 363-4920. The telecommunication number (TTY) for the hearing impaired is TTY 674-5900.

Weinstein Brothers
1300 W. Devon, 60660; 761-2400
111 Skokie Blvd., Wilmette 60091; 256-5700

Myron Weinstein is the contact for the Jewish Free Burial Society of Chicago.

Additional Funeral and Burial Resources

Chevra Kadisha
Rabbi Schaje Abramovitz
743–0074

Originally organized by AFTA, the Chevra Kadisha provides ritual washing and dressing at no charge. CK also is a resource for information about burial and mourning customs. All services are performed on a voluntary basis, and more volunteers are needed for this sacred work.

Jewish Burial Society
Dr. Gary Siegel, President
346-7950

A nonprofit corporation assisting Jews in obtaining dignified, reasonably priced, traditional Jewish funerals. Founded in 1975 as an alternative funeral program to meet soaring costs. Services are available to all Jews, whatever branch of Judaism. Tahara—Jewish ritual washing and dressing—through the Chevra Kadisha is available as an option. JBS encourages use of the synagogue for funeral services. Each time a synagogue is used, the congregation will receive a $150 contribution from JBS. Funerals may also be at graveside or in a nonsectarian, licensed funeral home. No officer of the JBS is a funeral director, and no advance membership is required for participating in this plan.

Jewish Free Burial Society (Gomle Chesed Shel Emeth)
Myron Weinstein, 256-5700 or 761-2400

This society provides free burial of indigent Jews and maintains those cemeteries in which indigent Jews have been buried. They also assist in maintaining abandoned Jewish cemeteries. More than 8,000 men, women, and children have been buried by the JFBS down through the decades.

United Synagogue of America, Midwest Region
72 E. 11th St., 60605; 939-2351

The Chicago-based office of the United Synagogue has a funeral-plan package that is available to affiliated Conservative congregations. One price covers services and facilities of a Jewish funeral director, all preparation, casket (wooden), and limousine. Prices may vary within $25 among four participating funeral directors. The twofold purpose of this plan is to minimize the mental anguish of the grieving family while also assuring traditional Jewish burial practices. This office has also published a booklet, *Guide to the Traditions, Rituals and Value of Jewish Funeral Practice.*

Some congregations have their own funeral plans. A sampling: B'nai Torah of Highland Park; Congregation Solel, Highland Park; Am Shalom, Glencoe; Am Yisrael, Northfield; and Congregation Bene Shalom of the Deaf, Skokie.

Chicago's few remaining verein organizations and fraternal societies (such as the Free Sons of Israel) still offer a funeral-protection plan for members and own sections of Jewish cemeteries. Going through the designated names of sections of the Jewish cemeteries is like reading a Yartzeit list for hundreds of verein and congregations and fraternal organizations that no longer exist.

The German Chevra Kadisha, founded by German Jews who escaped Hitler, was established in 1940 in Chicago and continues to provide members with all necessary burial arrangements and final rest in a section the society owns in Jewish Oakridge Cemetery, Hillside.

The Agudath Israel has its own Agudah Benevolent Society, which provides funeral protection to its citywide membership.

Cemeteries

The best resource available on the location of Jewish cemeteries in the Chicago area is a little book with a long title, published from time to time by Piser Memorial Chapels as a public service: *Piser Memorial Chapels, Gratch-Mandel, Hartman-Miller: Cemetery Guide of Jewish Cemeteries and Non-Sectarian Cemeteries with Jewish Sections in the Chicago Area and Map of Jewish Waldheim Cemeteries.*

B'nai B'rith Cemetery
Mt. Jehoshua Cemetery
Mt. Isaiah Israel Cemetery
6600 W. Addison St., 60634; 545-0044

A complex of old Jewish cemeteries near Mt. Mayriv Cemetery.

Jewish Waldheim Cemetery
1800 S. Harlem Ave., Forest Park 60130; 366-4100
Irv Lapping, Resource Contact, 366-2445

Actually a conglomerate of over 300 cemeteries bearing names of past and present congregations, fraternal organizations, family circles, and landsmanshaften verein. Jewish Waldheim extends south from Roosevelt Rd. to Cermak Rd. and west from Harlem Ave. to the Des Plaines River. Jewish Waldheim is separate from, but immediately south of, nonsectarian Waldheim Cemetery (where Emma Goldman is buried), which is north of Roosevelt Rd. Jewish Waldheim is a rich source for Chicago Jewish history.

The following are cemetery sextons at Jewish Waldheim:

Barnett Joseph & Son
1400 S. Des Plaines, Forest Park 60130; 366-2445

Silverman & Weiss
378-2838

Mt. Mayriv Cemetery
3600 N. Narragansett Ave., 60634; 545-0001

The third location of Chicago's first cemetery, founded in 1845 in Lincoln Park. Among many historic discoveries to be made here is the grave of Governor Henry Horner. The magnificent red marble column atop architect Dankmar Adler's grave came from the entrance to the Central Music Hall, his favorite commission, which was demolished in 1900, the year of his death, to make way for Marshall Field's State Street store.

Shalom Memorial Park
Rand Road (U.S. 12) at Rt. 53, P.O. Box 549, Palatine 60067;
255-3520 or 274-2236

Worth visiting for its art (tapestries by Siona Shimski of Israel and a twenty-foot mosaic by Pincus Shaar of Israel), SMP is the site of the periodic Geniza ceremony sponsored by the Chicago Rabbinical Council. During this ceremony, a communitywide accumulation of religious items, too worn to be of any further use, is buried. Jewish tradition forbids destroying such items. SMP also has information about the abandoned Jewish cemetery in Niles, at Hamilton and Shermer roads on the border of Morton Grove, including records of the original organizations of the Niles cemetery and of the reinterment of some of the graves from Niles to SMP.

■ **Irwin Lapping**
Barnett Joseph & Son
1400 S. Des Plaines Ave., Forest Park 60130
A resource on Jewish Waldheim and Jewish burial customs. Officer of the General Care Foundation for Jewish Cemeteries, Inc., and president of Metropolitan Chicago Cemetery Officials.

■ **Joseph Levinson**
175 E. Delaware Pl., 60611; 337-2609
An authority on Chicago's early Jewish cemeteries, Levinson traced the site of the original Jewish cemetery to what is now a baseball diamond in Lincoln Park. Levinson is also an expert on the history of KAM Congregation, Chicago's oldest, and on Mt. Mayriv Cemetery.

Alan D. Whitney
545 Lincoln Ave., Suite 12, Winnetka 60093
President of the Hebrew Benevolent Society of Chicago cemetery at 3919 N. Clark St., 60613, sometimes called Jewish Graceland. Hebrew Benevolent Cemetery, founded in 1851, is the oldest extant Jewish cemetery in the city. Whitney knows a great deal of history about HBC and about the people buried there, who include not only all his grandparents and one great-grandmother, but also the grandparents of writer Edna Ferber.

■ **Lewis M. Lazarus**
5755 N. Fairfield Ave., 60659
Lazarus is a professional genealogist who will search cemetery inscriptions and records for lost graves.

Chicago Jewish Historical Society
618 S. Michigan Ave., 60605; 663-5634
CJHS has sponsored two different cemetery tours: a tour of Jewish portions of Rosehill and Mt. Mayriv cemeteries, presented by Charles Bernstein, Dr. Edward Mazur, and Rachel Heimovics; and a tour of

Jewish Waldheim, by Irwin Lapping with input from Sidney Sorkin and Mark Mandle.

New Light Society—Chevra Or Chodosh
Charles Adler
525-0224

This unusual organization has as its singular purpose owning and maintaining the New Light Cemetery at Pratt Blvd. and E. Prairie Rd., in Lincolnwood. The organization assembles for one social function each year. Most of the members are German Jews who came to Chicago in the 1930s to escape Hitler. The cemetery was founded in the 1890s by earlier immigrants from Germany. The four original families were Florsheim, Frankel, Frank, and Rickersberg.

Monuments

Katz-Goldman Memorials
4350 N. Harlem, 60634; 625-2470

Kornick Monuments
3058 W. Devon Ave., 60659; 764-7600

Leve Monuments
3000 W. Peterson, 60659; 761-3334

Lieberman Monument Works Inc.
3012 W. Devon Ave., 60659; 743-1903

Soroka
7739 W. Roosevelt, Forest Park 60130; 366-1155

Wulkan Monument Co.
2116 W. Devon, 60659; 743-8066

Resources on Jewish Burial Customs

Contact Jewish funeral directors for resource persons on the subject of burial customs.

- **Rabbi Schaje Abramovitz**
  Chevra Kadisha, 743-0074

CK has a speakers' bureau that provides information on the Jewish attitude toward death, laws of mourning, and burial.

- **Dr. Gary Siegel**
  President, Jewish Burial Society
  346-7950

A speaker on Jewish death, burial, and the Jewish Burial Society.

See "Death in Jewish Folk Religion" by Rabbi Joseph L. Baron, Ph.D. dissertation, University of Chicago, 1932. A historic survey and analysis of Jewish folk customs and superstitions: in response to the approach of death, demons and magic, spiritual healing, and preparedness and the last struggle.

Resources on Grieving

Response Center
7457 N. Western Ave., 60645; 338-2292

The Project on Adolescent Mourning Experience is directed toward teens and families who are grieving the loss of a significant person or are anticipating such a loss. In addition to counseling, the RC provides educational programs on this subject.

Chicago Board of Rabbis
72 E. 11th St., 60605; 427-5863

Has prepared a booklet, *Help and Comfort,* which includes prayers, Psalms, and readings for all kinds of stress situations.

Self-help groups are listed in Chapter 2, under Support and Self-Help Groups. See also Chapter 3, under Pastoral Counseling, and Chapter 7, under Mental Health, for further suggestions regarding aid to the grieving.

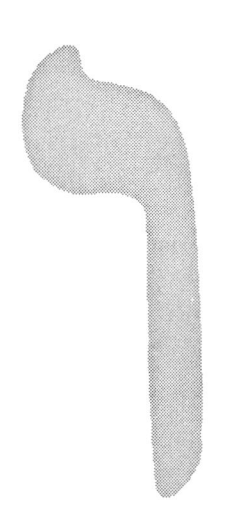

6
Education

Boards and Associations

Associated Talmud Torahs
2828 W. Pratt Blvd., 60645; 973-2828
Rabbi Harvey Well, Superintendent

The central agency for all Orthodox and Traditional religious schools, including day schools, after-school and weekend programs, community Hebrew schools, and high schools. Also provides preschool programs, Russian tutorial programs, and special education. Licenses and places teachers. Produces various publications. Sponsors Givat Ram, a day camp, in cooperation with the Horwich JCC. Extensive filmstrip library for teachers available in the pedagogic library named in honor of Rabbi Leonard Mishkin, Superintendent Emeritus.

Board of Education, City of Chicago
228 N. LaSalle St., 60601; 641-4141

The subject of the Holocaust has been introduced into Chicago public schools along with other examples of genocide and ethnic repression in a curriculum called Man's Inhumanity to Man. A number of Jews and Jewish organizations have assisted, particularly the Anti-Defamation League, which has also provided teacher workshops.

Board of Jewish Education
72 E. 11th St., 60605; 427-5570
Dr. Samuel Schafler, Superintendent

The central agency for Jewish education for Reform, Conservative, Reconstructionist, and Independent religious and secular afternoon, weekend, and day schools in the Chicago metropolitan area. Serves

16,000 students, from preschool age through high school.

Under the umbrella of the BJE are the High School of Jewish Studies, the largest supplementary Jewish high school program in the country; a network of Early Childhood Centers; Sabra, a school for Israeli children in Chicago that has been certified by the Israel Ministry of Education; Institute for Jewish Study; Institute for Jewish Leadership; and Family Education Association. Other programs include a testing program in Hebrew; the Philip and Elsie Heller Center for Innovative Education; the Frank G. Marshall Media Center; professional placement and the Professional Growth Institute, a professional continuing-education program for teachers; a broad music and music-training program; and day camps. Among various publications from the BJE is the new semiannual *SAFRA*, an evaluation of Jewish textbooks, issued jointly with the American Association for Jewish Education. The Teachers Reference Library with over 16,000 volumes is open to the public.

CATE (Chicago Association of Temple Educators)
Barbara (Cookie) Gross, President
c/o Temple Sholom religious school, 525-4707
CATE is the local chapter of the National Association of Temple Educators (NATE) composed of administrators of religious schools in the Reform movement.

Educators' Lodge B'nai B'rith
Marvin A. Pearlman, Executive Vice President and Chaplain
2945 Lilac Lane, Northbrook 60062; 564-3023
An organization of Chicago-area teachers and administrators of Jewish faith. Membership includes elementary, high school, and college instructors in the public, parochial, and private school systems. Monthly meetings, socials, field trips, theater parties. The lodge awards a scholarship to a deserving youth each year.

Hebrew Principals Association of Chicago
Rabbi David Brusin, President, 675-4141
A professional organization of full-time religious-school educators in Conservative and Reform congregations.

JUF Educators Division
1 S. Franklin, 60606; 346-6700
One of the Trades, Industries, and Professions Divisions of the Jewish United Fund. Educators organized for JUF fund raising.

Jewish Educators' Assembly
Dr. Irving Skolnick, National President
Board of Jewish Education, 72 E. 11th St., 60605
The national organization of the Conservative movement.

Joint Commission on Reform Jewish Education
100 W. Monroe, Rm. 312, 60603; 782-1477

Created in 1980 to deal with concerns of Reform Jewish education. Includes representatives from the Union of American Hebrew Congregations Chicago Federation, Chicago Association of Reform Rabbis, and CATE.

Educational Resources

The Board of Jewish Education and the Associated Talmud Torahs have virtually unlimited resources in the field of education: curriculum materials, publications, libraries, and filmstrip collections for teacher use. They each certify or license and then place teachers.

The Summer Institute for Teachers and Principals is held jointly by the BJE and the ATT in August of each year, with four intensive days of workshops, discussions, professional presentations, and brainstorming, often revolving around a theme. In 1980 the theme was Jewish Education in Chicago: An Agenda for the 1980s. The summer institute is held at the BJE facilities in Skokie.

Professional Growth Institute for Teachers and Principals
Board of Jewish Education
72 E. 11th St., 60605; 427-5570

The professional continuing-education program for educators sponsored by BJE. A year-long series of professional classes concerning all aspects of Jewish education—pedagogy, Hebrew, early-childhood education, multimedia for the classroom, primary, middle grades, high school, etc. The Professional Growth Institute also sponsors an annual Teacher Idea Fair, which is summarized in an issue of the BJE *Kivunim*.

■ Sarah S. Shapiro
Director, Department of Professional Growth
Board of Jewish Education
72 E. 11th St., 60605; 427-5570

Illinois Consultation on Ethnicity in Education
55 E. Jackson Blvd., Suite 1880, 60604; 663-5400

Associated with the American Jewish Committee and its Institute on Pluralism and Group Identity. Publishes an excellent free newsletter, *Heritage*, which covers news and opinions and happenings in ethnic education throughout the state and particularly in the Chicago area. Also reports on Title IX Ethnic Heritage Studies Programs and Projects in the region. Subscriptions go to members of the ICEE and others by request.

Institute for Computers in Jewish Life
845 N. Michigan Ave., Rm. 843, 60611
Rabbi Irving Rosenbaum, Director

Originally affiliated with Hebrew Theological College, the institute is now a separate organization to develop computer applications to Jewish life, particularly through its educational institutions.

Jewish Children's Bureau
1 S. Franklin, 60606; 346-6700

Provides educational services to professionals who are in the field of child welfare.

Jewish Vocational Service
1 S. Franklin, 60606; 346-6700

Provides educational as well as vocational counseling.

Kohl Jewish Teachers Center
161 Green Bay Rd., Wilmette 60091; 251-6950
Dolores Kohl Solovy, Founder
Besty Dolgin Katz, Curriculum Coordinator

One is tempted to call this special place unique, but it isn't—because Solovy also operates a nonsectarian Teachers Center up the road in Wilmette and two Jewish Teachers Centers in Israel. She also has been consultant to about twenty others that have opened throughout the country using her model. Founded in 1975, the KJTC is primarily aimed at the needs of teachers, but its rich resources are also available to parents, professionals working with seniors or handicapped, JCCs, etc. Emphasis is on the process of creativity in education rather than on any particular final product.

The center operates on three levels: as a drop-in center where teachers can take advantage of a wide availability of resources—books, ideas, games, materials, models, multimedia, and curriculum aids and units; as a workshop program wherein teachers attend scheduled one-time or continuing in-depth programs; and through support groups, open to newcomers, which have evolved from workshops. Currently, there are ongoing support groups in three areas: for teachers of children with learning disabilities, for teachers of Soviet children, and for Hebrew teachers.

A continually growing file of resource people is also available. Raw materials are for sale. Teacher Center in a Tube and Teacher Center in a Bag, made of recycled materials, are crammed full of ideas on teaching such subjects as Passover, Israel, and Zionism, and are available on a subscription basis. What is not for sale—but best of all—are the unanticipated nuggets of inspiration that come from simply being there and exchanging thoughts and concerns. The KJTC is open Sunday through Friday: 8:30 A.M. to 5 P.M. Mondays, Wednesdays, Thursdays; noon to 9 P.M. Tuesdays; 8 A.M. to 1 P.M. Fridays; noon to 5 P.M. Sundays.

Yosef Arye Schub—Friends of Jewish Education
Dr. Norman Silverstein, President
4403 W. Greenleaf, Lincolnwood 60646; 674-2737
An organization dedicated to furthering Jewish education and perpetuating the memory of Yosef Arye, who was associated with the Board of Jewish Education. The group itself preceded Arye's death. It originally was founded in the middle 1960s out of a PTA associated with the Board of Jewish Education Hebrew High School. There are about 150 members, and newcomers are welcome. Monthly meetings feature programs of Jewish content, usually held in the home of Dr. and Mrs. Silverstein. Contributions are made annually to the Board of Jewish Education and CASE, a program that benefits underprivileged Israeli youths.

■ Eliezer Berkman
125 Hawthorne, Glencoe 60022; 835-4158
A curriculum consultant who has developed Jewish curriculum "happenings" such as The Pesach Happening.

Preschools

Schools Associated with the Board of Jewish Education

Akiba-Schechter Jewish Day School
5200 S. Hyde Park Blvd., 60615; 493-8880
Half-day nursery classes for 3- and 4-year-olds and full-day kindergarten for 5-year-olds.

Anshe Emet Day School
3760 N. Pine Grove, 60613; 281-1858
Half-day classes: nursery for 3-year-olds; junior kindergarten for 4-year-olds. Full-day senior kindergarten for 5-year-olds.

Anshe Sholom a Beth Torah
20820 Western Ave., Olympia Fields 60461; 748-6010
Half-day nursery for 3- and 4-year-olds.

Beth Emet
1224 Dempster, Evanston 60202; 869-4230
Half-day nursery classes for 3- and 4-year-olds.

B'nai Torah
2789 Oak St., Highland Park 60035; 433-7100
Half-day nursery classes for 3- and 4-year-olds. Parent-toddler group for 2-year-olds meets once a week.

Maine Township Jewish Congregation
8800 Ballard Rd., Des Plaines 60016; 297-2006
Half-day nursery classes for 3- and 4-year-olds. Parent-toddler group for 2-year-olds.

Moriah Congregation
200 Hyacinth Lane, Deerfield 60015; 948-5346
Parent-toddler group.

Niles Township Jewish Congregation
4500 Dempster, Skokie 60076; 675-4141
Half-day classes for 3- and 4-year-olds. Parent-toddler group for 2-year-olds.

North Suburban Synagogue Beth El
1175 Sheridan Rd., Highland Park 60035; 432-8900
Half-day classes for 3- and 4-year-olds. Parent-toddler group for 2-year-olds.

Northwest Suburban Jewish Congregation
7800 Lyons, Morton Grove 60053; 965-0900
Half-day nursery classes for 3- and 4-year-olds. Parent-toddler group for 2-year-olds.

Sager Solomon Schechter Day School
350 Lee Rd., Northbrook 60062; 498-2100
Full-day kindergarten for 5-year-olds.

Solomon Schechter Day School–Skokie
9301 Gross Point Rd., Skokie 60076; 679-6270
Full-day kindergarten for 5-year-olds.

West Suburban Temple Har Zion
1040 N. Harlem, River Forest 60305; 366-9000
Morning classes for 3- and 4-year-olds.

Model Early Childhood Centers Operated by the Board of Jewish Education

Beth Judea Congregation
P.O. Box 763, Buffalo Grove 60090; 634-3640 or 427-5570
Half-day nursery for 3- and 4-year-olds. Parent-toddler for 2-year-olds.

Beth Tikvah Congregation
300 Hillcrest Blvd., Hoffman Estates 60195; 885-1600 or 427-5570
Half-day nursery for 3- and 4-year-olds. Parent-toddler group for 2-year-olds.

B'nai Tikvah Congregation
795 Wilmot, Deerfield 60015; 948-5320 or 427-5570
Half-day nursery for 3- and 4-year-olds.

Other Preschools

Anita M. Stone JCC
18600 Governors Highway, Flossmoor 60422; 799-7650
Nursery school programs: two days a week for 2- to 3½-year-olds, three days a week for 3-year-olds, and five days a week for prekindergarten 4-year-olds.

Arie Crown Hebrew Day School
8150 N. Tripp, Skokie 60076; 982-9191
Prenursery for 3-year-olds, nursery for 4-year-olds, and kindergarten for 5-year-olds.

Bais Yaakov Hebrew Parochial School
6526 N. California, 60645; 465-5761
Three-year-olds attend three times a week; 4-year-olds, five mornings a week; 5-year-olds, five full days a week.

Bernard Horwich JCC
3003 W. Touhy, 60645; 761-9100
Mommie and Me for 1½-year-olds meets once a week. Mom-Tot Workshop for 2-year-olds, once a week. Funtimers, for 2½-year-olds, meets twice weekly, and mothers are not required to stay with children. Nursery school for 3-year-olds and older available two, three, or five days a week.

Chicago Sinai Congregation Nursery School
5350 S. South Shore Dr., 60615; 288-1600
Reopened after several years, this nursery school has a Jewish orientation but an open policy. Children may attend two, three, or five mornings a week.

Henry N. Hart JCC
2961 W. Peterson, 60659; 275-8445
Parents and tots classes for children from walking age to 20 months, and for children 20 months to 3 years. Nursery school, playgroups,

and many activities for preschoolers 3 to 5, two or three mornings a week or three afternoons a week.

Hillel Torah North Suburban Day School
7120 Laramie, Skokie 60077; 674-6533

Prekindergarten and kindergarten programs.

Hyde Park JCC
1100 E. Hyde Park Blvd., 60615; 268-4600

Parent-toddler classes for 1½- to 3-year-olds, mornings or afternoons twice a week. Nursery school for 4-year-olds, five mornings a week, includes swimming. As part of its cooperative efforts with Michael Reese Hospital, has run preschool programs for Reese families.

KINS Nursery School
2800 W. North Shore Ave., 60645; 761-4000
Rabbi Michael Azose, Administrator

A morning nursery-school program.

Mayer Kaplan JCC
5050 Church, Skokie 60077; 675-2200

The Pearl Goodman Schoen Preschool and Day Care Center operates at the Skokie address; a west branch is at B'nai Jehoshua Beth Elohim, 901 Milwaukee Ave., Glenview 60025. For 3- to 5-year-olds. Also, mother-toddler groups for 2-year-olds.

William Lavin Educational Center
Associated Talmud Torahs
3545 Walters, Northbrook 60062

Preschool for 3- and 4-year-olds. Also has parent-toddler play workshop for 2-year-olds. A special Jewish Holiday Celebrations class for 3- and 4-year-olds meets once a week; this program is separate from the preschool.

Additional Resources

- **Marvell Ginsburg**
  Director, Department Early Childhood Jewish Education
  Board of Jewish Education
  72 E. 11th St., 60605; 427-5570

- **Fern Kamen**
  Director, Preschool Programs
  Bernard Horwich JCC
  3003 W. Touhy, 60645; 761-9100

A resource on all matters pertaining to preschoolers and preschool education.

Day Schools
Elementary Schools

Akiba-Schechter Jewish Day School (boys, girls)
5200 S. Hyde Park Blvd., 60615; 493-8880
Formed through a merger of the Orthodox Akiba Day School of South Shore and the Conservative Solomon Schechter Day School of Hyde Park. Programs are administered by both the Associated Talmud Torahs and the Board of Jewish Education.

Anshe Emet Day School (boys, girls; Conservative)
3760 N. Pine Grove, 60613; 281-1858
An independent elementary school affiliated with the Board of Jewish Education, founded in 1946 and privately financed and supported through tuitions and contributions.

Arie Crown Hebrew Day School (boys, girls; Orthodox)
8150 N. Tripp Ave., Skokie 60076; 982-9191
Founded in 1947.

Bais Yaacov Hebrew Parochial School (boys; Orthodox)
6526 N. California Ave., 60645; 465-5761

Bais Yaacov Hebrew Parochial School (girls; Orthodox)
2447 W. Granville, 60659; 465-3770

Hillel Torah North Suburban Day School (boys, girls; Orthodox)
7120 Laramie, Skokie 60077; 674-6533

Sager Solomon Schechter Day School (boys, girls; Conservative)
350 Lee Rd., Northbrook 60062; 498-2100
Kindergarten through 6th grade.

Solomon Schechter Day School–Skokie
 (boys, girls; Conservative)
9301 Gross Point Rd., Skokie 60076; 679-6270
All inquiries and registration: 350 Lee Rd., Northbrook 60062; 498-2100
Some of the younger grades held at the Sharp Corner School, which is also the location of the high school.

Solomon Schechter Secondary School (boys, girls; Conservative)
9301 Gross Point Rd., Skokie 60076; 679-6270
The junior high school, from 7th grade, is at this location.

South Suburban Hebrew Community Day School (boys, girls)
160 Westwood Dr., Park Forest 60466; 747-9513
Independent. For kindergarten through 3d grade.

High Schools

Brisk Talmudic Academy (boys; Orthodox)
9000 Forest View, Skokie 60203; 674-4652

Preparatory high school affiliated with the Brisk Rabbinical College.

Hebrew Theological College High School (boys; Orthodox)
7135 Carpenter Rd., Skokie 60077; 674-7750

Also called Yeshiva High School; attended by boys from all over the Western Hemisphere. Secular studies plus preparation for entrance into the seminary.

Ida Crown Jewish Academy (boys, girls; Orthodox)
2828 W. Pratt, 60645; 973-1450

Ida Crown Hanna Sacks Girls School (girls; Orthodox)
3021 W. Devon, 60659; 338-9222

Founded in the 1960s by the Associated Talmud Torahs for students whose parents preferred a separate education for girls.

Solomon Schechter Secondary School (boys, girls; Conservative)
9301 Gross Point Rd., Skokie 60076; 679-6270

Includes 7th grade through high school.

Telshe Yeshiva High School (boys; Orthodox)
3535 W. Foster Ave., 60625; 463-7738

After-School and Weekend Schools

High Schools

High School of Jewish Studies
Board of Jewish Education
72 E. 11th St., 60605; 427-5570

Sponsors an after-school and weekend High School of Jewish Studies at various locations; largest high school of Jewish studies in the country with about 800 students. Branches include Buffalo Grove, Deerbrook, Hyde Park, Lake Shore, North Shore, Northwest Suburban, Northwest–Maine Suburban, Skokie, South Suburban, and West Suburban. Also Waukegan, Rockford, and Northwest Indiana. Offers Advance Placement classes in association with Hebrew Theological College, Roosevelt University, College of Lake County, and Oakton Community College. Besides academic courses, the high school sponsors a basketball team that participates in league play.

Zaronsky-Katzman Consolidated Hebrew High School
Associated Talmud Torahs
2828 W. Pratt Blvd., 60645; 973-2828

The after-school high school of the ATT meets Mondays through Thursdays at the Ida Crown Jewish Academy and at regional schools. Provision is made for high school students who have not had an Orthodox preparatory education. The high schools have regular class sessions plus a "drop-in" program. The regional schools are Chicago-Evanston, Lincolnwood-Skokie, Woodfield-Hoffman Estates, and Morton Grove-Niles.

Other Schools

Associated Talmud Torahs
2828 W. Pratt, 60645; 973-2828

The ATT administers one dozen Hebrew schools, or Talmud Torahs, in an after-school program. Some of these are associated with congregations, but most are on a regional-community basis, such as the Southwest Community Hebrew School and Northbrook Community Hebrew School. These are the Orthodox and Traditional schools of the Chicago Jewish community.

Board of Jewish Education
72 E. 11th St., 60605; 427-5570

The BJE administers over 50 elementary weekday schools and over 50 weekend schools. Most of these are in association with a Conservative, Reform, or Reconstructionist congregation. Also under the BJE administration are two secular Jewish schools and a special school for Israeli children:

The North Shore School of Jewish Studies
5050 Church St., Skokie 60077

A secular school of Jewish studies for kindergarten through 9th grade, offered on Sundays at the Mayer Kaplan JCC.

South Side School of Jewish Studies
5715 S. Woodlawn Ave., 60637; 752-5655

An alternative school founded by secularists but no longer limited to that viewpoint. Meets at Hillel-University of Chicago.

Sabra School
5050 Church St., Skokie 60077; 675-2200

A school for Israeli children living temporarily in Chicago who are not enrolled in a day school. Provides Hebrew-language and Bible instruction and is fully accredited by the Ministry of Education of Israel. Sessions are held Sundays at the High School of Jewish Studies at the Kaplan JCC.

168 The Chicago Jewish Source Book

Jewish Institutions of Higher Learning

Brisk Rabbinical College (Yeshivas Brisk)
9000 Forest View Rd., Skokie 60203; 674-4652
Rabbi Aaron Soloveichik, Dean, President, and Founder
Rabbi Arthur Levin, Executive Director

Founded in 1974, BRC is named for Brisk, Lithuania, a great center of Jewish learning. Education of the highest quality is the main goal of BRC. At the same time, the program helps each graduate to prepare for a practical career. BRC divisions include the Rabbinic, the Kollel Graduate School, and the Brisk Institute for Women. The Joseph and Faye Tannenbaum Academy is an accredited preparatory high school for boys. Dormitories with board are available.

In formation are a School of Halachic Medical Ethics, a Holocaust Studies Center, and, eventually, a women's teachers college and a girl's preparatory school.

Rabbinic ordination at Brisk Rabbinical College may qualify a man to be rabbi, teacher, communal worker, scribe, ritual meat slaughterer, or chaplain.

Hebrew Theological College
7135 N. Carpenter Rd., Skokie 60077; 674-7750 or 267-9800

HTC, founded in 1921, is sometimes called the Jewish University of America. HTC provides the following programs: Yeshiva-Rabbinic, leading to ordination; Division of Liberal Arts, offering classes in humanities, sciences, social sciences, and business administration; Jewish Studies Program, a two-year program in basic Hebrew and Jewish studies for the student with a limited Judaic background; Anne M. Blitzstein Teacher Institute for Women, a program of advanced Hebrew courses for women leading either to a Bachelor of Hebrew Literature or Hebrew Teacher's Certificate, or both; and Yeshiva High School, a fully accredited four-year preparatory division of Hebrew Theological College. HTC also provides extension classes especially aimed at Chicago's young-adult Jewish population with limited background in Jewish studies. The Seymour Abrams Chair of Pastoral Counseling is open to graduate rabbis and qualifies a graduate for state licensing. HTC has a credit exchange program with Northeastern Illinois University.

Yeshiva Women of HTC, founded in 1949, is represented by many of the sisterhoods of Orthodox and Traditional congregations in the community. This auxiliary supports Jewish education and HTC in particular.

For interesting history and anecdotes about Hebrew Theological College and the Orthodox rabbinate, see "After Fifty Years, an Optimist," by Rabbi Oscar Z. Fasman, *American Jewish History*, vol. LXIX, no. 2 (December 1979).

■ **Roslyn Berlat**
8808 Dee Rd., Des Plaines 60016; 827-2594
Is in the process of completing her doctoral dissertation on the history of Hebrew Theological College. Her introductory chapter can be seen by appointment. She can also help in locating Yiddish periodicals and other research materials.

Spertus College of Judaica
618 S. Michigan Ave., 60605; 922-9012
Dr. David Wolf Silverman, President

The Ratner Center, dedicated in 1974, contains the classrooms and administrative offices of the college, the library, Maurice Spertus Museum of Judaica, the Museum Store, and Bederman Auditorium.

Spertus College of Judaica, founded in 1925 as the College of Jewish Studies, was renamed in 1970. This is the only nondenominational institution in the Middle West specializing in Judaic and Hebraic studies. The college is a fully accredited liberal arts institution granting bachelor's and master's degrees through a unique consortium agreement with eighteen other colleges and universities in the metropolitan Chicago area, with courses offered in six metropolitan locations. The college will hold its 53d commencement exercises in 1981. Courses are offered in Hebrew, Bible, Jewish Literature, Jewish History, Jewish Thought, Talmud, Yiddish, Arabic, Communal Service, and Education.

The Norman Asher and Helen Asher Library contains the largest Judaica and Hebraica collection in this region of the United States, some 70,000 volumes. It also houses the Chicago Jewish Archives.

For information about the Spertus Museum, see the section on Museums in this chapter.

■ **Dr. David Weinstein**
Chancellor, Spertus College of Judaica
618 S. Michigan, 60605; 922-9012
Lectures on Spertus College, Judaic studies, and other topics.

Telshe Yeshiva
3535 W. Foster Ave., 60625; 463-7738
Telshe Yeshiva is affiliated with an older seminary with the same name in Cleveland. In addition to its college-level and rabbinical degree programs, Telshe includes a preparatory high school for boys and a community outreach program for men in various locations within the city and in Highland Park. CITY (Community Institute of

Telshe Yeshiva) is another adjunct to the Yeshiva, providing an evening study session in learning Torah at a synagogue in Rogers Park. There is an auxiliary, Telshe Yeshiva Women.

Yeshiva Migdal Torah
5665 N. Jersey, 60659; 583-9535
Rabbi Yosef T. Heisler, Dean

Established in 1978 with one goal: to give the Jew of college age and older an opportunity to understand more about Judaism, and through this learning to be motivated to remain within Judaism, marry a Jewish partner, raise a Jewish family, and be an active asset to the Jewish community. Attempts to counter the effects of cults, intermarriage, and unsuccessful searching for Jewish identity. Classes—including some for high school students—are held at various locations. The Kesser Institute (which is related) provides instruction for couples. Courses are usually aimed at students with mixed backgrounds, some of whom have very limited backgrounds in Jewish learning or observances. Some suburban classes are being offered. Classes are also offered in the Lakeview area of Chicago.

Other Chicago-Area Institutions of Higher Learning

B'nai B'rith Hillel Foundations Jewish Federation
College Age Youth Service
1 S. Franklin, 60606; 346-6700
Rabbi Yehiel Poupko, Director

This agency directs the Jewish student organizations on college campuses throughout the Chicago metropolitan area. For answers to questions about Jewish student activities on any particular campus, call this office.

Barat College
700 E. Westleigh Rd., Lake Forest 60045; 234-3000
A small Catholic women's liberal arts college offering courses on Jewish-Christian Thought, Hebrew Bible as Literature, Judaism in the Time of the Birth of Christianity, and Contemporary Jewish Thought.

Chicago State University
95th and Dr. Martin Luther King Dr., 60628; 995-2523
Offers a year abroad at Hebrew University.

Chicago Theological Seminary
Center for Jewish Christian Studies
5757 S. University Ave., 60637; 752-5757
Dr. André Lacocque, Director

One of the doctoral centers of the CTS, the CJCS was founded in 1967 to train scholars and teachers in areas of Old Testament, New Testament, Intertestamental Literature, Rabbinica, and related disciplines. The program has a double purpose: to bring scientific study of the Jewish/Judaic background to both Testaments and to increase understanding between Christians and Jews. CTS is one of a cluster of nine theological schools that are part of the Spertus College consortium, a credit transfer system.

City Colleges of Chicago
Loop College
64 E. Lake St., 60601; 269-8000

Hebrew course is taught by Dr. Irving Skolnick of the Board of Jewish Education.

City Colleges of Chicago
Truman College
1145 W. Wilson Ave., 60640; 878-1700

Hebrew, Jewish History and Culture, and other Jewish-content courses are offered to senior adults through the Adult Continuing Education Program, which is approved by the Illinois Community College Board.

College of Lake County
19351 Washington, Grayslake 60030; 223-6601

Advanced placement credit for BJE High School of Jewish Studies courses.

DePaul University (Undergraduate School)
25 E. Jackson Blvd., 60604; 321-8000

A member of the Spertus College consortium. Course offerings have included Hebrew, History and Literature of Zionism, Russian Jews, Israel, Ancient Israel Archaeological Sources, Contemporary Jewish Thought, and Liturgy of the Jewish People. There is a Jewish Student Association.

DePaul University Law School
25 E. Jackson Blvd., 60604; 321-7700

Has a chapter of the Student Decalogue Society, which is a Jewish law organization.

George Williams College
555 31st, Downers Grove 60515; 964-3100
A collection of Judaica was presented to the library in 1974 by the Jewish Chautauqua Society of the National Federation of Temple Brotherhoods.

Illinois Institute of Technology
3300 S. Federal St., 60616; 567-3000
Alpha Epsilon Pi fraternity is located on campus at 3350 S. Michigan Ave., 60616; 842-8766.

Illinois Institute of Technology-Chicago Kent College of Law
77 S. Wacker Dr., 60606
Has a chapter of the Student Decalogue Society. Participant in year abroad at the Hebrew University.

John Marshall Law School
304 S. State St., 60604; 427-2750
Has a chapter of the Student Decalogue Society.

Kendall College
2408 Orrington Ave., Evanston 60201; 866-1300
A member of the Spertus College consortium.

Lake Forest College
E. Deerpath Rd. and N. Sheridan Rd., Lake Forest 60045; 234-3100
Course in Holocaust taught in Philosophy Department by Professor Abba Lessing. Philosophical and Theological Implications course will be added. Course offerings have also included Judaism, Biblical Heritage and Archaeology with a sponsored summer archaeological excavation internship in Israel. Am Yisrael Chai is the Jewish student organization. One of its offshoots, the Torah Study Group, meets every Friday afternoon. The best resource for Jewish offerings at Lake Forest College is Dr. Lessing.

Loyola University (Undergraduate)
6525 N. Sheridan Rd., 60626; 274-3000
Jewish Student Association. Participant in year abroad at the Hebrew University.

Loyola University
Graduate School of Social Work
820 N. Michigan Ave., 60611; 670-3180
A member of the Spertus College Consortium.

Loyola University Institute of Pastoral Studies
6525 N. Sheridan Rd., 60626; 274-3000
Has cosponsored lectures by Elie Weisel with Moriah Congregation.

Loyola University Dental School
2160 S. First, Maywood 60153
Has a chapter of Alpha Omega, the Jewish dental fraternity.

Mundelein College
6363 N. Sheridan Rd., 60660; 262-8100
A member of the Spertus College consortium. Some classes offered by Spertus College are taught. An ecumenical seder is given here.

Northeastern Illinois University
5500 N. St. Louis, 60625; 583-4050
NIU and Hebrew Theological College have a credit-exchange program. NIU is a member of the Spertus College consortium, and some Spertus College courses are taught here. Students at NIU have participated in the year abroad at the Hebrew University. An Introduction to Judaism course has been offered for credit, and Hebrew has been offered for noncredit.

There are three Jewish organizations on campus: Klal Yisrael and Students for Israel/Hillel, two student organizations; and the Northeastern Illinois University Jewish Forum, an organization that attempts to speak to faculty and staff and to service them. Advisers to all three groups are Dr. Stanley Newman, Professor of Anthropology, and Sophie K. Black, Associate University Librarian for Public Services. Newman and Black have also taught Jewish-content noncredit courses through the campus Jewish organizations.

Northwestern University
Evanston Campus
About 2,000 Jewish students attend Northwestern's Evanston campus. Jewish-content courses in the History of Religions department are taught mainly by Professors Manfred Vogel and Mordecai I. Mantel. An Introduction to Eastern European Jewish Culture has been taught by Dr. Irwin Weil, Slavic Languages and Literature Department. The annual James H. Becker lectureship, usually held in May, brings to the Evanston campus a Jewish scholar of international renown (e.g., Gershom Scholem, leading authority on Jewish mysticism). Northwestern has a foreign-study program affiliated with the Hebrew University, Jerusalem.

B'nai B'rith Hillel Foundation–Northwestern University
1935 Sherman Ave., Evanston 60201; 328-0650
Rabbi Michael Balinsky, Director

The center of Jewish religious activities on campus, with a lounge, library, kosher dining facilities, and rooms for meeting and relaxing. Ongoing noncredit courses offer Yiddish, Hebrew, and a rotating variety of classes in Talmud, Jewish history, and philosophy. Chevra is a group that plans Israeli-content programs on campus. The Kosher Dining Club provides five kosher dinners a week, and interested students can be released from board contracts to participate. Throughout the year, Hillel offers Sunday lox and bagel brunches and deli dinners. There are celebrations for all holidays and weekly Israeli folk dancing.

Religious services are as follows:
Traditional Friday evening services, followed by Shabbat dinner
Creative services, held after dinner
Traditional Saturday morning services, followed by Shabbat luncheon
Havdalah services (concluding the Sabbath) with Israeli folk singing, held every Saturday evening in dorms
Reform services, held Friday evenings with educational, social, and social-action programs

Northwestern University Dental School
303 E. Chicago Ave., 60611

Has a chapter of Alpha Omega, the Jewish dental fraternity.

Northwestern University Law School
357 E. Chicago Ave., 60611

Has a chapter of the Student Decalogue Society.

Northwestern University Medical School
301 E. Chicago Ave., 60611

Has a Jewish student organization.

Oakton Community College
Des Plaines 60016; 635-1600

A member of the Spertus College consortium. Some classes offered by Spertus College are given here. Gesher Hillel is the name of the Jewish student organization. Advanced placement credit for BJE High School of Jewish Studies.

Roosevelt University
430 S. Michigan Ave., 60605; 341-3500

A member of the Spertus College consortium. Jewish-content courses at Roosevelt are most often offered in association with Spertus. Has participated in the year abroad at the Hebrew University, Jerusalem. Advanced placement credit for BJE High School of Jewish Studies. There is an Association of Jewish Students; for information contact Student Activities, Herman Crown Center, Rm. 118; 341-2015.

Roosevelt has three satellite campuses: Arlington Heights, Glenview, and Waukegan. A noncredit course on the Holocaust was offered in 1980 at the Arlington Heights campus.

Seabury-Western Theological Seminary
2122 Sheridan Rd., Evanston 60201; 328-9300
This Episcopalian Seminary has a distinguished Old Testament library of 10,000 volumes.

University of Chicago
753-1234
No Judaica department, but there is an independent undergraduate and graduate degree program in Jewish Studies. The Fuerstenberg Scholarships, administered by Hillel, are available to students pursuing Jewish studies. Bible, Hebrew, Jewish history, and a variety of courses in Rabbinics are offered in departments of Divinity, Middle Eastern Studies, and Humanities. Also taught are the Sociology of Ancient Judaism, Biblical Aramaic, and courses in Akkadian, Arabic, Babylonian, Syriac, and Ugaritic. Hebrew has been part of the U of C scene since 1893, when Hebrew scholar William Rainey Harper came to serve as first president.

B'nai B'rith Hillel Foundation–University of Chicago
5715 S. Woodlawn, 60637; 752-1127
Rabbi Daniel I. Leifer, Director
Hillel is the center of Jewish religious and cultural life on the U of C campus. The house, given in memory of Lt. Raymond Karasik, who died in World War II, was given to Hillel by his parents, Yetta and Max Karasik. It has a library with a wide selection of Jewish magazines and periodicals, as well as a music listening lounge, kosher kitchen, and dining rooms. The program includes lectures, films, and classes in such subjects as Hebrew, Yiddish, Talmud, Hebrew calligraphy, Jewish and Hebrew literature, and Israel studies. Other activities are Adat Shalom, a Shabbat evening meal co-op, subsidized by a grant from AFTA; a kosher meat co-op; Israeli folk dancing; and a monthly faculty luncheon program.

There are Reform, Conservative, and Orthodox worship services on Sabbaths, High Holidays, and Festivals:
  Reform-Progressive services, 5:30 P.M. Fridays, cosponsored by the
  Chicago Conference of Temple Brotherhoods Sambatyon Program

Conservative-egalitarian services, offered by the Upstairs Minyan, 9:30 A.M. Saturdays

Orthodox services, Yavneh, held Fridays at sundown and Saturdays at 9:15 A.M.

Oriental Institute
1155 E. 58th St., 60637; 753-2475 or 753-2474

A research center and museum relating to Near Eastern antiquities. Dr. Norman Golb, voting member of the Oriental Institute, is Professor of Hebrew and Judaeo-Arabic Studies, Department of Near Eastern Languages and Civilizations. He is chairman of the Aronberg Judaica Lectureship Committee.

Joseph Regenstein Library
Department of Special Collections
1100 E. 57th St., 60637; 753-4366
Robert Rosenthal, Curator

In 1980, the Ludwig Rosenberger Judaica Library of approximately 20,000 volumes was donated to the University of Chicago, Joseph Regenstein Library. A special room will hold the extraordinary collection; target date for completion, 1981. The collection is largely of secular works on the life of Jews and their literature and social and political thought, more than half being in German and the remainder in Latin, English, French, Italian, and Spanish.

University of Chicago Bookstore
5750 S. Ellis, 60637; 753-3311

Food for the stomach as well as food for thought: prepackaged kosher sandwiches are sold in a vending machine on the second floor.

University of Chicago Business School
Organization of Jewish Business Students
For information, call 753-1792.

University of Illinois–Chicago Circle
601 S. Morgan, 60680; 996-3000

A member of the Spertus College consortium, offering a major in Judaic studies and an M.A. in Jewish Education. Credit also for courses taken at Hebrew Theological College and for study abroad in Israel. There are about 2,000 Jewish students on campus. Campus food service provides prewrapped kosher sandwiches, kosher potato chips, and drink. All food vending machines have at least one kosher soup selection. Kosher candy is sold at stands, and Dannon Yogurt is sold in various places. Call Hillel for information, 996-3385. During Passover, there is a kosher l'Pesach coffeehouse.

Hillel at the Circle
516 Chicago Circle Center, UICC, 60680; 996-3385
Miriam Prum, Director

Hillel is the center of Jewish activity on this commuter campus. Three programs function under the Hillel umbrella: Hillel itself, which provides Jewish programming, religious and holiday observances, bimonthly Torah study group, lectures, and miniclasses; Associated Movements for Israel (AMI), which coordinates all political action regarding Israel on campus; and Israeli Students Organization, which provides nonpolitical Israeli programming such as Israeli folk dancing. There is also a Jewish fraternity on campus, Sigma Alpha Mu, which offers only limited Jewish content but definitely identifies itself as Jewish and overlaps in membership with Hillel.

University of Illinois Dental School
996-7520
Has a chapter of Alpha Omega, the Jewish dental fraternity.

University of Illinois Medical Center
996-7000
Kosher prepackaged sandwiches are sold in the medical school cafeteria and in the bookstore at 750 S. Halsted. There is a Jewish student group in the medical school.

■ **Dr. Harold Wechsler**
Department of Education, University of Chicago
5835 S. Kimbark Ave., 60637
Dr. Wechsler is a resource person and lecturer on Judaic studies in universities. He is also an expert and lecturer on the history of Jewish quotas in American universities.

Adult Education

An ongoing parade of adult-education courses is offered by congregations, the Jewish Community Centers, the Jewish institutions of higher learning, and organizations such as the Brandeis University National Women's Committee, Lubavitch Chabad, and Agudath Israel. Regular series include the following:

Spertus College of Judaica Friday luncheon series, 922-9012

Annual Chicago Jewish Community Forum, sponsored by the Zionist Organization of Chicago and the *Sentinel*, 973-3232

North Shore Institute of Jewish Studies, sponsored by six congregations; provides courses in Hebrew, history, literature, Judaism, philosophy; 835-4800

The Joint Adult Education Council Forum, cosponsored by seven city congregations, 764-8320

The Northwest Suburban Institute of Jewish Studies, celebrating twelve years of continuing classes in 1981; sponsored by eleven congregations; call Niles Township Jewish Congregation, 675-4141

178 The Chicago Jewish Source Book

Some Specialized Resources

Rabbis in Chicago have many areas of expertise, covering all phases of Jewish history, texts, theology, and social thought. For referral to a rabbinical expert, contact the Chicago Board of Rabbis, 427-5863; the Chicago Rabbinical Council, 764-0259; Brisk Rabbinical College, 674-4652; Hebrew Theological College, 674-7750; or Telshe Yeshiva, 463-7738.

Arabic and Islam

The American Jewish Committee
55 E. Jackson, Rm. 1870, 60604; 663-5500

Provides investigation and discussion of growing Arab influence on the United States and its impact on energy policy and economics. Publishes a monthly newsletter, *Petro Impact*.

■ **Dr. Nahman Bar-Nissim**
Professor of Hebrew and Arabic
Spertus College of Judaica
618 S. Michigan Ave., 60605; 922-9012

Besides teaching, Dr. Bar-Nissim lectures in Hebrew, Arabic, and English on various subjects, including Egyptian theater and Middle Eastern music.

Center for Middle Eastern Studies
University of Chicago
5848 S. University Ave., 60637; 753-4548

■ **Dr. Fazlur Rahman**
Department of Near Eastern Languages and Civilization
University of Chicago
c/o Oriental Institute, 1155 E. 58th St., 60637; 753-4318

An Islamic scholar.

Chutzpah
P.O. Box 60142, 60660

The Mideast work group of Chutzpah occasionally offers panels of Jewish-Arab dialogue.

Archaeology

■ **Dr. Dan P. Cole**
Professor of Religion and Near Eastern Archaeology

Lake Forest College
Lake Forest 60045; 234-3100

Dr. Cole has been associate director of Lahav Research Project excavations at Tel Halif, Israel, since 1976. He presents slide lectures on current digs in Israel.

- Rachel Dulin
  Instructor of Hebrew Language
  Spertus College of Judaica
  618 S. Michigan Ave., 60605; 922-9012

Lectures on the archaeology of ancient Israel.

- Dr. Lewis Hopfe
  First Congregational Church of Evanston
  1417 Hinman Ave., Evanston 60201; 864-8332

Slide presentations of his own archaelogical digs in Israel.

Bible

Local institutions of higher Jewish learning have courses for both matriculated students and the general public on biblical subjects.

- Dr. Stanley Kazan
  Professor of Hebrew and Biblical Studies
  Spertus College of Judaica
  618 S. Michigan Ave., 60605; 922-9012

Lectures on the Bible, narrative texts, and the Psalms.

- Prof. André Lacocque
  Old Testament Scholar, Chicago Theological Seminary
  Director, Center for Jewish Christian Studies
  5757 S. University Ave., 60637; 752-5757

Also a visiting professor at Spertus College. His lecture topics include the Bible and Intertestamental Literature. One of his latest books offers commentaries on the Book of Daniel and Zechariah 9-14.

- Dr. Paul Raccah
  7521 N. Albany, 60645

Teaches a private class in his home Thursday evenings on the week's Torah portion.

English Language Lessons

B'nai Zion Congregation
6759 N. Greenview, 60626; 465-2161

English lessons, sponsored by the JCCs, have been offered at this location.

Bernard Horwich JCC
3003 W. Touhy, 60645; 761-9100

Classes in English for new Americans have been offered weekday evenings at the Horwich JCC by the City Colleges of Chicago. Classes open to all newcomers. Call for information.

Rogers Park JCC
7101 N. Greenview, 60626; 274-0920

English is taught to Soviet Jewish newcomers to Chicago. A special teen-age drop-in center at the Coach House, 2 to 3 P.M. Sundays and Monday and Tuesday evenings, will help teens and others who are having difficulty with the English language. Check with Soviet Jewry staff for other English lessons available.

Hebrew

- **Claire Roberta Aronson**
  4300 Marine Dr., 60613

A lecturer and writer on the Hebrew language, education, and culture. Aronson and her late husband established the Hebrew Culture Council.

- **Dr. Warren Bargad**
  Professor of Hebrew Literature and Acting Dean
  Spertus College of Judaica
  618 S. Michigan Ave., 60605; 922-9012

Lectures on Israeli literature in Hebrew as well as in English.

- **Dr. Nahman Bar-Nissim**
  Professor of Hebrew and Arabic
  Spertus College of Judaica
  618 S. Michigan Ave., 60605; 922-9012

Teaches Hebrew and lectures in Hebrew.

- **Rivka (Rosalie) Becker**
  465-4026

A qualified Hebrew teacher who has lived in Israel, has had experience with translating Hebrew, and has prepared translations of Hebrew poetry.

- **Chug Ivri**
  Sara K. Bassan, Contact
  5650 N. Sheridan Rd., 60660

A 25-year-old organization dedicated to the advancement of Hebrew culture. All eight yearly meetings are conducted in Hebrew.

- **Rachel Dulin**
  Instructor of Hebrew Language
  Spertus College of Judaica
  618 S. Michigan Ave., 60605; 922-9012

- **Frances Pearlman Finstad**
  4431 Trailside Ct., Hoffman Estates 60195; 991-3279
  Hebrew teacher, tutor, translator. Also a resource in programming for youth and youth groups.

- **Lauren Frank**
  281-0930
  Hebrew teacher, tutor, translator. Translating Hebrew songs is a specialty. Lived in Israel for 2½ years.

- **Dr. Norman Golb**
  5813 S. Blackstone, 60637; 324-7858
  Professor of Hebrew and Judaeo-Arabic Studies at the University of Chicago.

  Hebrew Culture Council of Metropolitan Chicago
  4300 Marine Dr., 60613
  Founded in 1948 by Robert and Claire Aronson. Worked for and achieved the reintroduction of Hebrew language and culture into the Chicago public schools in 1953.

  Histadrut Ivrit, Chicago Chapter
  Sara K. Bassan, Contact
  5650 N. Sheridan Rd., 60660
  The local chapter of Histadruth Ivrith of America, the Hebrew Language and Culture Association, headquartered in New York. Membership drawn from all over the Chicago area meets three times a year.

  Dr. Saul Kasman
  432-7404
  Hebrew teacher and translator—Hebrew to English.

- **Dr. Stanley Kazan**
  Professor of Hebrew and Biblical Studies
  Spertus College of Judaica
  618 S. Michigan Ave., 60605; 922-9012

  Kohl Jewish Teachers Center
  161 Green Bay Rd., Wilmette 60091; 251-6950
  Has an ongoing support group for Hebrew teachers.

Bonnie Levy
831-4288
Teaches Hebrew privately to adults and children.

Meyer Shisler
262-3047
Private tutoring and instruction in Hebrew. Shisler also teaches at North Shore Congregation Israel, Torah School of Congregation Solel, and has a very special following with several generations of students. He is the creator of a magnificent Rube Goldberg–style contraption for executing Haman, which is a feature at the annual Purim Carnival of North Shore Congregation Israel.

Dr. Irving Skolnick
Board of Jewish Education
72 E. 11th St., 60605; 427-5570
A BJE resource for Hebrew-language tests and for Hebrew teachers; has developed curriculum materials especially for 8- to 13-year-olds. Professor of Hebrew at Loop College.

Izrael (Dick) Taubenfligel
1324 W. Touhy Ave., Apt. 2C, 60626; 274-1562
Teaches elementary Hebrew as well as many other languages, including Polish and Russian.

■ **Dr. David Weinstein**
Chancellor, Spertus College of Judaica
618 S. Michigan Ave., 60605; 922-9012
Dr. Weinstein is a professor of Hebrew and Language Education.

Hebrew courses are offered at several high schools, including Evanston Township, Niles Township, and Highland Park. Noncredit Hebrew instruction is offered at the B'nai B'rith Hillel Foundations at Northwestern University and the University of Chicago. The Bernard Horwich, Rogers Park, and Mayer Kaplan JCCs also have instruction in Hebrew. Hebrew for college credit is offered at the institutions listed in the sections on institutions of higher learning.

Russian

Rogers Park JCC
7101 N. Greenview, 60626; 274-0920
For resources on the Russian language—instructors, translators, etc.—contact the Soviet Jewry program at the Rogers Park JCC.

Izrael (Dick) Taubenfligel
1324 W. Touhy Ave., Apt. 2C, 60626; 274-1562
Russian language teacher.

Talmud

- **Dr. Martin J. Goldman**
  Maxwell Abbell Professor of Talmud
  Spertus College of Judaica
  618 S. Michigan Ave., 60605; 922-9012
  Lectures on the Talmud.

- **Rabbi Oscar Lichtman**
  Dean, Talmudic Department
  Hebrew Theological College
  7135 N. Carpenter Rd., Skokie 60077; 674-7750

For resources for Judaeo-Arabic, Ladino, and Yiddish, see Chapter 4, "Cultural Judaism."

Independent Study

Hamasmid Institute
4721 N. Bernard, 60625; 478-6010
An advanced institute of Jewish studies, which emphasizes programs of independent study. Some of the HI activities are held at the Young Israel Congregation, 4931 N. Kimball.

Correspondence Courses

Academy for Jewish Study Without Walls
American Jewish Committee, 663-5500
A national home-study program of courses on Jewish subjects. Has sponsored a five-day summer seminar at Northwestern University.

United Synagogue Youth
72 E. 11th St., 60605; 939-2353
The USY Home Study course will earn High School of Jewish Studies credits from the Board of Jewish Education.

Jewish Effectiveness Training

JET (Jewish Effectiveness Training)
Barbara Hoffman, 174 Hazel, Highland Park 60035; 432-1173
Cara Madansky, 645 Sheridan Rd., Highland Park 60035; 433-6120

JET I and II are a series of classes for adults that provide practical, how-to information for Jewish holidays, customs, and ceremonies. JET I is concerned with the biblical and historical approach. JET II delves into the Jewish Life Cycle. Included are arts, crafts, books, records, and cooking. *The Jewish Catalog,* by Richard Siegel, Michael Strassfeld, and Sharon Strassfeld (Philadelphia: Jewish Publication

Society, 1973), is the basic textbook. JET has been presented at congregations and Jewish Community Centers.

Scholarships

Jewish Vocational Service
1 S. Franklin, 60606; 346-6700

The Academic Scholarship Committee of the Jewish Federation is administered by the JVS. Various categories of financial assistance are available. For information call the JVS.

B'nai B'rith and Women's American ORT are two of the Jewish organizations offering scholarships locally. Scholarships are offered for Jewish studies by Spertus College, the three seminaries, and through Hillel–University of Chicago.

Special Education

Associated Talmud Torahs
2828 W. Pratt, 60645; 973-2828

Provides a special-education program for day school or afternoon Talmud Torah Hebrew School for children with learning disabilities. P'TACH (Parents for Torah for All Children) is a parent/professional organization dedicated to fostering programs within the Jewish day schools for 1st-through-4th-grade children with learning disabilities who find it difficult to function in the regular classroom.

Temple Chai
Rt. 1, Box 271, Long Grove 60047; 537-1771

An outstanding IL (Individualized Learning) program for children with learning disabilities—perhaps one of the best synagogue-related learning-disabilities programs in the country. Experts say the success of such programs is due to the leadership of a dedicated professional. In this case credit goes to Jill Kirschner, who can be reached through the temple. Children begin in the Hebrew program at age 9.

Jewish Vocational Service
1 S. Franklin, 60606; 346-6700

A wide variety of programs for persons with all kinds of disabilities.

Kohl Jewish Teachers Center
161 Green Bay Rd., Wilmette 60091; 251-6950

Has an ongoing support group for special-education teachers.

Tikvah Institute for Childhood Learning Disabilities
2451 N. Kedzie, 60647; 384-8200
Carolyn Brenner, Director

A nonsectarian school with kosher kitchen for children with severe learning disabilities. All children are offered an opportunity for religious education, including bar and bat mitzvah preparation. Accredited by Cook County and State of Illinois. The Tikvah summer camp-school is operated similarly to the day school. For ages 8 to 18, the Tikvah Youth Center, staffed primarily by trained volunteers, operates on the first Sunday of each month. For a full description of the program, call or write for the brochure *Tikvah Means Hope—the Story of the Tikvah Institute for Childhood Learning Disabilities.*

Dr. Richard Malter and Associates
15 S. Dryden Pl., Arlington Heights 60004; 398-6640
A consultant in many areas of mental health, Dr. Malter has established learning-disabilities programs in Jewish schools and has been an adviser to both the Board of Jewish Education and Associated Talmud Torahs.

Several camp programs for children with learning disabilities are listed in Chapter 2, "Community Life."

Libraries

Associated Talmud Torahs
Rabbi Dr. Leonard C. Mishkin Jewish Historical Research Library
2828 W. Pratt Blvd., 60645; 973-2828
A library of pedagogy and Jewish history.

Board of Jewish Education
Teachers Reference Room
72 E. 11th St., 60605; 427-5570
A collection of books, pamphlets, and filmstrips. Open daily 9 A.M. to 5 P.M. This may be the largest Jewish educational library in the Middle West, with 16,000 to 17,000 volumes on pedagogy and related fields.

Chicago Public Library
Central Library
425 N. Michigan Ave., 60611; 269-2900
Temporarily housed in the former Mandel Brothers Warehouse, a building recently owned and sold by the Jewish Theological Seminary. The following are five Chicago Public Library branches of special interest:

Albany Park Branch
5150 N. Kimball, 60625; 588-3901
Yiddish and Hebrew books that circulate.

Bezazian Branch
1226 W. Ainslie, 60640; 561-1864
A small collection of Russian-language books.

Lake View Branch
644 W. Belmont, 60657; 281-7565
A small collection of Russian-language books.

North Town Branch
6435 N. California, 60645; 465-2292
Has 60 to 70 fiction titles each in Hebrew and Yiddish language. Collection circulates and is updated from time to time.

Rogers Park Branch
6911 N. Clark, 60626; 764-0156
Circulating collection includes some titles in Hebrew and around 50 books in Yiddish.

Glenview Public Library
1930 Glenview Rd., Glenview 60025; 724-5200
In addition to Hebrew and Yiddish dictionaries, this library has a few books of Yiddish poetry.

Hebrew Theological College
Rabbi Saul Silber Memorial Library
7135 N. Carpenter Rd., Skokie 60077; 267-9800
Leah Mishkin, Librarian
Collection includes Judaica, Hebraica, Rabbinics, ethics, philosophy, Jewish history, biblical literature, and Zionism. Special collections also cover Holocaust, halacha, and Hebrew periodicals. Open to public. Interlibrary loans.

Highland Park Public Library
494 Laurel, Highland Park 60035; 432-0216
This library has begun a mini-CAP (Coordinated Acquisitions Program) collection of Americana Judaica: historical, biographical, and sociological titles designed to dovetail but not duplicate synagogue library collections in the area. An excellent and broad assortment of periodicals of Jewish interest, and a growing collection of Yiddish and Hebrew titles that circulate.

Mayer Kaplan JCC
Anna and Charles Gollay Library
5050 Church, Skokie 60077; 675-2200
Contains basic books and periodicals of Jewish interest, some not readily available elsewhere, on such subjects as art, Bible, biography,

history, holidays, mysticism, and music. Reference encyclopedias and juvenile books are also available. Volunteer help is welcomed.

Park Forest Public Library
400 Lakewood Blvd., Park Forest 60466; 748-3731
In 1980 this library sponsored an Israeli Culture Fest with films and exhibits. An Israel bibliography prepared for this occasion is currently located in the pamphlet file; books listed in the bibliography are in the card file. In addition, the collection includes Hebrew and Yiddish grammar books, dictionaries, poetry, and literature.

Skokie Public Library
5215 Oakton, Skokie 60077; 673-7774
This collection, which includes about 100 Yiddish titles and 100 Hebrew titles, is constantly being updated. Some of the distinctive aspects of the material that can be found here are a large collection of writings on the Holocaust, including an annotated list and supplement; an annotated list of Israeli writers; a collection of classics on immigration, mostly in reprint on the shelves; and a noncirculating documentation of national media coverage of the 1978 Nazi march crisis (which is listed under National Socialism). Skokie Public Library cooperates with the Kaplan and the Horwich JCCs in supplying book materials for various programs.

Spertus College of Judaica
Norman Asher and Helen Asher Library
618 S. Michigan Ave., 60605; 922-9012
Richard Marcus, Librarian
This library contains 70,000 volumes and occupies four floors. Considered the second largest library of Hebraica and Judaica in the Middle West, after the library of Hebrew Union College–Jewish Institute of Religion in Cincinnati. Currently the Asher Library collection includes the Leaf Reference and Bibliographic Collection; a distinguished rare-book collection; the Chicago Jewish archives; Israeli publications received under the Public Law 480 program; the Badona Spertus Library on Art in Judaica containing over 1,000 volumes on Jewish art, artists, and archaeology; a periodical collection that includes subscriptions to more than 600 current publications and 1,000 titles that are no longer published; audiovisual facilities for reading and copying microfilm and for listening to tapes and records; and the Katzin Rare Book Room, which provides appropriate facilities for rare-book exhibits. Under Richard Marcus's direction the library has started to establish a network of Judaica libraries and collections throughout the metropolitan area.

Jewish Book Council of the Jewish Welfare Board
15 E. 26th St., New York, NY 10010

The JBC certifies libraries housed in Jewish institutions, including synagogues, schools, and JCCs, which meet the minimum criteria for a Jewish library. These standards include a full- or part-time librarian who spends at least ten hours a week in the library, a fixed annual budget and purchase of at least 100 books of Jewish interest within the previous year, and a special room set aside for use as a library. The following libraries have been certified by the JBC since 1948:

Anshe Emet Synagogue Library

Jordan E. Feuer Library, Congregation KINS of West Rogers Park

J. S. Hoffman Memorial Library of Congregation Rodfei Zedek
This library of more than 10,000 volumes is a public lending library located at the synagogue, 5200 Hyde Park Blvd.

Covenant Club of Illinois Library

Ner Tamid Congregation Library

Rose Chezewer Library, Temple Menorah

Bruce Gordon Memorial Library, Beth Emet The Free Synagogue, Evanston

North Shore Congregation Israel Library, Glencoe

North Suburban Synagogue Beth El Library, Highland Park

Temple Judea-Mizpah Library, Skokie

Philip A. Newberger Memorial Library of Judaica, Hillel Torah North Suburban Day School, Skokie

Temple Anshe Sholom Library, Olympia Fields

Abraham M. Warren Memorial Library, Congregation Beth Sholom, Park Forest

Hillman Library, Niles Township Jewish Congregation, Skokie

Museums and Collections

Art Institute of Chicago
Adams at Michigan, 60603; 443-3600

One of the world's great art museums, the AIC includes among its permanent treasures works by Jewish artists Marc Chagall, Camille Pissarro, Chaim Soutine, Amedeo Modigliani, and Ben Shahn. Woodcuts by Todros Geller and etchings by Ben Zion may be seen by appointment in the Print and Drawing Collection. Among the works of Jewish content are *Rabbi of Vitebsk (The Praying Jew)*, by Chagall; *Rebecca Welcomed by Abraham*, by Barent Fabritius (a follower of Rembrandt); and *The Synagogue*, a curious painting by Allesandro Magnasco (1667–1749) that reveals either the artist's ignorance or his anti-Semitism. In 1979 Hadassah presented the AIC with three color lithographs by Jacques Lipchitz, prepared by the sculptor at the age of 80 when he was creating the *Tree of Life* for the Hadassah Hospital in Jerusalem.

The AIC, founded in 1879, moved into its present building following the World's Columbian Exposition of 1893, when the structure housed the World Parliament of Religions. Some of the greatest Jewish leaders of the period assembled in Chicago at that time to meet with delegates of other world religions. The Jewish Women's Congress, chaired by Hannah Greenebaum Solomon, was the first national assembly of Jewish women and the beginning of the Council (later, National Council) of Jewish Women.

Hull House
800 S. Halsted St., 60680; 996-2793
A continuing exhibit: Ethnic Groups in the Hull-House Neighborhood 1850-1914.

Kol Ami Museum
North Suburban Synagogue Beth El
1175 Sheridan Rd., Highland Park 60035; 432-8900
Changing exhibits are usually organized around a central theme and often display rare Jewish items owned by congregation members or others in the community.

Museum of Science and Industry
57th and S. Lake Shore Dr., 60637; 684-1414
Originally enabled by a large gift from Julius Rosenwald (and still called by some the Rosenwald Museum), MSI has presented several exhibits of Jewish interest, including *My Brother's Keeper*, a Bicentennial exhibit, and, more recently, the *Children of the World Paint Jerusalem*, sponsored by the American Jewish Congress with paintings from children in 43 countries.

Oriental Institute Museum
1155 E. 58th, 60637; 753-2475 or 753-2474 (recorded message)
An extensive collection of Near Eastern antiquities from 5000 B.C. to around A.D. 1000. Permanent displays include treasures from Mesopotamia, Egypt, and ancient Palestine. Open Tuesdays through Sundays. Tour guides by appointment. Volunteer docent program. Archaeological expeditions also sponsored.

Frank F. Rosenthal Memorial Museum
Temple Anshe Sholom a Beth Torah
20820 Western Ave., Olympia Fields 60461; 748-6010
Appointments are necessary to see this museum of artifacts collected by the late Rabbi Rosenthal—about 1,000 pieces dating from 5000

B.C. to the Holocaust. Rabbi Rosenthal, an archaeologist, unearthed many of the artifacts himself. Included are medical instruments from 700 B.C., a Maccabean oil lamp, and a coin collection covering the centuries of Jewish experience.

Spertus Museum of Judaica
618 S. Michigan Ave., 60605; 922-9012
Arthur M. Feldman, Director
Grace C. Grossman, Curator

Founded in 1967 by Maurice Spertus, a trustee of the college. Permanent exhibits in this beautifully presented Jewish museum include Jewish ceremonial art, the Bernard and Rochelle Zell Holocaust Memorial, and the Heder Hadorot family history of Milton and Rosemary Ehrenreich Krensky. Included in the ceremonial art collection are objects, ethnographic materials, sculpture, paintings, graphics, textiles—all spanning the centuries of Jewish life and culture. Excellent traveling exhibits are also shown. *Play It Again, Solomon!*, through February 1981, focused on biblical archaeology. *Danzig: Treasures from a Destroyed Community*, in the spring of 1981, features ceremonial objects and heirlooms from immediately prior to World War II. *Among the Nations*, a traveling exhibition of the Museum of the Diaspora of Tel Aviv University, will open in the summer of 1981 and continue into fall.

Members receive discounts in the Museum Store. Volunteer docents are needed. Hours are 10 A.M. to 5 P.M. Mondays through Thursdays; 10 A.M. to 3 P.M. Fridays; 10 A.M. to 4 P.M. Sundays. Closed on Saturdays. Members and students (of Spertus or consortium schools) free admission; adults, $1; children, students, and senior citizens, 50¢. Free admission on Fridays.

Sydney and Julia Teller Copper Collection
Perlstein Hall, Illinois Institute of Technology
567-3000

A collection of over 2,000 items, including many Jewish ritual objects.

Morton B. Weiss Museum of Judaica
KAM–Isaiah Israel Congregation
1100 E. Hyde Park Blvd., 60615; 924-1234

Occupying a small room off the sanctuary, exhibits are displayed in glass cases arranged in the form of a six-pointed star. European and Asian Jewish artifacts as well as congregational archives are exhibited. Many items (such as ketubot) are related to marriage; a 300-year-old white-jade Chinese mezuzah and some jewelry are included as well. Groups should call in advance. Admission is free.

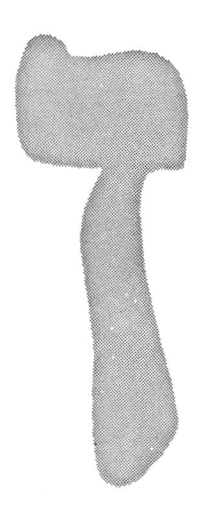

7
Health

Hospitals

Michael Reese Hospital and Medical Center
29th St. and Ellis Ave., 60616; 791-2000

One of two hospitals affiliated with the Jewish Federation of Metropolitan Chicago. A comprehensive medical center founded in 1880 as a result of a bequest by non-Chicagoan Michael Reese to his Chicago relatives. A facility of 1,000 beds for treatment, teaching, and research. More than half the beds are devoted to specialized programs or intensive care. Extensive outpatient services. Operates a shuttle-bus service until 8:45 P.M. between the hospital and three areas of the city—Hyde Park, downtown (including train stations), and north to Irving Park.

The Department of Public Affairs, 791-2330, has prepared material on the services of the hospital and will provide medical information to any publication in the U.S. or Canada. Community outreach services include slide programs, tours, and speakers.

The Council of Contributing Organizations is an association of the many auxiliaries and community organizations that support the work of the medical center.

High Holiday services for patients, visitors, and staff are usually held in the Mandel Lounge, Kaplan Pavilion. Since 1978 Reese has operated a Russian Immigrant Health Care Center, 2341 W. Devon, which provides basic examinations and referrals for Soviet Jews.

Hospital in Action by Lucy Freeman (Chicago: Rand McNally & Co., 1956) combines history with anecdotes about the individuals who created the medical center.

For access to emergency child care and treatment, dial 791-2840, the Tot Line Emergency Health Service of Michael Reese. Phone consultations with doctors can be had from 8 A.M. to midnight.

Mount Sinai Hospital Medical Center
15th St. at California Ave., 60608; 542-2000

Affiliated with the Jewish Federation of Metropolitan Chicago. Founded in 1910 as Maimonides Hospital to serve the needs of Eastern European Orthodox immigrants, Mount Sinai was financially reorganized and renamed in 1918. The hospital ministers to the people in the immediate area, which is no longer Jewish, while at the same time maintaining its ties to the Jewish community through specific programs such as the Touhy Satellite located at 2901 W. Touhy, 60645; 973-7350. Shuttle service from the Touhy Satellite to the West Side campus is available.

Mount Sinai has approximately 500 beds and is served by 23 auxiliaries and affiliated organizations. It is involved in many areas of research. Affiliations include a number of hospitals throughout the metropolitan area.

The hospital publishes an informative summary of health news, entitled *Check-up*, which is available at no charge. Jewish programming has included several symposia on Jewish law pertaining to ethical aspects of medical practice.

Weiss Memorial Hospital
4646 N. Marine Dr., 60640; 878-8700

This nonsectarian hospital founded in the 1950s has a strong identification with the Chicago Jewish community through its staff, large number of Jewish patients, and support auxiliaries. The Jacob M. Arvey Clinic for the medically indigent and the Free Bed Fund, whose primary target is the Uptown community, are supported by the Women's Auxiliary through various means, including a gift shop. Kosher meals are available upon request.

Health Agencies and Services

Council for Jewish Elderly
1415 W. Morse Ave., 60626; 973-6065

Provides health services for senior adults at its Morse Avenue drop-in center from 1 to 4 P.M. Sundays, and at the center at Temple Menorah, 2800 W. Sherwin Ave., from 9 A.M. to 5 P.M. Mondays through Fridays. Nurses and psychiatric staff assess health problems and make referrals to doctors when necessary.

Drexel Home
6140 S. Drexel Ave., 60637; 643-2384

An agency of the Jewish Federation providing a Medicare-certified skilled nursing facility for Jews age 60 and older who require posthospital care, either on a short-term basis or as permanent residents. Physicians are affiliated with Michael Reese Hospital. Under Reform Jewish auspices; not kosher.

Jewish People's Convalescent Home
6512 N. California, 60645; 743-8077

Since its founding in 1932 on South Albany on the West Side, facing Douglas Park, the JPCH has sought to provide convalescent care to needy persons. Capacity is limited to 40 beds. There are a number of supporting auxiliaries.

Michael Reese Health Plan, Inc. (HMO)
Des Plaines Health Center
1400 E. Touhy Ave., Des Plaines 60018; 297-8100; after hours: 791-2050
Lake Shore Health Center
3055 S. Cottage Grove Ave., 60616; 842-7117

A fully certified HMO (Health Maintenance Organization) providing prepaid medical and hospital health services on a group basis. All physicians have staff privileges at Michael Reese Hospital and Medical Center.

Mount Sinai Hospital HAP (Health Assurance Program) (HMO)
15th St. at California Ave., 60608; 542-2692

A fully certified HMO providing a prepaid, group medical plan serviced by physicians who are associated with Mount Sinai.

National Jewish Hospital and Research Center/National Asthma Center
189 W. Madison St., Suite 700, 60602; 726-4228

This nonsectarian hospital in Denver takes patients from all parts of the United States. Applications and referrals may be made through the Chicago office. Local auxiliaries support the institution. The hospital specializes in treating hereditary respiratory disorders, asthma, and cystic fibrosis.

Response Center
7457 N. Western Ave., 60645; 338-2292

Mount Sinai Hospital staff members provide clinical services for adolescents from 7 to 10 P.M. Tuesdays and Thursdays, including testing and counseling for venereal disease, pregnancy, and birth control.

Rush-Presbyterian St. Luke's Medical Center
1753 W. Congress Parkway, 60612; 942-5000
Sheridan Road Pavilion, 6130 N. Sheridan Rd., 743-2600
Affiliated with Mount Sinai Hospital Medical Center.

Selfhelp Home Health Care Facility
908 W. Argyle, 60640; 271-8182
Established in 1951 by German Jews who had escaped Hitler in the 1930s and early 1940s, this is a home for men and women in need of sheltered or intermediate nursing care. Minimum age is 62. Jewish dietary laws and holidays are observed. Shares a facility with the Selfhelp Home for the Aged.

Home care services are listed in Chapter 2, "Community Life."

Health Clubs

Physical fitness is one of the significant program areas of the Jewish Community Centers of Chicago. While all the JCCs have access to swimming pools, two—the Mayer Kaplan and the Bernard Horwich JCCs—have swimming pools on their own premises as well as facilities for personalized physical-fitness programs. The Hyde Park JCC has a reciprocal arrangement with Michael Reese Hospital and Medical Center whereby the hospital's pool and health-club facilities are used by the JCC in exchange for membership privileges and special programs for Reese staff and their families.

Health-Support Organizations

There are many health-support organizations that have been founded by or supported almost exclusively by members of the Chicago Jewish community. It is not the purpose of this book to identify projects, however worthy their purposes, simply because they have Jewish support. The health-support organizations listed here are just a few of the many that have specific ties to the Jewish community, perhaps through programming, history, or linkage with Jewish organizations.

AMC Auxiliaries
AMC Cancer Research Center and Hospital
6401 W. Colfax Ave., Lakewood, CO 80214
Attn: Mary Samora

Five Chicago-based auxiliaries support this institution, originally the Jewish Consumptive Relief Society, founded in 1904. In 1954 the name became the American Medical Center at Denver, and in 1975 it was changed to AMC. An oncology ward is open to patients from throughout the country. Chicago auxiliaries are the Helen Claire, Bea Duboe, Goodwill, Mildred Kulwin, and Diane Waller chapters.

Aaron Fox Foundation
180 N. Wabash, 60601
Harry Rosenthal, President

Dedicated to aiding diabetic children and a living memorial to Aaron Fox, this organization supports programs at Michael Reese Hospital and Medical Center and Children's Memorial Hospital, as well as a camp for diabetic children in Wisconsin. At the present time the entire membership is Jewish, although it is not necessarily a Jewish organization. Some programming at meetings has featured Jewish content.

B. Friendly Ladies' Aid Society
Fanny I. Chern

Founded in 1912 as a landsmanshaften organization (the B Stands for Berditchover, a town in Russia) that used to send money to the old country, the group later changed its name and purpose. Most recipients in recent years were hospitals such as Michael Reese, St. Joseph's, and Schwab Rehabilitation Hospital.

Chicago Ivreyoth
Florence Erlich
677-5330

A 45-year-old organization of approximately 100 women who raise funds for cancer research and equipment at Michael Reese, Mount Sinai, Weiss Memorial, and the Portes Cancer Prevention Center. Membership is open, and women with personal experience with cancer are especially welcome. Year-round programs and fund raisers include a fall rummage sale, a boutique Gift-Court, and a special pre-Thanksgiving sale.

City of Hope
4747 W. Peterson, 60646; 725-3170
William Kaufman, Midwest Regional Director
Pearl Friedman, Director of Auxiliaries

The City of Hope is a free, national, nonsectarian medical center, seeking to influence medicine and science through pilot programs in patient care, research, and education in cancer, leukemia, diseases of the heart, blood, and chest, and basic investigations in genetics and the neurosciences. The twenty Chicago area chapters are closely identified with the Jewish community. Fund-raising projects vary. For example, the Bobby Blechman Chapter has a travel club and the Howard S. Golden Chapter, an annual carnival. Several sell kosher Nosh-n-Rye, home-delivered deli boxes. Howard S. Golden also has a traveling boutique with gift items, purses, and jewelry at substantial discounts. All money goes to City of Hope. For information, call Marion Bromberg, 673-2740.

Jacob Blumberg Memorial Blood Bank
1350 N. Sheridan Rd., Waukegan 60085; 662-1899

Established by the family of Jacob Blumberg in his memory; provides free blood to individuals and groups who have donated blood to the bank. Jacob Blumberg was a founder of Congregation Am Echod where his son and grandson eventually held the presidency.

Little City Foundation
4801 W. Peterson, 60646; 282-2207

Since its inception in 1957 Jews have been closely associated with this nonsectarian residential and training facility for mentally retarded children, some of whom are also blind. Several auxiliaries have a predominantly Jewish membership.

Schwab Rehabilitation Hospital Women's Board
1401 S. California, 60608; 522-2010

As years pass, this historic institution has less and less association with the Jewish community. The once-Jewish women's auxiliaries are no longer exclusively so. The Isidor Chern Chapter Auxiliary, named after Fanny Chern's husband, who died in 1931, is still functioning. The hospital, formerly called Rest Haven Rehabilitation Hospital, was founded in 1912 and incorporated in 1921. It was originally established by a Jewish women's organization, the Sarah Greenebaum Lodge, United Order True Sisters. The Sarah Greenebaum Lodge was absorbed by the Johanna Lodge years ago, and all association with Rest Haven was severed.

Jewish Diseases

Illnesses that occur more frequently among Jews than among the general population are often called Jewish diseases. Some have a proven genetic cause; others are merely suspected of being genetic, though thus far proof has been inconclusive. It should be emphasized that Jewish diseases are extremely rare, even among Jews.

Dystonia muscularum deformans

Occurs with greater frequency among Ashkenazic (Central and Eastern European) Jews and cannot be detected by prenatal screening. In Chicago, treatment is provided by Dr. Harold Klawans, who may be contacted at the Department of Neurological Science, Rush University, 1725 W. Harrison; 942-8010.

Dysautonomia, Familial Dysautonomia, or Riley-Day Syndrome

Dysautonomia Foundation Chicago Chapter
550 Frontage Rd., Suite 2085, Northfield 60093; 441-5653
Affiliated with the national foundation, the local chapter was established in 1979 by parents and friends of children afflicted with this disease, which is of genetic origin and affects the autonomic nervous system. Chapter serves as a clearinghouse for information and resources as well as a self-help support group.

Tay-Sachs

The best known of the Jewish diseases; can be detected by prenatal screening. Several National Council of Jewish Women sections sponsor community screening. The West Valley Section, for example, has a program in connection with Glenbrook Hospital. For information, call 729-8800, x115. Ninety percent of all affected children are of Ashkenazic Jewish descent, primarily from Lithuanian and Polish provinces.

Tourette Syndrome

May or may not be a Jewish disease. Dr. Harold Klawans, who treats this disease locally, believes that it is. Dr. Klawans may be contacted at the Department of Neurological Science, Rush University, 1725 W. Harrison; 942-8010.

- Dr. Eugene Pergament
  Director, Division of Medical Genetics
  Michael Reese Hospital and Medical Center
  791-3848

Dr. Pergament is a resource for general information and possible treatment, screening, or referral concerning Jewish genetic diseases and any other diseases that may be genetic in origin.

- Dr. Harold Klawans
  Department of Neurological Science
  Rush University
  1725 W. Harrison, 60612; 942-8010

Available to speak to groups on the subject of genetic diseases.

Mental Health

AMHAI (Association for Mental Health Affiliation with Israel)
P.O. Box 357, Wilmette 60091; 251-0065
Works to improve mental health in Israel and sponsors local programs on mental health issues.

Chicago Coalition on Group Identity and Mental Health
Institute on Pluralism and Group Identity
55 E. Jackson Blvd., 60604; 663-5400
One of the divisions of the IPGI founded by the American Jewish Committee. Its purposes are to prepare mental-health professionals to understand the needs of ethnically diverse communities, to offer educational opportunities, to provide information sharing, and to develop model community-health centers.

Council for Jewish Elderly
1015 W. Howard, Evanston 60202; 973-4105
Provides some mental-health and counseling services.

Jewish Children's Bureau
1 S. Franklin, 60606; 346-6700
Provides a variety of mental-health services, counseling, and referrals, including some residential options with special housing for emotionally handicapped youths.

Jewish Family and Community Service
1 S. Franklin, 60606; 346-6700
Offers a variety of mental-health services and referrals for clients.

Virginia Frank Child Development Center of JFCS
3033 W. Touhy, 60645; 761-4550
Day-care centers for emotionally, socially disturbed young children.

Jewish Vocational Service
1 S. Franklin, 60606; 346-6700
Offers a wide variety of services, including counseling and training for persons with emotional handicaps, rehabilitation, and placement.

Michael Reese Hospital and Medical Center
29th St. and Ellis Ave., 60616; 791-2000
A comprehensive medical center with many services for adults and children with psychiatric problems. Four specialized programs are listed below.

Wexler Psychiatric Clinic
2960 S. Lake Park Ave., 60616; 791-3900
Outpatient psychiatric evaluation, treatment.

Institute for Psychosomatic and Psychiatric Research and Training
2959 S. Cottage Grove Ave., 60616; 791-3800

Pritzker Children's Psychiatric Unit
800 E. 55th St., 60615; 643-7300
A comprehensive outpatient center offering psychiatric diagnosis and treatment for children ages 3 to 17 years.

David T. Siegel Institute for Communicative Disorders
3033 S. Cottage Grove, 60616; 791-2900
A psychiatric service for deaf adults and children and their families.

Mount Sinai Hospital Medical Center
15th St. at California Ave., 60608; 542-2000

■ **Dr. Richard Malter**
15 S. Dryden Pl., Arlington Heights 60004; 398-6640
Available for training teachers and mental-health or family-service workers in various areas of interest and concern, including issues of grief and loss, and dealing with the Holocaust. Malter and his wife, Rosalie, have done extensive work in therapy with Jewish clientele, relying in part on cultural and religious materials as part of the therapy process. They also use art therapy and Gestalt techniques that they believe will help in dealing with problems and conflicts related to the Holocaust.

■ **Paul Reizen**
741 St. Johns, Highland Park 60035; 433-0770
Speaks on Mental Health in Israel. Named honorary vice-president of AMHAI.

■ **Joan Rosner, R.N.**
Ravenswood Hospital School of Nursing
Wilson at Winchester, 60640; 878-4300 x5270
Gives workshops and lectures; has small private practice dealing with holistic health, response to stress, and therapy with cancer victims. Lectures to Jewish audiences and applies Jewish values to what she teaches.

■ **Dr. Alfred Soffer**
729-6722 (home) or 698-2200 (office)
Cardiologist and executive director of American College of Chest Physicians. Speaks on Jewish Medicine and Magic, Maimonides, Philosopher and Physician, and Medicine in Israel.

Pastoral counseling is included in Chapter 3, "Religious Life."

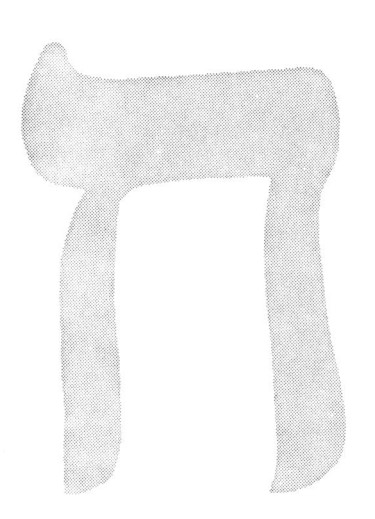

8
The Arts

Greater Chicago Jewish Folk Arts Festival
Jewish POCET
1710 Madison, Evanston 60202; 864-5557
Michael and Susan Lorge

The second annual GCJFAF held Sunday, June 14, 1981, in Centennial Park, Evanston. Auditions held for artists, dancers, musicians, and other performers, particularly those for children's audiences. Filled with Jewish music and dance, a juried art exhibit and sale, Israeli-Jewish food, and an array of ongoing exhibits and celebrations of Jewish life. Free admission. The Lorges dubbed the organization that established the first fair in 1980 as Jewish POCET—Jewish Production Organization for Cultural Events and Theater.

Artists and Artisans

Anita Alexander
2032 N. Point St., 60647

Has assembled a portfolio of etchings of old Chicago synagogues, originally commissioned by Spertus Museum.

Bee Arons
959 Oak Dr., Glencoe 60022; 835-0042

An artist and printmaker inspired by patterns, textures, and shapes of the land of Israel. Represented in the Art Rental and Sales Gallery of the Art Institute of Chicago, Deerpath Gallery, etc.

James Axelrod
59 E. Van Buren St., 60605; 922-4800 (studio)
7540 N. Claremont, 60645; 764-6683 (home)
Artist, painter, illustrator; Jewish subjects, realistic style. Gold Medalist, Art Directors Club of Chicago.

Joseph Badalpour
Circle Studio
5600 N. Western Ave., 60659; 275-5454 (studio) or 267-5621 (home)
Stained-glass creations, often dealing with biblical themes. His *Promised Land* hangs in the lobby of Spertus Museum.

Irene Baer
6101 N. Sheridan Rd., Apt. 10C, 60660; 274-4531
Oil paintings and linoleum-block prints of Jewish subjects. Greeting cards made from block prints. Represented in the Art Rental and Sales Gallery, Art Institute of Chicago. Call for private showing.

Iris Barchechat
4522 N. Ashland, 60640; 769-4529
Graphic artist, Jewish arts and crafts educator, and resource person.

Marcia Bartenes
4001 Greenleaf, Skokie 60076; 675-8939
Ceramist with Nessia Frank (see below). Mezuzot, plaques, and plates in honor of bar/bat mitzvah and all other special occasions.

Richard Bitterman
1701 W. Chase Ave., 60626; 743-1511
Sculptor, jewelry designer, silversmith, and metalsmith whose innovative blending of brass, copper, and steel has been displayed and sold by Marshall Field & Co., Neiman-Marcus, and other fine stores. Also produces a line of religious art: mezuzot, kiddish cups, spice boxes, seder plates, chala trays.

Russell W. Blanchard
1162 Dartmouth Lane, Deerfield 60015; 945-7605
Studied with Mark Tobey; designer of Temple Jeremiah's 20th anniversary tapestry. Commissions in tapestry design; also painting, drawing, and graphic design.

Barbara Bleckman
Fiber Focus
254 Red Oak Lane, Highland Park 60035

Original macramé creations blending natural fibers with earth and sea objects; uses spiritual-ecological motifs for wall hangings and table sculptures.

Abby Block
1773 Ridgelee Rd., Highland Park 60035; 831-3622
Wall hangings, quilts, and possibly a chupah (wedding canopy) by commission. Her appliqué-tapestry of Jerusalem hangs at B'nai Tikvah congregation. In honor of a bat mitzvah, Block created a wall hanging with the celebrant's Torah portion.

Paula Buchwald
6139 N. Francisco Ave., 60659; 262-0924
Pen-and-ink drawings—some with Jewish themes, including recent drawings on the Holocaust theme. Has exhibited at the Art Rental and Sales Gallery, Art Institute of Chicago, for seven years. Assistant Dean, Chicago Academy of Fine Arts.

Yochanan Center
c/o Mrs. E. Najarian, 22 South Chase, Lombard 60148
Artist and Hebrew calligrapher. Works include paintings, greeting cards, and ketubot (Jewish marriage contracts).

Rose Ann Chasman
6147 N. Richmond, 60659; 764-4169
Hebrew calligraphy, graphics, Jewish needlework, paper arts, ketubot. By commission. Teaches Hebrew calligraphy.

Bryna Cytrynbaum
9400 N. Lincolnwood, Evanston 60203
Jewish macramé; instructor for children and adults.

Hetty de Leeuwe
1528 Sheridan Rd., Highland Park 60035; 433-6557
Jewish embroidery; member of Pomegranate Guild, Embroidery Guild of America, and North Suburban Embroiderers Guild. Has embroidered a set of Torah mantels and Torah wrappers. Coauthoring a book on crocheting kipot (skull caps) with Rosie Kaz (see below). Also has preserved an antique parochet, a curtain that hangs in front of the Ark.

Hannah Dresner
920 E. 61st St., 60637; 955-2882
Painter, graphic artist, Hebrew calligrapher: ketubot, invitations.

Bonnie Ferdman
475-6386

Artist and arts and crafts consultant. Graduate of Art Institute who has developed kindergarten-through-8th-grade arts and crafts curriculum projects with Jewish content. Watercolors, drawings.

Milt Fink
6820 N. Francisco Ave., 60645; 262-5071 or (815) 629-2094

Sculptor. To date he has erected eighteen public sculptures, including a 60-foot wallpiece on Mayer Kaplan JCC, Skokie, plus sculptures at Emanuel Congregation, North Shore Congregation Israel, Temple Jeremiah, Beth Emet, Bene Shalom, and B'nai Yehuda.

Nessia Frank
1642 Linden Ave., Highland Park 60035; 432-6668

From Bezalel School of Art, Jerusalem. Hebrew calligraphy: invitations. With ceramist Marcia Bartenes, creates mezuzot, plaques, and plates, personalized for special occasions.

Curt Frankenstein
2112 Old Glenview Rd., Wilmette 60091; 256-4764

Considered one of the best draftsmen working in etching and paintings; has his own etching press in his Wilmette studio and printshop. Surrealistic works, some on strictly Jewish themes, others with a Jewish flavor.

Marla Gassner
337 Sumac Rd., Highland Park 60035; 831-9116

Creates jewelry combining fiber with precious and semiprecious metals, stones, and antique glass beads. Will use Jewish jewelry motifs. By commission.

Stuart Gootnick
8877 Grand St., Niles 60648; 299-0249

As a painter, Gootnick has developed the technique of reverse stained glass, a takeoff from old Pennsylvania Dutch form, and has used Jewish thematic material. Available for commissions. As a miniaturist, he is currently creating a major miniature replica (1 inch = 1 foot) of the Touro Synagogue, Newport, RI. Made from drawings obtained from the Library of Congress, it will measure 50 square inches, and will be available for viewing in 1981.

Judith Gordon
2608 W. Farwell Ave., 60645; 743-4369

Weaver. Wool, silk, cotton. Tallitim (prayer shawls), tallit bags, chala covers. Hebrew alphabet a frequent motif. Creates new and different designs by transposing English or Hebrew phrases into a weaving. Work has been published. Works with Sharon Shattan (see below).

Steve Grubman
442 N. Wells St., 60610; 787-2272
Photographer. All aspects of commercial photography. His architectural photography was exhibited at the Spertus Museum in the Faith and Form Bicentennial exhibit of synagogue architecture in Chicago and Illinois.

Annette Hirsh
4126 N. Ardmore Ave., Milwaukee, WI 53211
Although not a local artist, Hirsh is frequently represented in Chicago shows and regularly at the North Suburban Synagogue Beth El Festival of the Arts and the Oakbrook Art Festival. Silversmith, metalsmith, jewelry designer: Torah crowns, breastplates, mezuzot, eternal lights, sterling-silver dreidls. North Shore Congregation Israel and Emanuel Congregation have commissioned her work.

Sol Hoffman
677-0573
Metal sculpturing by welding and brazing. Jewish content. Art Rental and Sales Gallery, Art Institute of Chicago.

Milton Horn
1932 N. Lincoln Ave., 60614; 664-2550
Internationally eminent Chicago sculptor whose Jewish-content work adorns West Suburban Temple Har Zion and Kol Ami. His *Job*, a life-size bronze, was acquired by the National Collection of Fine Arts, Smithsonian Institution, Washington, D.C. He is a Fellow of the National Sculpture Society. (His secular work in Chicago may be seen at the Federal Building and at the Central District Filtration Plant.)

Etta Japha
2526 Jackson Ave., Evanston 60201; 328-0498
Etchings using Jewish themes and Hebrew calligraphy: birth announcements, bar/bat mitzvah cards, invitations. Art Rental and Sales Gallery, Art Institute of Chicago.

Henry Jelen
262-7296
Creates greeting cards based on original drawings.

■ **Judith Kanin**
833 W. Buckingham, 60657; 348-8432
Fine-art Hebrew calligraphy: custom invitations, ketubot. Sculptural paintings with Hebrew content. Slide program: Hebrew Calligraphy through the Ages.

Betsy Katz
325 Prospect, Highland Park 60035; 432-3844
Designs wimples. (A wimple is a Torah binder made from swaddling cloth used at the circumcision ceremony, often decorated with the child's name, date of birth, and the ritual formula recited during the circumcision ceremony. The custom of the wimple came from southern Germany in the sixteenth century.)

Rosie Kaz
367 Laurel, Highland Park 60035; 433-6535
Judaic needlepoint. Member of Pomegranate Guild. Coauthoring a book on crocheting kipot (skull caps) with Hetty de Leeuwe.

Mazala Kolman
Antiquities Inc.
930-8 Shady Way, Arlington Heights 60005 *or*
P.O. Box 580, Wilmette 60091; 593-1008
Jewelry designer who re-creates ancient amulets originally supposed to ward off evil. These authentic reproductions of antique Jewish (and other) jewelry, including some Kabbalistic, come with a written explanation. Kolman, whose work has been exhibited, has made an extensive study of the symbology of magic and served as consultant to Spertus Museum for an exhibit on Magic and Superstition.

Darryl Rotman Kuperstock
6636 N. Newgard, 60626; 743-6888
Hebrew calligraphy, manuscript design: ketubot, invitations, certificates, and gifts for special occasions. Also teaches Hebrew calligraphy at Hillel-University of Chicago. Knowledge of reading and writing Hebrew is a requirement for enrollment. Each commission is one of a kind. Only permanent watercolor paints or metallic enamel and 100-percent rag papers or real parchment are used.

Philip Kupritz
c/o Barbara Palatnik, 2841 W. Estes, 60645; 743-2032
Designs wall hangings with Judaic themes, with Mike Palatnik (see below).

Edith LeVee
2712 W. Greenleaf Ave., 60645; 761-1107
Artist, sculptor. One-of-a-kind ceramic sculptures: Chassidim, rabbinic figures in work, play, study, dance. Designed plaque for Women's Division-JUF. Work displayed at the Chicago Public Library Cultural Center for the 1977-78 Yiddish Exhibit: Tradition—The Hasidim in America.

Barbara Lewis
920 Elmwood, Evanston 60202; 869-9472
Macramé, knitting, crocheting as art forms. Her Torah mantle, a satin-cord gold-metallic wound Tree of Life, was commissioned by Emanuel Congregation for its centennial in 1980.

Jerry Lidsky
1011 Whitfield Rd., Northbrook 60062; 498-3306
Artist and art therapist. Paintings, etchings, watercolors, most of which have Jewish content. Very much affected by three-year stay in Israel. Uses art therapy in treating disabilities. Activities Therapy Director, Highland Park Hospital.

Al Lieberman
9525-E Gross Point Rd., Skokie 60076; 676-9347
Photographer, Jewish arts and crafts educator. Copper enamels, Judaic jewelry.

■ **Phyllis Mandler**
3020 N. Sheridan Rd., 60657; 281-2909
Stained-glass design and execution. All work is of original design and is suitable for architectural-scale projects including synagogues and Jewish institutions. Stained glass completed for Congregation B'nei Ruven. Slide lectures presented on the history of stained glass and stained glass in Jewish architecture.

Robert Saul Markovitz
4 E. Ohio, Rm. K, 60611; 787-9656
Gouache, oil, pen-and-ink, and pencil studies of Jewish subjects, many based on impressions of Eastern European Jews as they lived before the Holocaust.

Northfield Pottery Works
Elaine Kessler and Jill Grau
1741 Orchard Lane, Northfield 60093; 446-3470
Provides classes for beginners and advanced potters. Studio rentals to advanced potters. Commissions and sales include menorahs, seder plates, kiddish cups.

Mike Palatnik
c/o Barbara Palatnik, 2841 W. Estes, 60645; 743-2032
Designs wall hangings with Judaic themes, with Philip Kupritz.

Wendy Rabinowitz
5548 S. Kenwood, 60637; 947-0173
Weaver-designer inspired by Jewish mystical tradition as it reflects women and the world. Also uses the mystical interpretation of the

letters of the Hebrew alphabet. Her work *God's Female Aspect: The Shekhinah of Jewish Mystical Tradition* or *Female Presence, I–XXVIII* is a series of woven works out of the experience of "being with child, giving birth, and mothering, 1977–80." Exhibited at the Monroe Gallery, Chicago, January 1980.

Dr. Fred Rappaport
345 W. Belden Ave., 60614; 348-5991

Viennese born, twice president of the American Jewish Arts Club, he creates at least one work of Jewish content each year. Medium: woodcuts. Rappaport's work hangs in the Museum of Modern Art, Jerusalem, and the Museum of Modern Art, Eilat, Israel.

Judith Roth
220 Moraine, Highland Park 60035; 433-0468

A visual artist working in various drawing media (graphite, charcoal, etc.) and in oil on canvas and paper. Her work is figurative, with an emphasis on the human form, and often draws upon biblical concepts and characters.

Rita Sargen-Simon
606 Florence Ave., Evanston 60202; 475-0605

Sculptor. Will accept commissions to develop sculpture with Jewish themes. Works with bronze, stoneware, Plexiglas. Her ceramic lamps were part of the 1980 Chicago Ceramic and Glass Show, Chicago Historical Society.

Molly Schiff
262-4959 or 262-1409

Painter and printmaker. Accepts commissions on Jewish subjects and will be happy to make referrals to other artists, especially those working in other media. Portraits, landscapes, scenic paintings. Variety of prints, paintings, drawings represented by Joy Horwich Gallery and the Art Rental and Sales Gallery of the Art Institute of Chicago.

Susan Shapiro
5550 S. Dorchester, Apt. 1003, 60637; 955-7472 or 281-1287

Works with handpainted porcelain decorated with medieval Jewish manuscript motifs and designs. Seder plates, bowl and pitcher for traditional mayim achronim (washing after meals), and porcelain wine cups. Studied in Switzerland with specialist in porcelain motifs design. May be the only artist to apply Jewish design to porcelain decoration.

■ Sharon R. G. Shattan
c/o Judith Gordon, 2608 W. Farwell Ave., 60645; 743-4369

Designs and weaves textiles for Judaic rituals and celebrations including prayer shawls, chala covers, matzo covers, Passover pillows. Involves client in the design and execution of finished product. Brides-to-be participate in creating chupah (wedding canopy). Bar mitzvah child learns to tie tzises, the knotted fringe on his prayer shawl. Mothers and grandmothers have added their own embroidery. Samples and slides are available. Work by commision. Member Pomegranate Guild. Works with weaver Judith Gordon. Slide lecture: Jewish Decorative Textiles from Synagogue and Daily Life, from Biblical Times to the Present.

Herb Slobin
433-1459
A graphic designer; designs books, posters, brochures, other graphics; wide experience with material of Jewish content.

Alice Sostrin
2540 W. Morse Ave., 60645; 262-4920
Painter, sculptor. Woodcuts with Jewish content.

Sarah Stiebel
432-0156
Extraordinary Havdalah candles sold across the country, from Natick, MA, to Palo Alto, CA. Locally available at the Spertus Museum Store, Schwartz-Rosenblum Hebrew Book Store, and the gift shop of North Suburban Synagogue Beth El. Stiebel learned the art from her grandmother, who had learned it from hers; now she teaches her granddaughters and nieces. One of her mother's candles is in the permanent collection of the Spertus Museum.

David Wolfe
9106 Ewing Ave., Skokie 60203; 676-9106
Metal sculptor. Creates variety of Jewish subjects: menorahs, figures, wall decors. Commission work for religious institutions.

Louise Dunn Yochim
676-3187
Painter, sculptor, art educator, and author. Her paintings include Jewish content. Among many other subjects, she has written about Chicago Jewish artists.

Gershon Yudkowsky
2927 W. Touhy Ave., 60645; 262-5700
Commercial artist who does Hebrew calligraphy and illumination. Invitations, testimonial plaques, certificates, ketubot.

American Jewish Arts Club
c/o Michael Karzen, President, 761-1382

An organization of Chicago-based Jewish artists working with various media and thematic subjects, not necessarily Jewish. Catalog of the 50th anniversary annual exhibit at Spertus Museum (1978) included a historical essay by Louise Dunn Yochim, who traced the beginnings to the Around the Palette group at the old Jewish People's Institute. In 1940, in response to Hitler, the organization changed its name to the American Jewish Arts Club. Early membership is a who's who of the great Chicago Jewish artists. Annual exhibit held at the Spertus Museum in spring.

- **Michael Karzen**
761-1382

Artist and president of the AJAC presents slide lectures: Jewish Artists of the Twentieth Century; Jewish Ceremonial Art; and, available soon, Jewish Artists of Chicago.

- **Grace C. Grossman**
Curator, Spertus Museum of Judaica
618 S. Michigan Ave., 60605; 922-9012

Illustrated lectures on many subjects, including Fakes and Forgeries in Jewish Art, The Wedding in Jewish Art, and Tribute to Marc Chagall.

- **Arthur M. Feldman**
Director, Spertus Museum of Judaica
618 S. Michigan Ave., 60605; 922-9012

Lectures on The Jewish Museum, Jewish Artists, and Survey of Jewish Art and Architecture from Biblical Times to the Present. Also lectures on individual shows at the Spertus Museum.

- **Lenore Pressman**
168 Lakewood Pl., Highland Park 60035; 432-5838

Art historian, teacher, lecturer, writer on such subjects as Marc Chagall and His Time, Jewish American Artists, and Jewish Themes in Contemporary Art.

Public Art and Sculpture

Yaacov Agam
Israeli kinetic sculptor

A newly commissioned monumental kinetic sculpture is in the lobby of the Avondale Centre, 20 N. Clark St. The 10-foot-high by 20-foot-long sculpture, though stationary, appears to move and completely change in design and color as the viewer changes position. Another kinetic sculpture by Agam hangs in the lobby of the Harris Trust and Savings Bank, 111 W. Monroe. Both works are visible from the street.

Henri Azaz
Israeli artist and sculptor
The Form Makers, an 80-foot sculpture that once occupied the lobby of the former Sherman House, is now on the campus of Rosary College, 7900 W. Division, River Forest. The sculpture *Hands of Peace* is on the facade of the Chicago Loop Synagogue, 16 S. Clark.

Marc Chagall
The Four Seasons, a 70-foot mosaic wall, is in the First National Bank Plaza, along Dearborn just north of Monroe. Dedicated in September 1974 with the artist in attendance, this work, completed by the artist at age 87, includes stones from all over the world. The *America Windows* are on view at the Art Institute of Chicago.

Moses Ezekiel
Christopher Columbus, in Victor Arrigo Park, Lexington and Lytle streets, was originally executed by Ezekiel for the 1893 World's Columbian Exposition and later decorated the front of the Columbus Memorial building at State and Washington. This is the only Chicago public work of this great American sculptor, who was a Jew and whose father helped found the Hebrew Union College in Cincinnati.

Milt Fink
His 60-foot, stainless-steel wallpiece is on the Mayer Kaplan JCC in Skokie. His 6-foot cement menorah is in Mount Sinai Hospital. Numerous works by Fink are in area synagogues. For more information on Fink, see listing above under Artists and Artisans.

Milton Horn
A locally based, world-recognized sculptor whose work has been reproduced in many publications. His bas relief *Jewish Philanthropy* is on the Madison Street side of the Jewish Federation building, 1 S. Franklin. He also is represented in several local synagogues, including West Suburban Temple Har Zion and Kol Ami. For more information on Horn, see listing above under Artists and Artisans.

A memorial bust of German playwright Gotthold Lessing, author of *Nathan the Wise* and friend of Moses Mendelssohn, is in the Rose Garden of Washington Park, 57th and Cottage Grove. Presented to the city in 1930 by Henry L. Frank.

Fabric of Our Lives
3003 W. Touhy, 60645
For information, contact Chicago Mural Group
2261 N. Lincoln Ave., 60614; 871-3089
Miriam Socoloff and Cynthia Weiss, Artists

A Jewish-subject mural commemorating immigrant and labor history is on the exterior of the Bernard Horwich JCC. It was created in the summer of 1980 and dedicated in November of that year. The large ceramic-tile mosaic was assembled in the Dolnick Center by the artists and their volunteers. Depicted are the Eastern European Jewish immigrant to Chicago, specifically to Maxwell Street of the 1880s to 1920s, and the emergence of Jewish and Yiddish culture in Chicago. Men and women workers, the sweatshop intellectual, union organizer, Yiddish actress, and musician are all there.

Synagogue Art and Architecture

- **Marian Despres**
  1220 E. 56th St., 60637
  A resource on the synagogue architecture and other work of her father, Alfred S. Alschuler, Sr.

- **Rachel B. Heimovics**
  P.O. Box 524, Highland Park 60035
  A resource on the synagogue commissions and other architecture of Dankmar Adler and Adler and Sullivan.

- **Philip Kupritz**
  233 N. Northwest Highway, Park Ridge 60068; 692-6166
  Presents slide lectures on Synagogue Art and Architecture.

A scale model of the Second Temple of Jerusalem is in the lobby of the Associated Talmud Torahs, 2828 W. Pratt Blvd. Model is by Rachmani, Israeli artist and architect.

Spertus Museum of Judaica
618 S. Michigan Ave., 60605; 922-9012

The Bicentennial exhibit of the Spertus Museum was Faith and Form: Synagogue Architecture in Illinois. A slide program based on that exhibit may still be available. The catalog (for sale in the museum store) contains 150 photographs, a historiography of synagogue architecture in Illinois, a list of the many congregations in Chicago and Illinois, and a diagram that traces their origins. The catalog also includes "The Roots and the Branches: A Survey of the Chicago Jewish Community 1845-1976" by Morris A. Gutstein.

Some Distinctive Synagogues

B'nei Ruven
6350 N. Whipple, 60659; 743-5434
Award-winning building completed in 1960. Stained glass by Phyllis Mandler.

Chicago Loop Synagogue
16 S. Clark, 60603; 346-7370
Designed by Richard Bennett, who incorporated innovative features, including ramps for the handicapped and elderly and an unusual seating arrangement in the sanctuary. Outstanding features are the dramatic east-wall window by Abraham Rattner and the Ark and exterior sculpture by Henri Azaz.

Emanuel Congregation
5959 N. Sheridan Rd., 60660; 561-5173
Facade sculpture by A. Raymond Katz. Chapel, with benches around walls, was inspired by Dura Europas, a fourth-century building with a unique spiral plan. Chicago sculptor Mike Fink is represented inside by a fourteen-foot screen, a three-dimensional Magen David, and a Torah pointer. In honor of Emanuel's centennial observance in 1980, Barbara Lewis created a Torah mantle and Annette Hirsh, a Torah pointer.

Ezra-Habonim
2620 W. Touhy, 60645; 743-0154
Displays ceremonial and synagogue objects saved from synagogues in Germany destroyed on Crystal Night, including an original parochet made in 1745.

Lakeside Congregation for Reform Judaism
1221 County Line Rd., Highland Park 60035; 432-7950
A modern synagogue designed by Fitch, Larocca, and Carrington, Inc. Cited by Chicago chapter AIA (American Institute of Architects) for architectural excellence.

Moriah
200 Hyacinth Lane, Deerfield 60015; 948-5340
Within the sanctuary (formerly the gymnasium of a public school) is an impressive mural by Jordan Krinstein. Bimah designed by Philip

Kupritz, and bimah cover by Americana quilt-designer Ed Larson of Libertyville.

North Shore Congregation Israel
1185 Sheridan Rd., Glencoe 60022; 835-0724

This architectural landmark by Minoru Yamasaki received an award from the local Chicago chapter AIA when completed in 1964. Light is the central architectural principle of the design. Ark is teakwood overlaid with gold. Altar is white marble. Open to visitors 10 A.M. to 4 P.M. Mondays through Thursdays. On the patio there is a life-size sculpture, *Jacob Wrestling with the Angel*, by Evanston sculptor Egon Weiner.

Rodfei Zedek
5200 S. Hyde Park Blvd., 60615; 752-2770

Award-winning windows in the chapel by Adolfas Valeska depict the unity of God, Torah, and Israel. There are other fine windows in the sanctuary, including a three-dimensional Magen David.

Temple Sholom
3480 N. Lake Shore Dr., 60657; 525-4707

Architects went back to the first century for inspiration for this synagogue with its octagonal sanctuary and octagonal roof. Designers were Coolidge and Hodgsen and Loebl Schlossman and Demuth architectural firms.

West Suburban Temple Har Zion
1040 N. Harlem, River Forest 60305; 366-9000

See the William Gropper floor-to-ceiling windows before the sun sets to get the full impact of these impressive works of art. Milton Horn's sculpture in the sanctuary shows the *Ascension of Rabbi Judah*, with the rabbi being lifted by angels. Horn's sculpture outside is reputed to be the first monumental figure sculpture on a Jewish house of worship in 1,500 years.

Historic and architectural landmarks are in Chapter 9, "History."

Performing Arts

■ **Roslyn Alexander**
433-2057 or 472-6550 (service)

This actress and narrator dramatizes literature, appears on stage and TV, and regularly reads on WFMT, where she has presented programs on Elie Weisel. Also presents narrations of contemporary and classical Jewish literature, Bible readings, Sholem Aleichem, and more.

■ Ruth Bise Alpert
5719 N. Virginia, 60659; 271-4265

Sings Yiddish and Hebrew songs; program tailored to each audience.

Am Chai Players
P.O. Box 60142; 60660

Presents Yiddish and English translations of Yiddish stories and songs. Part of Am Chai, the Alternative Chavurah. This performing-arts group has also prepared a dramatic presentation of fantasy and fun from Jewish folklore, *Spit Three Times.*

Anshe Emet Day School
3760 N. Pine Grove, 60613; 281-1858

A 7th- and 8th-grade musical production is given annually under the direction of Leona Molotsky and Pearl Harand.

■ Marlene Baron
4845 W. Kirk, Skokie 60077; 674-3982

Mezzo-soprano. Presents a variety of musical programs tailored to the audience, including My People Sing, a treasury of old and modern Israeli and Yiddish classics.

■ Naomi Bayer
2842 Walnut Rd., Homewood 60430; 798-6496

Songleader. Teaches Jewish songs to groups of all ages and also performs at weddings, bar/bat mitzvah, and other functions.

■ Rivka (Rosalie) Becker
465-4026

Performs and teaches all kinds of Jewish music—Israeli, Yiddish, Chassidic, folk, and also liturgical. Has had wide experience as a soloist and group leader in singing the music of the Jewish worship service.

■ Eileen Berman
9830 N. Karlov, Skokie 60076; 674-0035

Lyric soprano. Offers various musical programs including a vast repertoire of classical and popular songs of Jewish origin. Performs cantorial liturgy. Has been soloist in synagogue choirs.

■ Joan Bernick
795 Vernon Ave., Glencoe 60022

Presents dramatic readings of Jewish literature, including Sholom Aleichem and Agnon, mostly from her own translations. Also, Jewish folk and art songs in Hebrew, Yiddish, and Ladino, and her own translations. Bernick also conducts sing-alongs with Jewish and international folk and old popular songs.

Beth Emet Players
1224 Dempster, Evanston 60202; 869-4230
A performing troupe from Beth Emet The Free Synagogue.

■ Joe Black
475-5514
Tiny Tov from television's *Magic Door* is a versatile free-lance song leader who also sings the music of the Jewish worship service. Presents song-and-dance programs with his wife, Haje.

Bill Bozin Orchestra
6318 N. Fairfield, 60659; 764-8202
Performs Chassidic and traditional Jewish and American music. May be the only local Jewish band using a male vocalist. Size of the band can be adjusted, depending upon the particular assignment or occasion. All arrangements done by Bozin, a versatile musician.

Temple Chai
Rt. 1, Box 271, Long Grove 60047; 537-1771
Welcomes nonmembers into its choir.

Chamber Ballet Ensemble
Marla Balaban
864-6721
Classical ballet group that will perform Jewish-content dances.

Chicago International Mandolin Orchestra
c/o Sonia Rockler, 262-9655
A nonprofessional, well-versed group that plays ethnic music, some Jewish, and some eighteenth-century chamber music. Participation in the orchestra is open. Group evolved out of the Jewish Folklore Mandolin Ensemble of the 1960s, which was associated with the Rogers Park JCC.

Chicago Pirchei Choir
Peretz Dissen, Director
4939 N. Central Park, 60625; 539-8505
Sponsored by Pirchei Agudath Israel of Chicago; performs for organizations, women's groups, senior adults—Chassidic songs primarily. Choir includes boys from 4th through 8th grades, but admission for newcomers is open only to 4th through 6th graders. Auditions arranged through Orthodox day schools in fall, but open to others as well. Choir members must read Hebrew. Rehearsals once or twice a week at the Agudath Israel Center, 3540 W. Peterson.

Der Driter Dor
Adar Rossman, Contact
1323 W. Albion, 60626
A small troupe of third-generation American Jews who perform Yiddish folk songs and poetry and will provide translations depending upon audience requirements.

■ **Rabbi Yechiel Eckstein**
222 W. Adams, Rm. 1449, 60606; 782-5080
Besides being director of Interreligious Activities for ADL, Rabbi Eckstein is a performer, storyteller, and singer who has four albums to his credit. He sings Chassidic and Israeli songs, lectures, presents music programs, and tells stories. He has performed throughout the United States, Canada, and Israel and has appeared with Theodore Bikel. During its 1973 war, the State of Israel invited him to entertain troops. Rabbi Eckstein is also a cantor and has performed for the High Holidays in area synagogues.

■ **Sharona Frantz Feller**
4250 N. Marine Dr., 60613; 929-8694
Musical director of Temple Jeremiah. Also performs as a song leader, music specialist. Programs of Hebrew, Yiddish, English, and Ladino songs vary in length from 20 to 40 minutes. She has also been involved in youth programming and is a composer of musical comedies.

Four Star Entertainers
Mayer Kaplan JCC
5050 Church St., Skokie 60077; 675-2200
A teen play-production company.

■ **Rabbi Reuven Frankel, Baritone**
Penina Frankel, Narrator
700 Wilmot Rd., Deerfield 60015; 948-5895
Rabbi and Mrs. Frankel present two multimedia works: The American Jewish Experience: From Minsk to Manhattan, a Multimedia Reminiscence; and An Echo of Eternity, a Multimedia Experience, based on an essay by Dr. Abraham Joshua Heschel, which includes 100 slides of Jerusalem. In addition, Rabbi Frankel performs concerts of liturgical and other Jewish music.

■ **Reuven Gold**
P.O. Box A3769, 60690; 227-3175
Storyteller, uses Chassidic stories for Jewish audiences. Also conducts experiential units for mental-health professionals, Jewish educators,

and teachers, which are concerned with humanistic, psychological, spiritual, and mystical elements all at once. Also lectures on The Art of Story Telling, The Story as Folk Art, and The Story Tie-in with Art—the latter offered at the Art Institute of Chicago.

Guild of Temple Musicians
Judith H. Karzen, National President
6636 N. Talman, 60645

A source for referrals to performers of Jewish music.

HATAV Orchestra
Shlomo Atlas, Director
Eileen Atlas, Pianist
539-1965

This professional orchestra, whose members belong to the Musicians Union, performs for a variety of Jewish audiences at religious affairs, weddings, bar mitzvah parties, banquets, and concerts; although they will not perform for social dancing, they will for circle dancing. Founded in 1975, the orchestra includes up to nine players, although more musicians can be added if needed. All kinds of Jewish music, but mostly Chassidic.

Habonim Israeli Dance Troupe
David Telman, Leader and Contact
9410 Lorel Ave., Skokie 60077; 966-4564

Israeli folk-dance group, semiprofessional. Will perform either for benefits or for small fee. Includes about fourteen teens.

Halevi Choral Society
David Politzer, Director
Board of Jewish Education
72 E. 11th St., 60605; 427-5570

Adult choir in residence at the Mayer Kaplan JCC, but also performs from time to time at Temple Menorah. Today's Halevi Choral Society is actually successor to a 50-year-old Chicago musical institution. New members are especially welcome.

■ **Dina Halpern**
c/o Danny Newman
Lyric Opera of Chicago
20 N. Wacker Dr., 60606; 346-6111 or 327-2914 (home)

Actress of the international Yiddish theater. Dramatic Yiddish theater presentations, play readings. Also presents a historical narrative of the Yiddish theater.

- **Sulie and Pearl Harand**
  708 Church St., Rm. 233, Evanston 60201; 864-1502
  Offer book talks, musical programs, and programs on Israeli and Jewish issues.

- **Julie Hartmann**
  1419 W. Cornelia, 60657
  Plays guitar and sings, has wide repertoire of Jewish and Hebrew songs. Work experience with Chicago Federation of Temple Youth and Olin-Sang-Ruby Union Institute summer camp.

Hatzabarim Israeli Folk Dancers
Marla Balaban, Director
864-6721
Semiprofessional Israeli folk-dance group.

Henry Street Players
Henry N. Hart JCC
2961 W. Peterson, 60659; 275-8445
Teen drama group; performs at senior adult centers, JCCs, and elsewhere.

Hyde Park JCC
1100 E. Hyde Park Blvd., 60615; 268-4600
The Jewish Adult Mobile Theater is a traveling troupe that performs Yiddish drama in English translation. Through various scenes the audience is shown changes in Jewish life-styles and values. Call the JCC for a booking. An adult chorus meets weekly. A new resident adult community theater was started at the end of 1980.

Imagination Theatre
7535 N. Washtenaw, 60645; 262-4102 or 262-4292
Nonprofit touring theater company provides some Jewish content for Jewish audiences. Performs for senior adults, schools, JCCs, and audiences of handicapped and mentally retarded. Special program for Purim.

- **Max Janowski**
  KAM–Isaiah Israel
  1100 E. Hyde Park Blvd., 60615; 924-1234
  Congregation music director Janowski is also cantor, composer, organist, and music director for choral ensembles assembled for specific performances.

Jewish People's Choral Society
Philip Fox, 673-8748
Sonia Matz, 262-4863
Rehearses and performs at the Bernard Horwich JCC under the auspices of the Mayer Kaplan Senior Adult Center. Repertoire includes Yiddish, English, Hebrew songs. Open to new members; rehearsals 7:30 to 9:30 P.M. Thursdays. Founded in 1914.

- **Shelley Kaplan**
  5206 S. Dorchester, 60615; 493-2767

Kaplan is really Shellebelle the Jewish Clown. Both Jewish and general programs for children, families, senior adults. A poet and teacher with a circus background. Special material for holidays and festivals, including a Purim Spiel.

- **Sonia Kass**
  679-3965

Primarily a pianist and accompanist, Kass is also the organist and choir director for B'nai Torah congregation and choir director for North Suburban Synagogue Beth El. She frequently accompanies cantors and other soloists. Wide repertoire includes all varieties of music, Jewish and non-Jewish.

- **Jerry Kaye**
  782-1477

When he is not directing youth and camp activities for the local office of the Union of American Hebrew Congregations, Kaye presents programs as a storyteller of Chassidic tales.

- **Letty Kipen**
  4414 N. Francisco, 60625; 539-4461

Performer, singer of Yiddish melodies and other Jewish-content songs. She is a free-lance liturgical singer available for Sabbath and High Holiday services.

- **Avrohom Levin**
  6421 N. Richmond, 60645; 743-0750

Chassidic accordionist; also performs some Israeli music.

- **Cantor Dale Lind**
  272-0252

Available for concerts, weddings, programs.

- **Anita Borcia Malina**
  7506 N. Kedvale, Skokie 60076; 679-6881

Humorous and dramatic programs from Jewish folklore and literature in English and Yiddish.

■ **Marcus/Price Puppets**
251-7611 or 869-6360

Susan Bass Marcus and Marilyn Lieb Price work together but also independently, with each creating her own style of puppets from a variety of materials. Together they have been consultants for Puppet Weeks at the Art Institute of Chicago. Some programs are designed for older children and adults, others for younger children. Programs for Jewish audiences include Shabbat stories, Chanukah shows (*Goose Candles; A Chanukah Party*), *Close Encounters of the Purim Kind*, and programs for other Jewish festivals and special occasions.

■ **Renee Matthews**
761-8541 or 676-4435

A singer whose performances span the musical spectrum from contemporary to camp, from intimate songs to international favorites. She includes a great deal of Jewish music—Yiddish, Hebrew, Israeli—as well as an entire segment of songs from the Yiddish theater. Appears with accompanist Dorraine Heftel.

■ **Sonia Matz**
262-4863

A soprano who sings Yiddish, Israeli, English, and some Russian songs with accompaniment. Performs for organizations and is a soloist with groups such as the Jewish People's Choral Society.

■ **Aviva May**
864-8733

Has been called a "strolling troubador" in her presentations of Yiddish, Hebrew, Chassidic, and English songs. Israeli born, a musician and linguist, she is well known in this area as an Israeli-Yiddish folk singer and educator. Most often, she appears alone, accompanying herself on guitar, but she also has been vocalist with bands and orchestras. Teaches singing and guitar as well as Hebrew and Yiddish, and tutors for bar mitzvah. Has used her music with perceptually handicapped children.

■ **Arnold Miller, Music Director**
Sima Miller, Soprano
8610 Avers Ave., Skokie 60076; 673-6409

Arnold Miller accompanies his wife in her performances of Jewish music and conducts his orchestra for all kinds of audiences and celebrations. Their repertoire includes Israeli, Yiddish, Chassidic, liturgical, Jewish rock, and Jewish folk rock. He is also a composer and a composer member of ASCAP and has written compositions for the Yiddish theater and for Jewish worship settings. She has performed throughout the United States and Israel and for local organizations and audiences. Her recordings include *Sima Miller in Concert, Sima Sings, Presenting Sima Miller.* Arnold and Sima Miller are included in the Board of Jewish Education recording *The American Jewish Experience in Song.*

■ **Irene Nathan**
743-8421

Performs dramatic readings and dramatizations of Jewish and Israeli literature. The autobiography of S. Y. Agnon and *The Story of Joseph*, a moving dramatization of the Bible story, are current offerings.

National Council of Jewish Women North Shore Section
P.O. Box 234, Glencoe 60022; 663-9400

Two NCJW performing troupes have been displaying their musical-theater talents for nearly twenty years. One troupe performs for physically and mentally handicapped children; the other, for senior adults—at centers, retirement homes, and nursing homes. All performers are volunteers but highly professional. Each performance includes audience participation. All material is written by the women.

National Council of Jewish Women South Cook Section
c/o 53 W. Jackson, Suite 724, 60604; 663-9400

The Traveling Players is a children's theater troupe that goes to schools and centers to perform, often for the handicapped. Volunteers write a new play every year, geared to elementary-school level.

Nitzanim Dance Troupe
Phil Moss, Leader
2341 Meadow Lane S., Wilmette 60091; 251-2676

Semiprofessional Israeli folk-dance troupe available for hire.

Once Upon a Players
Bernard Horwich JCC
3003 W. Touhy, 60645; 761-9100

Children's theater troupe consisting of adults and children who perform for children.

Open Stage Players
Mayer Kaplan JCC
5050 Church St., Skokie 60077; 675-2200

Adult theater production group.

Junior Open Stage Players
Mayer Kaplan JCC
5050 Church St., Skokie 60077; 675-2200

A theater production group for 6th through 9th graders. Auditions are held in early September and late January for productions in December and June. Contact Janie Weisenberg.

Playreading Group
Bernard Horwich JCC
3003 W. Touhy, 60645; 761-9100

■ **Ruth Rubin**
6304 N. Central Park Ave., 60659; 539-0374
Dramatic presentations of biographies and best-sellers, largely with Jewish content.

■ **Anita Salzman**
5334 Wright Ter., Skokie 60077; 965-8390
Performer and songleader of folk music—original, Jewish, and traditional international.

Martin Scharaga Orchestra
300 W. Hill, Apt. 718, 60610; 266-7535
Martin Scharaga's orchestra has been performing for the Chicago Jewish community for over fifteen years. All members of the orchestra belong to the Chicago Federation of Musicians Local 10-208.

■ **Ruth Shallett**
9 Martha Lane, Evanston 60201; 866-6254
Soprano performing concerts of Jewish music. Knows Jewish liturgical music and has been associated with synagogue music as soloist and music director for about twenty years. Shallett and partner Jo Minds, a mezzo-soprano, perform musical comedy and Jewish songs tailored to audience requests.

Shir/Chicago Ensemble
1416 W. Winnemac, 60640; 271-3810
Gerald Rizzer, Director
Shir is an ensemble of singers and instrumentalists who perform sacred and secular music related to Jewish culture. Usually Shir performances include one to four singers with flute and piano, but other combinations are available. Only "serious" music is performed, dating from the works of Rossi, who composed the first choral music for the synagogue around 1600, to music by modern Israeli and American composers. Programs usually include sophisticated arrangements of folk melodies, including Sephardic, Eastern European, and Israeli. Rizzer, a pianist, is director of Shir and the Chicago Ensemble of which Shir is a subsidiary.

■ **Ruth G. Silverman**
837 Lehigh Lane, Buffalo Grove 60090; 398-2019
Dramatic reader on subjects pertaining to the Holocaust, Soviet Jewry, and other Jewish topics. Has also performed in Jewish religious services.

Sing-a-long for the Blind
Opportunities Unlimited
c/o B'nai B'rith Council
8 S. Michigan Ave., 60603; 346-8555

Solel Congregation Choir
1301 Clavey Rd., Highland Park 60035; 433-3555
Bernhard Ebstein, Director
A performing choir open to members of the community.

Teen Footlighters
Bernard Horwich JCC
3003 W. Touhy, 60645; 761-9100
Teenage theater production troupe.

Tzlilim Band
Peretz Dissen, 539-8505
Yisroel Levin, 463-5451
A group of young Chicago Jewish musicians who perform Chassidic and Israeli music. For bookings contact either Dissen or Levin. They will perform for bar mitzvah parties and other family celebrations.

■ **Carol Wechter**
675-7383
Sings Hebrew and Yiddish show tunes and other kinds of music.

■ **Dr. Irwin Weil**
c/o Leigh Bureau
77 W. Washington, 60602; 236-3541
Although Weil is known principally as Professor of Slavic Languages and Literatures at Northwestern University, he is also a talented musician who performs the folk music and other songs of Russia and Russian Jewry.

Wise Men of Chelm
Bernard Horwich JCC
3003 W. Touhy, 60645; 761-9100
Scheduled a production for spring 1981 as the first of a series to be presented by the newly organized adult theater troupe at Horwich Center.

■ **Helen Zachary**
267-7213
Presents a musical variety show, sings Yiddish songs, old theater pieces, and old Jewish songs in translation.

Zimriya
Board of Jewish Education
72 E. 11th St., 60605; 427-5570
The annual music and dance festival of the Board of Jewish Education, under the direction of David Politzer. The 1980 performance included a combined community choir of 300 voices, three junior choirs, two dance companies, and two instrumental ensembles, all representing seventeen congregations and schools.

For names of Soviet Jewish performers now living in Chicago, call the Jewish Immigrant Center, Rogers Park Jewish Community Center, 274-0920.

Performing Arts Resources
Dramatics

■ **Anne Richmond Lefkovitz**
1001 Hull Ter., Evanston 60202
Has worked with creative dramatics and children's theater for over fifteen years, mainly in Jewish camps, community centers, and synagogues. Gives teacher and staff training workshops in creative dramatics and is a consultant in the organization of children's theater groups and in the use of dramatics in the Jewish day school, religious school, or community center. A resource on the use of dramatics as a tool in the teaching of Hebrew and on dramatic presentations in the Hebrew language.

■ **Marilyn (Toddy) Richman**
525 Sheridan Rd., Glencoe 60022; 835-1910
A specialist in creative drama as a teaching modality for all ages. Has worked with Jewish religious-school students from kindergarten through 12th grade and has served as coordinator and drama therapist for the Institute for Therapy through the Arts, Music Center of the North Shore, Winnetka. Special activities have included numerous workshops for teachers for Board of Jewish Education and a weekend of arts for the High School of Jewish Studies.

Music

Board of Jewish Education
72 E. 11th St., 60605; 427-5570
David Politzer, Director, Department of Music Education

The Board publishes *Zemer*, a music newsletter issued twice each year for musicians and educators, with emphasis on the Chicago musical scene, Jewish music, and musicians. BJE also sponsors Jewish music courses, some in cooperation with the Northwestern University School of Music, some at the Old Town School of Folk Music. Also, BJE offers two annual music workshops at no charge to the public. The Halevi Choral Society, an adult choir, is affiliated with the BJE and directed by Politzer. The annual "Zimriya"—music and dance festival—features a combined choir of 300 boys and girls from congregations and schools across the metropolitan area.

BJE republished in 1980 the Rudolph Beck *Community Songs*, including words and piano accompaniment for 56 oldtime favorites. That and a new curriculum, *A Music Guide for Jewish Schools*, designed for all ages, are available separately, or together at a reduced rate, from the BJE.

Friends of Jewish Music
8252 S. Woodlawn Ave., 60619; 768-5274

Publishes Jewish music, almost exclusively the music of Max Janowski—composer, cantor, music director.

Guild of Temple Musicians
6636 N. Talman, 60645
Judith H. Karzen, National President

An organization of synagogue musicians working throughout the United States and Canada. Founded in 1974, GTM provides educational material and resources for members. Open to all forms of Jewish worship and all persons associated with Jewish music, including music directors, choir directors, organists, music teachers, musicologists, and performers on all levels. One purpose of this organization is to offer opportunities in Jewish music to persons with little or no Judaic background. Also offers assistance to congregations in filling music positions. A local source for Jewish music programs.

Jewish Musicians Club of Chicago
Robert Gordon
6241 N. Ridgeway, 60659; 267-7318

Founded in 1915 as the Hebrew Musicians Club, the JMC was probably the first of several ethnic clubs to form within the Musicians

Union, Local 10-208. This is not so much a source for music or for Jewish music as an organization for professionals who gather for social purposes. Meets at 9 P.M., the first Wednesday of each month, at the Zionist Organization of Chicago headquarters, 6238 N. California. Associate nonvoting memberships are available for non-Jews who are card-carrying members of the Musicians Union. Current membership tops 100, and the club is seeking more members.

Old Town School of Folk Music
927 Noyes St., Evanston 60201; 864-6664
909 W. Armitage, 60614; 525-7793
Occasionally sponsors workshops and concerts in Jewish music. When Shlomo Carlebach sings his way into Chicago, the Chassidic Rebbe folk singer faithfully appears at the OTSFM.

Olin-Sang-Ruby Union Institute Camp Song Book—*Shiron*
100 W. Monroe, Rm. 312, 60603; 782-1477
A broad collection of Jewish songs without musical accompaniment but including English and Hebrew with English transliterations. The new national song book of the Reform Jewish camp movement is also available through this office.

■ **Rivka (Rosalie) Becker**
465-4026
Music educator and consultant as well as soprano soloist and guitarist. Has conducted workshops for Jewish educators at the Old Town School of Folk Music, cosponsored by the Board of Jewish Education. Teaches guitar. Certified as a K–12 vocal and string educator. She is strong on Jewish content and proficient in Hebrew.

■ **Roz Ebstein**
1329 Lincoln Ave. S., Highland Park 60035; 433-0368
Teacher of Jewish music in both day schools and afternoon-weekend religious schools; director of children's choral groups and expert in music for preschool children. Musical leader of Sabbath services and musical consultant on bar/bat mitzvah. Song leader in Hebrew and Yiddish music with a special love for Yiddish. A good source of information concerning Jewish choral groups open to newcomers—some of which are led by her husband, Bernhard.

■ **Stephanie Ettelson**
300 Lincolnwood, Highland Park 60035; 433-4535
Lectures and leads courses on music with Jewish content. Examples include a ten-week course for Congregation Solel, The Jewish Idiom

in Classical Music, and individual lectures on Ernest Bloch, Leonard Bernstein, or particular compositions such as the *Jeremiah* Symphony and the *Kaddish* Symphony. Also covers music of Jewish content by non-Jewish composers such as Ravel and Prokofiev. Ettelson also writes program notes for local concerts of Jewish content.

- **Dr. Maxine Ribstein Kanter**
  741 Green Bay Rd., Highland Park 60035; 433-2853

Pianist, educator, author, lecturer. Kanter wrote her doctoral dissertation on the music of the Sephardic High Holiday Liturgy. Her topics include The Jewish Contribution to the Music of Western Civilization, History and Culture of Sephardic Jewry, The Music of the Jewish People.

- **Judith H. Karzen**
  6636 N. Talman, 60645

A choir leader and resource on music, Jewish music, and music programs. She is national president of the Guild of Temple Musicians.

- **David Politzer**
  Board of Jewish Education
  72 E. 11th St., 60605; 427-5570

Music consultant to the Board of Jewish Education and director of the Halevi Choral Society. One of the outstanding resources in Chicago on Jewish music.

- **Shulamit Ran**
  1455 N. Sandburg Ter., 60610; 266-2295
  May be contacted through the Department of Music, University of Chicago

Ran is a composer whose music is often based on texts related to the Jewish experience. Her work *O the Chimneys* is based on the poems of Nelly Sachs. She is available to speak about her music or to lecture on Jewish music. Her talks are illustrated with tapes and records. Ran is a native of Israel who came to the United States to further her music studies in 1963. Her work has been recorded, published, and performed in the U.S., Europe, and Israel. A concert pianist and composer, she has received many awards, fellowships, and honors.

- **Barry Serota**
  127 N. Dearborn, 60602; 332-0323
  3111 W. Chase, 60645; 761-3111

Serota is making a unique contribution—preserving cantorial and other Jewish music and performances that are in danger of extinction.

Through his Musique Internationale, he has published about 60 LP records, some of which preserve performances from the time of World War I. An annotated list is available. Some of his recordings feature the composers of the Jewish Folk Song Society of St. Petersburg, Russia, 1908–18. Serota also presents illustrated lectures on the music and personalities of cantors and others, many of whom are part of Chicago's history.

■ **Cantor Shlomo Shuster**
675-4141
In addition to being the resource person for the Cantors' Assembly and a performer, Shuster is also a good source on Jewish music and music programming.

Cantors' Assembly Midwest Region
c/o Cantor Shlomo Shuster
Niles Township Jewish Congregation
4500 Dempster St., Skokie 60076; 675-4141
Largest organization of its kind in the world; includes cantors from all branches of Judaism. The central resource for cantors in the Chicago area.

Dance

■ **Ann Barzel**
3950 Lake Shore Dr., 60613
A speaker and resource on Jewish Dance and the Dance in Israel. Board member, Dance Library of Israel.

Chamber Ballet Ensemble
Marla Balaban, Director
864-6721
This Evanston-based classical ballet troupe of six dancers is adding Jewish-content dances to its repertoire. Call for information about performances.

■ **Dr. Mayer Gruber**
Associate Professor of Biblical Studies
Spertus College of Judaica
618 S. Michigan Ave., 60605; 922-9012
Lectures on Dance in the Bible—an Academic Interpretation.

Israeli Folk Dance

■ **Becky Alexander**
677-9875
A dance leader and teacher.

■ **Marla Balaban**
864-6721
A choreographer of Israeli folk dance, director of Hatzabarim Israeli Folk Dancers. Also a teacher of classical ballet and director of the Chamber Ballet Ensemble. Balaban is available for hire on an individual basis as a leader and teacher.

■ **Shlomo Barchechat**
4522 N. Ashland, 60640; 769-4529
Israeli dance performer and teacher.

■ **Penny Brichta**
2707 W. Albion, 60645; 262-1569
Israeli folk-dance leader and teacher.

■ **Haje Brickman Black**
475-4517
Israeli folk-dance leader and all-around resource person on the local Israeli folk-dance scene—groups to join, groups for hire, qualified leaders.

■ **Fran Cohen**
c/o Sager Solomon Schechter Day School
350 Lee Rd., Northbrook 60062
Israeli folk-dance teacher for all ages. Teaches, leads at Mayer Kaplan JCC as well as at Solomon Schechter schools.

■ **Phil Moss**
2341 Meadow Lane S., Wilmette 60091; 251-2676
Director of Nitzanim Dance Troupe; leads and teaches weekly at Northwestern University. Either Moss or the dance troupe available for hire.

■ **David Telman**
9410 Lorel Ave., Skokie 60077; 966-4564
Israeli folk-dance leader for hire for single event (bar/bat mitzvah, wedding)—dancing, leading, and instruction. Spokesman for Habonim Israeli Dance Troupe.

Habonim Israeli Dance Troupe
David Telman, Leader
9410 Lorel Ave., Skokie 60077; 966-4564

A semiprofessional troupe that will perform benefits on occasion and charge a small fee on other occasions. Includes fourteen teens. Repertoire reflects the wide ethnic differences in Israel: Russian, Arab, Yemenite, Bedouin, etc. Meets 5 to 9 P.M. Sundays at the Habonim meeting place, 4155 Main, Skokie. Newcomers may join; membership in Habonim is preferred.

Hatzabarim Israeli Folk Dancers
Marla Balaban, Director
864-6721 or the Consulate General of Israel, 565-3300

Semiprofessional adult dance group, open to new members. Meets 7:45 to 10 P.M. Sundays at the Horwich JCC, 3003 W. Touhy. Sponsored by the Consulate General of Israel. Group is for hire for performances or to lead Israeli folk-dance parties. Its repertoire includes Yemenite, Chassidic, Rumanian, and Russian. Costumes reflect ethnic background of each dance. Many of the dances have been professionally choreographed by Balaban and others.

Nitzanim Dance Troupe
Phil Moss, Leader
2341 Meadow Lane S., Wilmette 60091; 251-2676

Semiprofessional Israeli dance troupe; has performed for many civic events and community celebrations. Meets 2 to 5 P.M. Sundays at the Kaplan JCC, 5050 Church, Skokie. Participation open to experienced folk dancers. Troupe is for hire for performances and also for group participation with Moss leading.

Am Chai
P.O. Box 60142, 60660

Am Chai has an ongoing Israeli folk-dance group for members. It has performed on occasion at the Rogers Park JCC.

B'nai B'rith Hillel Foundation–Northwestern University
328-0650

Sponsors Israeli folk dancing with Phil Moss Thursday evenings at Parkes Hall, located on southeast corner of Chicago Ave. and Sheridan Rd. in Evanston. Instruction from 8 to 9 P.M.; requests from 9 to 11 P.M. Special discount to Hillel members, but everyone is welcome for minimal fee.

B'nai B'rith Hillel Foundation–University of Chicago
752-1127
Regular Israeli folk dancing at 8 P.M. Tuesdays in Ida Noyes Hall, 1212 E. 59th St., third floor.

Lincoln Park–Lakeview JCC
524 W. Melrose, 60657; 871-6780
Israeli folk dancing for beginners and intermediates. Tuesdays, 8 to 10:30 P.M. Led by Steve Glushakow-Smith.

Mayer Kaplan JCC
5050 Church St., Skokie 60077; 675-2200
Israeli and international folk dancing offered 7:30 to 10:30 P.M. Tuesdays, led by Fran Cohen; and 7:30 to 10 P.M. Wednesdays, led by Dit Olshan. First hour on both evenings is for beginners who are welcome to stay for the more advanced dances. Series fees are available or pay at the door.

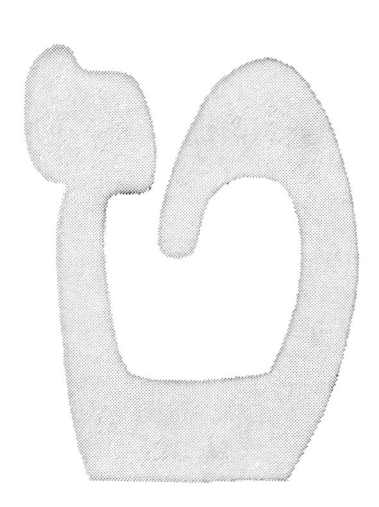

9
History

Archives and Historical Societies

Chicago Jewish Archives
618 S. Michigan Ave., 60605; 922-9012
Rabbi Morris Gutstein, Founder and Director
Richard Marcus, Librarian and Archives Administrator

Maintained in association with the Asher Library, Spertus College of Judaica, the CJA welcomes personal and institutional archives pertaining to any aspect of the local Jewish community. Among the holdings are archives of the Jewish Federation, Jewish Children's Bureau, Chicago Home for Jewish Orphans, Marks Nathan Home, Johanna Lodge, and the Jewish Training School. Among family collections are the family papers of Col. Marcus Spiegel, an officer in the Civil War. The CJA has received a federal matching grant from the National Archives for "A Survey and Accessioning Project for the Records of the Jewish Community of West Rogers Park."

Chicago Jewish Historical Society
618 S. Michigan Ave., 60605; 663-5634
Dr. Adele Hast, President

A membership organization, the CJHS was founded in 1977 to collect, preserve, and exhibit materials pertaining to the history of Chicago's Jews and the Jewish community and to encourage study and research, conduct programs, and disseminate information pertaining to this history. The society presents bimonthly public programs during the fall, winter, and spring and bus tours during the summer.

CJHS will pick up materials for processing and placement in the

Chicago Jewish Archives. Call Elsie Orlinsky, 643-9666. For information about bus tours, contact Leah Axelrod, 432-7003. Persons who are interested in collecting oral histories should call Dr. Curtis Melnick, 282-9583.

The following CJHS board members present lectures on Chicago Jewish history:
- Charles and Roberta Bernstein, 324-3089
- Dr. Irving Cutler, 251-8927 or 995-2186
- Rachel B. Heimovics, P.O. Box 524, Highland Park 60035
- Dr. Edward Mazur, 274-7720
- Sidney Sorkin, 221-4096

Rabbi Saul Silber Memorial Library
Hebrew Theological College
7135 N. Carpenter Rd., Skokie 60077; 267-9800 or 674-7750
Leah Mishkin, Librarian

Contains the record books, the pinkasim, from as many as 30 former Orthodox synagogues and schools. The books were rescued from buildings on the West Side. Special collections include those of J. Rapoport, R. Farber, Saul Silber, Rev. Newman, Max Shulman Zionist Library, Rabbi Simon H. Album Halakhah Collection, Rabbi and Mrs. L. C. Mishkin Holocaust Collection, and the Hebrew Periodical Collection. Open to the public most weekdays and Sundays.

American Jewish Archives
3101 Clifton Ave., Cincinnati, OH 45220

Located on the campus of the Hebrew Union College–Jewish Institute of Religion, the AJA has archives pertaining to Chicago Jews and congregations. Photographs in the AJA collection also include Chicago subjects. *American Jewish Archives*, an AJA semiannual publication, includes listings of acquisitions. The affiliated American Jewish Periodical Center of HUC-JIR is the outstanding repository of American Jewish periodicals.

American Jewish Historical Society
2 Thornton Rd., Waltham, MA 02154; (617) 891-8110
Morris Soble, Local Contact, 664-2227
Rachel Heimovics, Local Contact, P.O. Box 524, Highland Park 60035

Founded in 1892, the AJHS is the nation's oldest ethnic historical society. The AJHS building on the campus of Brandeis University contains a museum, library, and archival collection that includes holdings on the Chicago Jewish community. AJHS has an updated list of all local Jewish historical societies in the U.S. and Canada. The Rutenberg and Everett Yiddish Film Library contains a significant collection of American-made Yiddish films, fully restored and available for rent. *American Jewish History* is the quarterly publication of the society. Sponsors a speakers' service of academicians.

Rabbi Norman Berlat
Division of Pastoral Care, Lutheran General Hospital
1775 W. Dempster St., Park Ridge 60068; 696-2210
Has a 100,000-slide archive of American Jewish history. He will permit scholars and researchers to view the slides by appointment.

Chicago Historical Society
Clark St. at North Ave., 60614; 642-4600
All three divisions of the CHS Research Collections have materials related to the Chicago Jewish community. The Manuscript Collection contains the archives of the Jewish Community Centers, including the Jewish People's Institute and Max Straus Center, and of the Jewish Home for the Aged–BMZ, and the personal papers of Rabbi Jacob J. Weinstein. The Graphics Collection includes photographs of former synagogues, Jewish neighborhood scenes, and Chicago Jews. The Printed Collection includes titles and bound documents relating to Chicago Jewish history. An 1884 Jewish Directory of Chicago lists the rules for patients at Michael Reese Hospital:

> Patients must have a full bath once a week unless otherwise ordered by the physician; but never sooner than two hours after a full meal.

Chicago Public Library, Newspaper Room
425 N. Michigan Ave., 12th Floor, 60611
Foreign Language Press Survey has on microfilm English-translated excerpted articles from the following Chicago Yiddish publications: *Jewish Advance* (1881); *Jewish Daily Courier* (1906-28); *Jewish Daily Forward* (1919-32); *Jewish Labor World* (1908 and 1916-19); and *Jewish Standard* (1908-9). The University of Chicago Regenstein Library has the original typewritten copy from which the microfilms were made.

Hull House
800 S. Halsted, 60680; 996-2793
Hull House was founded in 1889 by Jane Addams and Ellen Gates Starr. The historic settlement and the personalities associated with it played an important role among Jewish immigrants. Only the original house was spared from demolition in the 1960s with construction of

the surrounding University of Illinois–Chicago Circle. Visit Hull House for its archives, library, and the continuing Bicentennial exhibit Ethnic Groups in the Hull House Neighborhood 1850–1914. For groups, advance reservations are expected. Groups are shown slide shows to accompany the exhibit. The Jewish portion of the elaborately documented exhibit was researched and mounted by Michal Finkelstein.

Illinois Labor History Society
20 E. Jackson, 60604; 663-4107

Lawrence J. Gutter Chicagoana Archive
1125 Oak Ridge Dr., Glencoe 60022; 835-4946
The most outstanding privately held collection of Chicagoana includes some 30 to 40 items of Jewish interest. Examples are the United Hebrew Relief Association reports for 1859 (year of founding) through 1862 and *Richards Magazine*, vol. I, no. 1 (March 1916) and vol. I, no. 2 (May 1916), two issues, perhaps the only issues of a magazine published by the precocious youth Richard Loeb. Scholars are welcome but must make an advance appointment.

Leo Baeck Institute, Chicago Chapter
Dr. Kurt Schwerin, 338-2799, and
Martin Mainzer, 1509 Edgewood Lane, Winnetka 60093;
  Cochairmen
The prime purpose of the Leo Baeck Institute is the research, study, and documentation of Central European Jewry. The Institute supports three educational-archival centers—in London, New York, and Jerusalem. The local chapter sponsors programs and supports international endeavors.

Michael Reese Hospital and Medical Center
29th St. and Ellis Ave., 60616; 791-2330
Archivist is Sally Gordon.

Municipal Reference Library
Rm. 1004, City Hall, 121 N. LaSalle, 60602; 744-4992
Collection includes old city directories, street-name change file, street-number change correlations, list of incorporations. Newspaper clipping file, started in 1957, includes 8,000 assorted subject headings. Direct Jewish queries to Clare Greenberg.

Newberry Library
60 W. Walton, 60610; 943-9090
A major humanities library, especially known for its genealogy materials and holdings in family and local history. Has archives pertaining

to Chicago Jews; its most recent major acquisition is the papers of author Ben Hecht and his wife, Rose—a collection totaling 68 boxes.

YIVO Institute for Jewish Research, Chicago Committee
Ezra Perkal, Chairman, 427-5570
Local committee supports YIVO's singular program of documentation and research pertaining to the Jewish communities of Eastern Europe and their move to America and other lands—their culture, organizations, and institutions. New York based, YIVO includes archives (no one is quite sure how many) from Chicago's Yiddish folk groups.

■ **Dr. Elliot Lefkovitz**
1001 Hull Ter., Evanston 60202
Author of *A History of Anshe Emet Synagogue;* available for research and writing on Jewish historical topics.

■ **Mark Mandle**
1619 W. Columbia, Apt. 2F, 60626; 262-8443
Local synagogue archivist, genealogist, and professional librarian.

Chicago Jewish Bibliography

Highland Park Public Library
494 Laurel, Highland Park 60035; 432-0216
This library has a mimeographed *Chicago Jewish History Bibliography,* which presents an excellent selection of titles for anyone interested in learning about the Chicago Jewish community. The bibliography indicates where each title can be found. It was compiled by Mark Mandle, November 1977.

Bibliography of Publications about Jews in America in Five Chicago Libraries: A Tercentenary Publication, published by the Jewish Historical Association of Chicago in Cooperation with the Chicago Jewish Tercentenary Committee, March 1955.

Contents include holdings in the Chicago Public Library, Newberry Library, University of Chicago, the College of Jewish Studies (now Spertus College), and Hebrew Theological College—books, commemorative booklets, theses, mimeographed reports, etc. It was compiled by Rabbi Leonard Mishkin and is available at any of the included libraries.

Bernheimer, Charles S. *The Russian Jew in the United States.* Philadelphia, 1905.

This classic work on immigration history describes the structure of Russian immigrant society by presenting various aspects of life (education, philanthropy, labor, religion, etc.) in three separate cities: Chicago, New York, and Philadelphia. The Chicago sections were written by local people. It is available in reprint from the Jerome Ozer Co., New York.

Gutstein, Morris Aaron. *A Priceless Heritage.* New York: Bloch Publishing Co., 1953.

The best available history of the nineteenth-century Chicago Jewish community, well footnoted, with a significant bibliography. Unfortunately, there is no counterpart for the twentieth century.

History of the Jews of Chicago. Jewish Historical Society of Illinois, 1924.

Commonly called the "Meites," after editor and publisher Hyman L. Meites, this is the rarest book about Jewish Chicago. This 854-page, gilt-edge, leather-bound book, a typical turn-of-the-century "mug-shot" history, has many photographs and biographies. As history it is undocumented, unfootnoted, and has certain gaps. At least two versions of the book were published, with some variation in the photographs and biographies. Each numbered volume (of 500) was dedicated to a subscriber. Libraries received unnumbered copies. Most of the writing was done by Associate Editor David E. Hirsch, now an octogenarian, who lives in Israel, where he and his wife, Valia (also a Chicagoan), have published a newspaper for American Israelis.

To be included in a "Meites" history inventory, owners are requested to send volume number and dedication name plus current owner's name to

Rachel B. Heimovics, P.O. Box 524, Highland Park 60035.

Holli, Melvin G., and Peter d'A. Jones. *The Ethnic Frontier: Group Survival in Chicago and the Midwest.* Grand Rapids, MI: William B. Eerdmans Publishing Co., 1977.

Includes a chapter by Dr. Edward Mazur entitled "Jewish Chicago: From Diversity to Community." Volume II, *Ethnic Chicago*, with a 1981 publication date, includes "The Jews of Chicago: From Shtetl to Suburb."

Jaret, Charles L. "Residential Mobility and Local Jewish Community Organization in Chicago." Ph.D. dissertation, University of Chicago, 1977.

"The Lakeville Studies"
Sklare, Marshall, and Benjamin Ringer. *Jewish Identity on the Suburban Frontier*. American Jewish Committee, 1967.
Sklare, Marshall, and Benjamin Ringer. *The Edge of Friendliness*. American Jewish Committee, 1967.
Sklare, Marshall, and Joseph Greenblum. *Jewish Identity on the Suburban Frontier: A Study of Group Survival in the Open Society*. 2d edition, 1979.

"The Lakeville Studies"—two original volumes and updated second edition—are a sociological study of Jewish movement into and acculturation within "Lakeville"—actually Highland Park with a thin slice of Glencoe. For purposes of projecting findings and conclusions, actual names of studied congregations and personalities have been changed, but they will be evident to persons who know the territory.

Langer, Jeffrey Ira. "White-Collar Heritage: Occupational Mobility of Jews in Chicago 1860-1880." B.A. thesis, University of Illinois, 1976.

More like a graduate thesis, Langer's study utilizes modern quantitative methods to study vocational patterns among Jews identified with early Chicago congregations and social clubs.

Mazur, Edward H. "Minyans for a Prairie City: The Politics of Chicago Jewry, 1850-1940." Ph.D. dissertation, University of Chicago, 1973.

An excellent review of Chicago Jewish political history; includes a significant bibliography of published and unpublished materials on Chicago's Jewish community.

Rosenthal, Erich. "Acculturation with Assimilation, the Jewish Community of Chicago, Illinois." *American Journal of Sociology*, vol. LXVI, no. 3 (1960).
Rosenthal, Erich. "This Was North Lawndale." *Jewish Social Studies* (April 1960), pp. 67-80.

Two fascinating historio-sociological studies by a former Chicago sociologist. These challenge some of the theories presented by Louis Wirth in *The Ghetto*.

Wirth, Louis. *The Ghetto*. Chicago: University of Chicago Press, 1928.

Kept in print, with the original woodcuts by Todros Geller, this classic was one of the great studies of the Chicago School of Sociology. An excellent portrait of Chicago's Jewish ghetto, although some of the projections of population disbursement and other theories were later disproven and are a reflection in themselves of social thought in the 1920s.

The Sentinel Publishing Company, which is celebrating its 70th anniversary in 1981, has published three books that belong in any bibliography of Chicago:

The Chicago Jewish Community Blue Book. Undated, published about 1918. Describes in detail the many organizations in the Jewish community.

The Sentinel Presents 100 Years of Chicago Jewry, 1948. Very well illustrated.

The Sentinel's History of Chicago Jewry 1911–1961. Included here is a lengthy bibliography of books in all fields, including fiction, by Chicago Jewish authors.

Chicago Metro History Fair
60 W. Walton, 60610; 943-9090
David Ruchman, Arthur Anderson; Codirectors

The first Metro History Fair was held in 1979, the second in 1980. Directed from the Newberry Library, the fairs were cosponsored and funded by the Illinois Humanities Council. Among finalist projects at both fairs were projects of Jewish content. The student historians may be regarded as resources and may be contacted through the Chicago Metro History Fair.

Among the Jewish subjects of the 1979 fair finalists were Jewish Customs Today; the abandoned and desecrated Jewish cemetery in Niles; a history of North Suburban Synagogue Beth El; various genealogy projects (Aldort-Kantoff, Eselevsky-Raizman, Schwartz-Gold, Ottenfeld); and several on subjects pertaining to specific Chicago Jews (the Leopold and Loeb murder; the Julius Rosenwald mansion).

In 1980, the winning project, The Synagogue That Wouldn't Die, by Irma Romero and Elsa Salazar of Bowen High School, told the story of Agudath Achim-Bikur Cholim synagogue at 89th and Houston. Among other finalists were projects on the Nazi march in Skokie; immigration (How to Escape a Pogrom); and genealogy projects (Fox-Saphier, Friedman-Tuler, Levy-Goldberg, Band-Kaplan, Motel-Miller, Mendez-Necheles, and Rugen families).

Illinois

The first Jewish interest in Illinois dates back to colonial days—to the 1760s and 1770s—when a group of Lancaster, PA, Jews financed several commercial expeditions to the Illinois-Indiana territory. For accounts of this history, see the following:

Alvord, Clarence Walworth. *The Illinois Country 1673–1818*. Originally published 1922. Reprinted. Chicago: Loyola University Press, 1965.

Baldwin, Edward Chauncey. "The Jewish Influence upon the Colonial Development of Illinois." Introduction to the *History of the Jews of Chicago* (the "Meites" book). Jewish Historical Society of Illinois, 1924.

The earliest known Jew to settle in Illinois was Isaac Levy, provisioner and physician, who preceded George Rogers Clark's 1778–79 expedition to the Illinois colony in Kaskaskia and Cahokia. In 1793, another Jew, John Hays, came to the territory. Hays served first as volunteer postmaster and then was appointed sheriff of St. Clair County. That Levy and Hays knew each other is borne out by the Land Claims Records of the Register's Office, Kaskaskia, November 29, 1815.

Historic and Architectural Landmarks

Agudath Achim-Bikur Cholim
8927 S. Houston, 60617; 768-7685
Millie Miller, Contact, 493-8880
Currently seeking landmark status as the oldest synagogue in continuous use. Congregation Bikur Cholim, founded in 1888, laid the cornerstone of this building in 1900. May be the first synagogue designed by Alfred S. Alschuler, Sr.

First Jewish services in Chicago
Site: Southwest corner of Lake and Wells. A group of early Jewish settlers convened for Yom Kippur, 1845. Later, KAM congregation began at this location—above the store that stood on the corner.

First synagogue in Chicago, KAM
Site: Clark St. and Quincy, now occupied by the Kluczinski Building of the Federal Center. Plaques on the wall designate the exact site. Dedicated in 1851, this location was on the edge of the "Jewish neighborhood" of the 1850s.

Heald Square
Wacker Dr., Wabash, and South Water
Declared a Chicago Landmark in 1971. Monument of George Washington, Robert Morris, and Haym Salomon, the most famous Jew of

the Revolutionary War period. Dedicated one week after the United States entered World War II—December 15, 1941—to commemorate the 150th anniversary of the ratification of the U.S. Bill of Rights. Designed by Lorado Taft, completed after his death by his protégé and associate, Leonard Crunelle. For their "Spirit of '76" fleet for the Bicentennial, the Chicago Transit Authority named a specially decorated rapid transit train the "Haym Salomon."

Henry Horner Monument
Horner Park, Montrose and California
In memory of the first Jewish governor of Illinois. The monument is owned and maintained by the Illinois Department of Conservation.

JPI (Jewish People's Institute)
(now Julius Hays Hess public school)
3500 W. Douglas Blvd.
Declared a National Historic Landmark by the National Park Service of the Department of Interior in 1978, 75 years after the founding of the organization that became the Jewish Community Centers of Chicago. The architect was Eugene Henry Klaber.

KAM Temple
Pilgrim Baptist Church
33rd and Indiana Ave.
Built by KAM in 1890 as its fifth home, this is one of the lesser-known extant works of the architectural firm of Adler and Sullivan. Architecturally, the building reflects the influence of H. H. Richardson. The Romanesque exterior was constructed of rusticated Joliet stone, and the gilt plaster ornament inside remains among the richest examples of Sullivan's work. Adler's father, Rev. Liebmann Adler, was the spiritual leader of KAM from 1860 through semiretirement at the time of his death in 1892. (A model of this building, constructed by Randy Noe, can be seen at the Rose Art Museum of Brandeis University, Waltham, MA.)

KAM-Isaiah Israel Temple
1100 E. Hyde Park Blvd.
Declared a Chicago Landmark in 1977. Built by Isaiah Israel congregation in 1924, the brick Byzantine-style structure, based on a second-century synagogue in ancient Tiberias, was designed by Alfred S. Alschuler, Sr.

Maxwell Street Market District
Maxwell and Halsted streets

Originally established in the 1850s, the district became the place of first settlement for Jews from Eastern Europe, beginning in the 1880s. The Maxwell Street area was the focus of *The Ghetto* by Louis Wirth (Chicago: University of Chicago Press, 1928). Nostalgia for the market was the basis for Ira Berkow's *Maxwell Street* (New York: Doubleday & Co., 1977). The market retained its Jewish character long after the area had ceased to be a Jewish residential district.

Jewish History

- **Sophie K. Black**
1026 Harvard Ter., Evanston 60202; 328-9286

Lectures on the Holocaust and Jewish life in Europe before the Holocaust. Black is Associate University Librarian for Public Services and Associate Professor in the Library, Northeastern Illinois University, 5500 N. St. Louis, 60625; 583-4050, x469. She presents book talks and is involved with Jewish student and faculty groups at Northeastern.

- **Dr. Isaac Daniel**
6708 N. Francisco, 60645; 761-1571

A resource on the Jews of Greece, especially from the area of Salonica. His slide presentations, Places of Jewish Interest around the World, include photographs of the ancient Jewish ghetto of Veria (Veroia) in Greece, where his own family originated.

- **Dr. Norman Golb**
Professor of Hebrew and Judaeo-Arabic Studies
Department of Near Eastern Languages and Civilizations
University of Chicago
5813 S. Blackstone Ave., 60637; 324-7858

Twice a Guggenheim Fellow, Dr. Golb has worked on the Cairo Genizah documents of Cambridge University as well as on materials relating to medieval Kiev, Sicily, and the Jews of medieval Rouen. He is a voting member of the Oriental Institute.

- **Jacob Gordon**
100 N. LaSalle St., 60602; 236-2155 or 835-2646

Lectures on Jewish historical subjects.

- **Judah L. Graubart**
321 N. Harvey Ave., Oak Park 60302; 383-0677

Lectures on American Jewish history, with emphasis on the years since 1881, the beginning of the great immigration from Eastern Europe. A resource for oral history.

- **Miriam Greenblatt**
 111 Hogarth Lane, Glencoe 60022; 835-4954
Author and lecturer on many aspects of Jewish history to both adult and children's audiences. When speaking to the latter, she uses props. Some topics have been Jewish Heroes of the Revolutionary and Civil Wars, Jews in the West, Jewish Peddlers, Jews in the Roman World, How Jews are Presented in Textbooks, and Jews in Science Fiction.

- **Rabbi Morris A. Gutstein**
 5830 N. Drake Ave., 60659; 539-9355
Author, historian, and founder of the Chicago Jewish Archives. Lectures on American and local Jewish history.

- **Dr. Monfred Harris**
 Professor of Jewish Texts and Institutions
 Spertus College of Judaica
 618 S. Michigan Ave., 60605; 922-9012
Lectures on holidays and other aspects of Jewish culture as they relate to history.

- **Rachel B. Heimovics**
 P.O. Box 524, Highland Park 60035
Author and lecturer. Slide presentations on immigration, equal rights, and other topics.

- **Dr. Elliot Lefkovitz**
 1001 Hull Ter., Evanston 60202
A lecturer on Jewish history and culture; has taught at Loyola and Spertus; consultant to Chicago Board of Education. Conducts social studies and history workshops. Special areas: history of anti-Semitism, history of Zionism, history of French and Russian Jewry, and American Jewish history.

- **Dr. Edward Mazur**
 2923 W. Birchwood, 60645; 274-7720
Professor, City Colleges of Chicago, 269-8000. The Jewish Response to Critical Periods in American Jewish History is one of his lecture topics.

- **Dr. Oscar Miller**
 4638 W. Dempster, Skokie 60076; 679-4077
Dean of Student Affairs, University of Illinois–Chicago Circle, consultant to the Board of Jewish Education, and active in many local and national academic and Jewish organizations. Lecture and resource topics include politics and history of the Middle East, of Jerusalem, of

Zionism, of anti-Semitism, of Israel; Jewish history generally; and Jewish education.

■ **Dr. Judith-Rae Ross**
8725 Springfield, Skokie 60076
Dr. Ross has a Ph.D. in history from the University of Illinois. She presents lectures on subjects relating to The History of the Holocaust; Voltaire and the Jews; The Pro-Semites—from Macaulay to Guizot; The Jewish Image in Fiction; The Evolution of the Jewish Mother; Israel and the Media; and The Pre-Cursor of Mastercharge—Aaron of Lincoln and Twelfth-Century Finance: Some Thoughts for Today. Dr. Judith-Rae Ross is also executive director of the Chicago Zionist Federation.

■ **Dr. Joyce S. Schrager**
475-8093
Teaches courses and presents individual lectures on topics related to twentieth-century Jewish history.

■ **Dawn Schuman**
1302 Forest Ave., Highland Park 60035; 433-3380
Speaker, lecturer, teacher, and seminar leader on Jewish history, from ancient times to today. Has accompanied groups on trips of Jewish content and adventure, including trips to Eastern Europe, and, in 1980, to the Soviet Union. Courses have covered ancient, medieval, modern, and Holocaust history.

■ **Dr. Moses A. Shulvass**
Distinguished Service Professor of Jewish History
Spertus College of Judaica
618 S. Michigan Ave., 60605; 922-9012
Lectures on many aspects of Jewish history.

■ **Dr. Irving Skolnick**
Board of Jewish Education
72 E. 11th St., 60605; 427-5570
A resource on social studies and history units for junior high school age. Has prepared or directed preparation of curriculum materials on Jewish Beginnings in America, Sephardic Jewry, East European Jewry, and other topics.

■ **Emily D. Soloff**
2325 W. Greenleaf, 60645; 262-7721
A writer and editor on Jewish history.

■ **Norma Spungen**
9011 N. Kildare, Skokie 60076; 676-0715

Teaches a course, The American Jewish Experience, and gives lectures on American Jewish history, such as The Colonial Experience; Zionism—American Style; and Up from the Sweatshops—The Jewish Labor Movement. Currently lectures to JCC groups and to seniors through the Adult Continuing Education Department of Truman College.

■ **Marillyn Tallman**
514 Jackson Ave., Glencoe 60022; 835-2688

Leads and teaches adult survey courses in Jewish history—ancient, medieval, and modern. Also presents educational programs: The Chain of Tradition of Jewish Women, Jews behind Walls (primarily the story of the remnant Jewish communities in Eastern Europe), and on the Holocaust, American Jewish immigrant history, and the sweep of ancient Jewish history. Also reports on trips to the Soviet Union to see Refuseniks. Tallman is cochairman of the Chicago Action for Soviet Jewry.

Terry Terracina
13 Webster Ave., Highwood 60040

Mr. Terracina, who himself is an Italian-born Jew, is a resource on the subject of Italian Jewry.

■ **Dr. Irwin Weil**
c/o Leigh Bureau
77 W. Washington St., 60602; 236-3541

Dr. Weil is a professor of Slavic Languages and Literatures at Northwestern University and author of several books and articles about Russian literature and Russian and Soviet culture. He lectures, leads discussions, and presents concerts and study groups on Jewish Life in the USSR, The Treatment of the Jew in Russian Literature, and related topics.

Labor History

Illinois Labor History Society
20 E. Jackson St., 60604; 663-4107

Archives and publications containing materials of Jewish interest.

Jewish Labor Committee Chicago Office
127 N. Dearborn, 60602; 641-5086
David Schacter, Executive Director

This office has programs available to organizations, including an audiovisual presentation tracing the history of Jews in the labor movement of Chicago. Also has a videotape of a speech presented by Irving Howe at the Institute of Labor and Industrial Relations, University of Illinois–Chicago Circle.

- Sol Brandzel
  c/o Amalgamated Clothing Workers of America
  333 S. Ashland, 60607; 738-6147

A member of the board of the Chicago Jewish Historical Society, Sol Brandzel is a resource person and lecturer on the history of labor in Chicago in general and of Jews in labor in particular.

- Peter Pero
  447 Marengo St., Forest Park 60130; 771-3990

Slide lectures on Jews in Chicago's Labor Movement. Guided tours of Chicago with emphasis on labor history, ethnic groups, and architecture. Has worked closely with other ethnic groups.

- Stanley Rosen
  Professor of Labor and Industrial Relations
  Institute of Labor and Industrial Relations
  University of Illinois–Chicago Circle
  P.O. Box 4348, 60680; 996-2623 or 274-0464 (home)

History professor and lecturer. His lectures reflect his appreciation for the ideologies, sometimes left-wing or radical, that motivated Jews in past generations. Topics include Labor, History of Jews in Labor, Politics and Political Ideologies. Lectures with or without slides.

For a historic review of the 1910 Hart, Schaffner & Marx clothing workers' strike, see N. Sue Weiler's "Walkout: The Chicago Men's Garment Workers' Strike, 1910–1911," *Chicago History*, vol. VIII, no. 4 (Winter 1979–80).

Oral History

Chicago Jewish Historical Society
618 S. Michigan Ave., 60605; 663-5634
Dr. Curtis Melnick, 282-9583

CJHS has an ongoing oral history project. Training sessions are held periodically. Volunteers are needed to interview subjects and to transcribe tapes.

Council for Jewish Elderly
1016 Howard, Evanston 60202; 973-4105

This agency prepared about one dozen oral histories for the 1976 Bicentennial observance. The tapes contain personal reminiscences by Jewish elderly about their own immigration experiences and about life in early Chicago. CJE uses the tapes in training others in oral history and for classroom and program resources.

Oral History Project in Labor and Immigration History
Roosevelt University
430 S. Michigan Ave., 60605; 341-3763
Dr. Elizabeth Balanoff, Associate Professor of History and
  Director of the Oral History Project

This oral history project includes interviews with Jewish people such as Lillian Herstein (12 hours), Chicago Teachers Union; Jacob Potofsky (1½ hours), Amalgamated Clothing Workers Union; Frank Rosenblum (3 hours), Amalgamated Clothing Workers Union; Joel Seidman (1 hour), University of Chicago Business School; Mollie Levitas (3½ hours), retired Secretary, Chicago Federation of Labor; Myrna Seigendorf Kassel (2 hours), former Executive Secretary, Community Services Chicago Industrial Union Council; Pearl Spencer (2 hours), retired garment worker; Jacob Woolfe (2 hours), retired laundry owner; and Irving Ross (2 hours), retired garment worker. A very long biographical interview with Ralph Helstein, former International President, United Packinghouse Workers Union, is under way.

■ **Judah L. Graubart**
321 N. Harvey Ave., Oak Park 60302; 383-0677

Graubart, an expert in the entire field of oral history, is also a member of the board of the Chicago Jewish Historical Society. He and his wife, Alice V., coauthored *Decade of Destiny* (Chicago: Contemporary Books, 1978) based on over 60 oral history interviews. A second collection is nearing completion.

■ **Dr. Edward Mazur**
2923 W. Birchwood, 60645; 274-7720

Conducts workshops on oral history techniques.

■ **Gertrude Steinberg**
256-5489

Caseworker for the Council for Jewish Elderly. She has prepared close to twenty oral histories of Chicago Jewish elderly, many in connection with her 1975 M.A. dissertation for Northeastern Illinois University, entitled "A Study of the Life Review Process in a Group of Older Adults."

Genealogy

■ **Rhea Adler**
251-3705

A member of the North Suburban Genealogical Society and other national and regional genealogy societies. A good guide through routes and byways in the search for family roots.

- **Charles B. Bernstein**
  5400 S. Hyde Park Blvd., 60615; 324-3089

A board member of the Jewish Genealogical Society as well as the Chicago Jewish Historical Society, Bernstein's passion is genealogy. He seems to know everyone's relationship to everyone else and has retained all diagrams, dates, and descendancies in his head. Lectures and provides general guidance on genealogy.

- **Judy S. Frazin**
  1025 Antique Lane, Northbrook 60062

Has spent ten years on her own family; now lectures and conducts workshops on Jewish genealogy that give guidance on organizing and documenting genealogical research and that include materials for each participant.

- **Rabbi Benzion C. Kaganoff**
  2901 W. Greenleaf Ave., 60645; 274-9034

Rabbi Kaganoff is a resource person, author, and lecturer on the subject of Jewish family names. See his book *A Dictionary of Jewish Names and Their History* (New York: Schocken Books, 1977). Rabbi Kaganoff also writes a column for the quarterly *Toledot: The Journal of Jewish Genealogy.*

- **Lewis M. Lazarus**
  5755 N. Fairfield Ave., 60659

Lazarus is a professional genealogist who will take on professional research assignments. He has spent seventeen years in genealogical research and advertises periodically in the "Directory of Professional Genealogists" of the *Genealogical Helper.*

- **Kenneth Lipman**
  764-0430

Has traced his father's Lodz (Poland) branch to the ninth century; now researching his mother's Stazow (Poland) branch.

- **Mark Mandle**
  1619 W. Columbia, Apt. 2F, 60626; 262-8443

Mandle is a professional librarian, archivist, and member of the board of the Chicago Jewish Historical Society who has been researching his own family genealogy for years. He is also available for genealogy assignments.

■ **Richard Sobel**
c/o 507 Lake Ave., Wilmette 60091

Sobel has been seeking information on the Sobel (Austria-Hungary) and Debs-Dobrowitz (Riga) families in Chicago.

Howard Tuber
6609 N. Campbell, 60645

Tuber prepared a 37-page family tree of his ancestor, Louis Tuber (1847–1929) from Popilon, Kovna Gabernia, Lithuania. Many of the descendants live in the Chicago area and gathered for a celebration in August, 1980, in Lincolnwood. Howard Tuber would like additional genealogical information from family members. Copies of the tree are available.

Church of Latter Day Saints
Branch Genealogy Libraries

Persons may view—or order—microfilms prepared by the Mormons that include vital statistics from former Jewish centers of population in Poland, Hungary, and Germany. Branches are open Tuesdays, Wednesdays, Thursdays, and Saturdays, but this is subject to change. Call for hours.

Chicago Heights Branch
402 Longwood, Chicago Heights 60411; 754-2525

Naperville Branch
Ridgeland and Naperville Rd., Naperville 60540; 357-0211

Wilmette Branch
2801 Lake Ave., Wilmette 60091; 251-9818

Genealogy Unlimited
789 S. Buffalo Grove Rd., Buffalo Grove 60090; 541-3175

Has materials relating to Jewish genealogy, including a Russian history atlas. Also offers courses in general and in Jewish genealogy, the latter taught by Stuart Feiler. Will restore and copy old photos and documents and preserve them in Mylar.

Newberry Library
60 W. Walton, 60610; 943-9090

This outstanding genealogy reference library is one of the top humanities libraries in the country. Has the 1880 Soundex of the Illinois-Indiana census.

Winnetka Public Library
768 Oak St., Winnetka 60093; 446-7220

In the Chicago area, this genealogy collection, begun in 1963, is second only to that of the Newberry Library. There are volunteer genealogists to assist.

The Krensky-Ehrenreich "Time-Line," Heder Hadorot
Spertus Museum of Judaica, 2d floor
618 S. Michigan Ave., 60605; 922-9012

This permanent exhibit is a documentary and pictorial history of the Krensky-Ehrenreich family, with pictures and diagrams tracing back 200 years, on the walls of the Milton J. Krensky and Rosemary Ehrenreich Krensky Conference Room. An excellent model for other family studies.

The Holocaust

Holocaust Memorials

New Light Cemetery
Pratt Blvd. and E. Prairie Rd., Lincolnwood 60645

This Holocaust memorial was dedicated September 22, 1974, with Rabbi Eric Friedland officiating.

Bernard and Rochelle Zell Holocaust Memorial
Spertus Museum of Judaica
618 S. Michigan, 60605; 922-9012

A permanent memorial to the victims and a record for history that includes photographs, other graphics, a film, and artifacts. On six pillars are inscribed the names of victims remembered by those living in Chicago. New names are added on the annual observance of Yom HaShoah. The brochure for the exhibit includes an extensive Holocaust bibliography, about 70 titles, covering all aspects and academic disciplines; all titles available at the Spertus College library.

Available at the Zell exhibit are Daf-Ed forms that are forwarded to the Yad Vashem Archives in Jerusalem. Daf-Ed—Page of Testimony—is an attempt to gather into Israel the permanent record of each Jew who died, fought, or rebelled against the Nazis or Nazi collaborators.

Dr. Janusz Korczak Playlot Park (#1090)
Southwest corner of Claremont and Granville, 60659

This park was named for a Jewish hero who sacrificed his life in the Holocaust. A pediatrician, Korczak chose to remain with 250 orphans rather than gain freedom for himself alone.

Dr. Janusz Korczak Memorial
Church St. and Dr. Korczak Ter., Skokie 60076
An eternal light.

Holocaust Observances

Yom HaShoah is the day designated for memorials and observances of the Holocaust on a community level. Many of the specific religious and secular observances take place on that date. Yom HaShoah will be observed on May 1 in 1981, April 20 in 1982, and April 10 in 1983.

Memorial Services are held in the Zell Holocaust Exhibit room of the Spertus Museum, conducted by the Chicago Board of Rabbis. The other groups participating vary slightly from year to year.

Chicago Yizkor Committee for Six Million Martyrs holds an annual ceremony to commemorate the anniversary of liberating concentration camps. It usually takes place in the afternoon, at a synagogue, following a morning observance at Shalom Memorial Park cemetery, Palatine. Sponsors include Shaarit Ha-Plita Jewish Camp Survivors.

The Anti-Defamation League and certain Christian groups sponsor a Christian Memorialization of the Holocaust.

The Hyde Park community has a Holocaust commemoration that is the combined effort of several groups, including synagogues, Hillel, and the JCC. It is coordinated by the JCC.

Mid-West Jewish Council sponsors a Commemoration of the Warsaw Ghetto Uprising and the Annihilation of Six Million Jews; usually a Yiddish-oriented program.

Congregation Ezra-Habonim includes the annual observance of Crystal Night in fall in its congregational bylaws.

Many congregations, individually and combined, have religious observances concerning the Holocaust.

Holocaust-Centered Organizations

American Federation of Jewish Fighters, Camp Inmates and Nazi Victims, Inc.
Sol Goldstein, Contact
7227 N. Hamlin, Skokie 60076

Association of Children of Holocaust Survivors
Miriam Schiller, 677-9239

ACHS is an organization of Chicago area men and women in their twenties and thirties whose parents survived the Holocaust. Founded in the late 1970s, this group serves as a bridge between survivors and the rest of the Jewish community. ACHS sponsors programs and support groups related to the Holocaust and children of Holocaust survivors. Their ultimate purpose is to use their own understanding and insight to influence the community at large.

Jewish Documentation Center, Vienna, Austria
Simon Wiesenthal
Gerald C. Bender, Midwest Representative
7 S. Dearborn, Suite 1324, 60603; 236-6333
Bender, an attorney, lectures and raises money on behalf of Wiesenthal's work in tracking down Nazi criminals.

Shaarit Ha-Plita (Concentration Camp Survivors)
Sol Goldstein, Chairman
7227 N. Hamlin, Skokie 60076
Umbrella organization for Holocaust survivors' groups in Chicago.

Witnesses to the Holocaust, Inc.
Route 4, Box 148, Elgin 60120
Robert O. LeRoy
This organization, established by survivor Robert O. LeRoy, is dedicated to furthering the inclusion of Holocaust studies in public schools and, through public appearances, publicity, and advertisements, keeping a continual awareness by the public of the Holocaust.

Other Survivors' Organizations

ACHS (Association of Children of Holocaust Survivors) will act as a liaison for anyone wishing to make contact with Holocaust survivors or any of the Holocaust survivors' organizations. Contact Miriam Schiller at 677-9239.

Dr. Janusz Korczak Unit of B'nai B'rith
Jewish Lithuanian Club
Kielczer Club (all members of this small club come from Kielcz, Poland)
L'Or
Midwest Chenstochower Society (Barbara Pryor, President, 465-7917)
New Citizens Club

Jewish Family and Community Service
1 S. Franklin, 60606; 346-6700
JFCS will assist victims of the Holocaust with filing claims for restitution from the German government.

Programming Resources

- **Rabbi Robert Addison**
  Board of Jewish Education
  72 E. 11th St., 60605; 427-5570

Rabbi Addison is the BJE resource person in all areas of Holocaust education, commemoration programming, curriculum materials, and teacher education in methodology of teaching the Holocaust and general materials on the Holocaust.

- **Minna Davis**
  Mayer Kaplan JCC
  5050 Church St., Skokie 60077; 675-2200

Coordinates support groups for children of Holocaust survivors. This program, offered at many of the JCCs, won the 1980 National Program Award presented by the Jewish Welfare Board.

- **Rabbi Yechiel Eckstein**
  Director of Interreligious Activities
  Anti-Defamation League Midwest Office
  222 W. Adams, Rm. 1449, 60606; 782-5080

Works especially in the context of interfaith programming regarding the Holocaust. Served as a consultant to the Chicago Board of Education on the development of Man's Inhumanity to Man curriculum.

- **Sol Goldstein**
  7227 N. Hamlin, Skokie 60076

Chairman of the Holocaust survivors' organization in Metropolitan Chicago. Headed "Stop the Nazi March" in Skokie. Member of the United States Holocaust Memorial Council.

- **Grace C. Grossman**
  Curator, Spertus Museum of Judaica
  618 S. Michigan Ave., 60605; 922-9012

Assisted in establishing the Zell Holocaust Memorial Exhibit.

- **Dr. André Lacocque**
  Chicago Theological Seminary
  5757 S. University Ave., 60637; 752-5757

Dr. Lacocque is director of the Center for Jewish Christian Studies of CTS and has been a visiting professor at Spertus. Among his lecture topics is Auschwitz and Its Impact on Judaism, Christianity, and the Modern World. He has a theological-philosophical work in progress that is a reflection on the Holocaust.

- **Dr. Abba Lessing**
  Professor, Department of Philosophy

Lake Forest College
683 Cherry Ave., Lake Forest 60045; 234-3649
Teaches a course on the Holocaust at Lake Forest. Speaker and adult-education class leader on this and other subjects primarily related to Jewish philosophy.

■ **Dr. Richard Malter**
15 S. Dryden Pl., Arlington Heights 60004; 398-6640
Psychological and mental-health aspects of dealing with the Holocaust. Dr. Malter has served as a consultant to both the Board of Jewish Education and Associated Talmud Torahs.

Hannah Messinger
Member, American Jewish Arts Club
Through graphics, this artist depicts the universality of human suffering reflected in the Holocaust.

National Conference of Christians and Jews
203 N. Wabash Ave., 60601; 236-9272
Has available a Holocaust Memorial Service for Christians—Yom Ha-Shoah. Lists bibliography and resources for Christian programming on the Holocaust, Christian efforts to rescue Jews, and anti-Semitism from the Christian viewpoint.

Dimensions of the Holocaust, lectures at Northwestern University by Elie Weisel, Lucy S. Dawidowicz, Dorothy Rabinowitz, and Robert McAfee Brown, was published in 1977 (Evanston: Northwestern University Press).

Miriam Rosenbush
6033 N. Sheridan Rd., Suite 43D, 60660; 271-2339
This producer's 23-minute, 16mm color film, *The Legacy: Children of the Holocaust*, is available for rental or purchase.

■ **Miriam Schiller**
677-9239
A general resource on survivors' groups in Chicago and a member of the Association of Children of Holocaust Survivors.

■ **Malke Seifert**
7919 Kilbourn Ave., Skokie 60076
A survivor and humanities teacher, Seifert speaks on the Holocaust and leads study groups on the subject.

- **Dr. Byron L. Sherwin**
  David C. Verson Professor Jewish Religious Thought
  Spertus College of Judaica
  618 S. Michigan Ave., 60605; 922-9012

Lectures on the Holocaust and how to approach study of the Holocaust. Editor with Susan Ament of *Encountering the Holocaust*, an anthology (Chicago: Impact Press, 1979).

- **Beverly Yusim**
  1620 Robin Hood Lane, Highland Park 60035; 831-4671

Book reviewer, writer, lecturer, study group leader; contributed to the anthology *Encountering the Holocaust*.

10
Social and Political Concerns

American Jewish Committee, Chicago Chapter
55 E. Jackson Blvd., 60604; 663-5500
Jonathan Levine, Midwest Regional Director
Founded in 1906, AJC is the oldest of the American Jewish defense organizations. AJC is dedicated to securing and protecting the full civil and religious rights of Jews and other minority groups everywhere. Its four operating commissions are Domestic Affairs, Foreign Affairs, Interreligious Affairs, and Jewish Communal Affairs. Among its concerns are civil rights, anti-Semitism, ERA, Arab influence in the U.S., energy, human rights around the world, Soviet Jewry, Jewish family life, intermarriage, and Israel. AJC established the Institute on Pluralism and Group Identity, Chicago Institute of Interreligious Research, Chicago Alliance for Shaping a Safer City, Chicago Task Force on Jewish Family Life, and Chicago Interreligious Task Force on Soviet Jewry. Sponsors discussion groups, singles groups, and an Academician's Seminar in Israel. A member of the Public Affairs Committee of JUF.

American Jewish Congress Midwest Region
22 W. Monroe St., Suite 2102, 60603; 332-7355
Shirley Sachs Mouratides, Midwest Director
Founded in 1918, the Congress is committed to the religious and cultural survival of the Jewish people; to civil rights, religious freedom, and separation of Church and State in America; and to security and peace in Israel. The local office has a legal staff person who initiates and participates in legal cases concerning civil and religious

liberties. Local members may join policy-formulation commissions and/or participate in chapters that meet for programs and discussions. Chapters exist for couples and individuals of different age groupings: post-college and under 40; 35 and older; 45 and older. In 1978, the Congress founded a Russian-American chapter that welcomes Soviet Jews into membership with Chicagoans. AJC initiates and supports Jewish cultural activities throughout the metropolitan area, including Yiddish programming and exhibits at public museums. The organization offers many international travel tours with some designed just for singles—both those under 40 and older, "sophisticated singles." The Midwest Region sponsors an annual family retreat at Camp Chi. The COJO-ERA coalition is administered from this office. A member of the Public Affairs Committee of JUF.

American Jewish Congress Chicago Women's Division
22 W. Monroe St., Suite 2102, 60603; 332-7355

The Women's Division has three chapters, with purposes and programs parallel to those of the American Jewish Congress. It supports the Louise Waterman Wise Youth Hostel in Jerusalem. The Women's Division is represented separately on the Public Affairs Committee of JUF.

Anti-Defamation League of B'nai B'rith Midwest Regional Office
222 W. Adams St., Rm. 1449, 60606; 782-5080

A. Abbot Rosen, Midwest Regional Director

Founded in Chicago in 1913 by Sig Livingston in his small, one-room law office to fight the growth of anti-Semitism in the United States. Today ADL's work can be divided into two broad categories:

1. Defensive measures in response to specific incidents, literature, and groups considered anti-Semitic or bigoted.

2. Positive programming aimed at preventing the spread of prejudice and anti-Semitism, through the development and dissemination of educational materials—books, pamphlets, reports, films, slides, etc.—and through conferences, seminars, and specific interfaith happenings such as the annual seder with Mundelein College cosponsored by the Catholic archdiocese and B'nai B'rith Council. Extensive programming suggestions and bibliographies available upon request. Also concerned with Jewish-Christian relations, women's issues, and struggles of other minorities. Locally, ADL also files Friend of Court briefs. A member of the Public Affairs Committee of the JUF.

Jewish Defense League of Illinois
18 S. Michigan, 60603; 236-0065

Dedicated to Jewish militancy as a way to combat anti-Semitism; has developed an activist program that operates under the motto Never Again!

Public Affairs Committee of the Jewish United Fund
1 S. Franklin, 60606; 346-6700
Peggy Norton, Director

This committee represents 34 Jewish organizations based in Chicago—Zionist, rabbinic, congregational, women's, defense, and local chapters of national or international bodies. The PAC speaks to the public with one voice on issues of concern and thus represents the widest forum of the Chicago Jewish community. There is no attempt to duplicate or parallel any work being done by other agencies. PAC does centralize efforts on issues that require unified action, such as support for Soviet Jewry, the threatened Nazi march in Skokie, reactions regarding Israel and anti-Israel threats, response to refugees, and issues concerning Jewish security wherever and whenever that security is threatened. PAC has also sponsored some community events—celebrations, observances, and demonstrations. Speakers are available.

■ **Joel J. Sprayregen**
3400 Xerox Centre, 55 W. Monroe St., 60603; 726-5700
Chairman of the PAC during 1979–80 and a member of the Executive Committee of the National Conference on Soviet Jewry. Speaks on topics concerning Soviet Jewry, the Middle East, and the Public Affairs Agenda of the Jewish Community.

Warsaw Ghetto Uprising Coalition
c/o Chutzpah
P.O. Box 60142, 60660

This is the name selected by groups formed to demonstrate and fight against the threatened Nazi march in Skokie in 1978. The participating organizations were primarily left-wing, consciousness-raising groups of young adults—not all Jewish—and without a direct voice in the Chicago Jewish establishment. They deliberately chose the name Warsaw Ghetto Uprising Coalition to affirm their Jewish identity in confronting the Nazis. More information on this group can be obtained from Chutzpah, organizer of this coalition.

Armed Forces—Active Servicemen and Veterans

Fort Sheridan and other military installations
Chaplain (Lt. Col.) Oscar M. Lifshutz, U.S. Army Ret., rabbi of Congregation Agudas Achim North Shore, sees to the chaplaincy needs of

military personnel of Jewish faith. His telephone number is 539-5454.

Chaplain Lifshutz is a member of the Chaplaincy Commission of the National Jewish Welfare Board and is the JWB liaison serving any military installation without a full-time Jewish chaplain. He assists in matters that arise among military personnel and between the military establishment and Jewish personnel. He makes referrals to appropriate agencies in response to inquiries from families and other civilians.

Glenview Naval Air Station
A volunteer civilian leads Jewish religious services monthly for Jews stationed at Glenview.

Great Lakes Naval Training Station
Rabbi Mitchel Schranz, Chaplain, 688-6765
Rabbi Schranz is the only full-time Jewish military chaplain in the Chicago area. His services at Great Lakes are open to visitors. Friday night services are held at 7 P.M.

Veterans Administration Medical Centers
Chaplain David Spitz
North Chicago VA Medical Center, North Chicago 60064;
  689-1900, x2542
Rabbi David Spitz, a civilian chaplain, serves three of the four local VA hospitals: West Side Hospital, Lakeside Hospital, and North Chicago Hospital.

Chaplain Lawrence H. Charney
7800 Lyons, Morton Grove 60053; 965-0900
Rabbi Charney is the chaplain at Hines VA Hospital.

Groups or individuals interested in volunteering services to hospitalized veterans should contact
Chief of Volunteer Services
North Chicago VA Medical Center
North Chicago, IL 60064; 689-1900, x2539.

A number of B'nai B'rith and ORT chapters, sisterhoods, and men's clubs assist in cheering up hospitalized veterans and also provide services for the active armed forces on local bases.

American Camp and Hospital Service
Sally Goldsmith, Former President
3100 N. Lake Shore Dr., 60657

Founded in 1943, ACHS serves hospitalized veterans of all faiths. Provides monthly visits to VA hospitals.

B'nai B'rith Council of Greater Chicago
8 S. Michigan, Rm. 2301, 60603; 346-8555

For over 30 years, B'nai B'rith has gone to Hines VA Hospital on the first Monday in December to entertain veterans and distribute gifts.

Jewish War Veterans of the United States
Department of Illinois
176 W. Adams St., Rm. 2011, 60603; 372-0262; 9 A.M. to 1:30 P.M. weekdays
Maurice Lepavsky, Adjutant

JWV has taken over the work of the former Armed Forces Council of Chicago in overseeing programs for active armed forces and hospitalized veterans in the area. Founded in the U.S. in 1898 and in Illinois in 1933, JWV assists all veterans, regardless of race, creed, or color, with their claims through the Veterans Administration and G.I. Bill of Rights. Also assists spouses, children, and parents of deceased servicemen and servicewomen and conducts parties at VA hospitals and at the USO. The Goodman Tunick Post and Ladies Auxiliary #347 hold services at cemeteries in memory of dead servicemen. They will honor requests for decorating graves with flags. There are about 25 men's units and 15 women's auxiliaries in the Chicago area.

Louis D. David Veterans of Foreign Wars, Post 235
4708 N. Kedzie Ave., 60625; 539-1166

Probably the only VFW Post in the Chicago area with a majority of Jews and with an opening prayer that is Jewish. The Louis D. David Post (reorganized in 1957) is actually an amalgamation of the Louis D. David Post, founded in 1934, and another from Lawndale. Probably 85 to 90 percent of the 300 members are Jews. Sophie Goldstein, a member of the women's auxiliary of this post, served as national president of the Ladies Auxiliary of VFW. This information is from a history of the post prepared by Dr. Edward Mazur, Chicago Jewish Historical Society, and placed in the Chicago Jewish Archives.

Mayer Kaplan Jewish Community Center
5050 Church, Skokie 60077; 675-2200

All classes and programs are open to all active servicemen at members' rates. All membership benefits are offered them without membership fees.

■ Marshall D. Krolick
Past President, Civil War Round Table
3126 Violet Lane, Northbrook 60062; 498-3126
Presents a first-class program, Jews and the Civil War, in which he appears dressed in the uniform of a Union soldier. Good for all ages.

Black-Jewish Relations

Chicago Conference on Religion and Race
111 E. Wacker Dr., Rm. 510, 60601; 565-1100
Dr. William White, Chairman

Founded in 1963, cosponsored by the Chicago Board of Rabbis, Catholic Archdiocese of Chicago, Episcopalian Diocese of Chicago, and the Church Federation of Greater Chicago, CCRR seeks to eliminate racial and religious intolerance and to make the Judaeo-Christian principles of social justice a reality throughout the metropolitan area.

Other organizations working to better relations between Jews and Blacks include the Jewish Council on Urban Affairs, Anti-Defamation League of B'nai B'rith, National Conference of Christians and Jews, as well as other social and political action groups, interfaith organizations, and the social-action committees of congregations.

For a review of Chicago Black-Jewish ties, see *The Chicago Reporter*, vol. VI, no. 8 (September 1977). Although dated, this article presents a historic perspective.

Civil Rights and Civil Liberties

The following organizations provide speakers and other programs concerning civil rights and civil liberties:

American Jewish Committee
55 E. Jackson, Rm. 1870, 60604; 663-5500

American Jewish Congress
22 W. Monroe, Rm. 2102, 60603; 332-7355

Anti-Defamation League of B'nai B'rith
222 W. Adams, Rm. 1449, 60606; 782-5080

Community Organizations

Chicago Board of Rabbis
72 E. 11th St., 60605; 427-5863
Rabbi Mordecai Simon, Executive Director

CBR represents Chicago Jewry in various community-based organizations such as the Chicago Conference on Religion and Race.

Jewish Community Centers
1 S. Franklin St., 60606; 346-6700

The JCCs provide a base for community-centered activities within their own particular neighborhoods.

Jewish Community Council of West Rogers Park
3003 W. Touhy Ave., 60645; 761-9100

Promotes stability and the Jewish presence and well-being in the West Rogers Park neighborhood. This is an advocacy organization that is involved in landlord-tenant relations, condominium issues, and all aspects of housing. Posts housing opportunities at the Horwich JCC.

Jewish Council on Urban Affairs
53 W. Jackson Blvd., 60604; 663-0960
Milton Cohen, Executive Director
Rabbi Robert Marx, Founder

A community organization, founded in 1964, providing a Jewish presence in areas of Chicago experiencing problems of racial, economic, and social change. Works closely with minority groups. A small staff provides expertise in community organizing for social services, human rights, and community action, through volunteer lawyers, doctors, architects, teachers, and businessmen and businesswomen. JCUA services any organized Chicago-area group engaged in improving community conditions, and services are provided at no charge. The organization is funded by individual contributions.

Discrimination Recourse

American Jewish Congress Midwest Region
22 W. Monroe St., Suite 2102, 60603; 332-7355

A legal staff member initiates and participates in legal action in cases regarding civil and religious liberties, including situations that may involve anti-Semitism or discrimination.

Anti-Defamation League of B'nai B'rith
222 W. Adams, 60606; 782-5080

Persons may report to the ADL office anything that they perceive to be an example of anti-Semitism in action, including anti-Semitic statements in broadcasting, discrimination in employment—both in seeking the job and on the job—scheduling of school exams on Jewish holidays or Sabbath, synagogue desecrations, dissemination of anti-Semitic literature in public places, and expressions of anti-Semitism, such as by remarks in commercial establishments. All complaints are investigated by a former Chicago policeman. If the complaint is justified, the appropriate action is then taken.

Bureau on Jewish Employment Problems
220 S. State, Rm. 1630, 60604; 663-9470
Sidney H. Silverman, Executive Director

The primary purpose of BJEP is to fight discrimination in hiring and employment practices against Jews and other minority groups. Advocates the principle of hiring in accordance with individual merit. Investigates complaints, conducts research into the Jewish labor market, and cooperates with labor, industry, commerce, and government agencies to develop and carry out fair-employment practices. Provides speakers to organizations. Created by B'nai B'rith, American Jewish Committee, American Jewish Congress, and the Jewish Labor Committee, which are represented on BJEP's board.

COLPA
Marvin Rosenblum, 236-4541

National Jewish Commission on Law and Public Affairs, an organization made up of lawyers, political scientists, and others concerned with protecting the civil liberties in America of Jews whose religious observances may be infringed upon in employment and other spheres of secular life.

Jewish Civil Service Employees of Chicago
Herman Fiarman, 973-6125

Will investigate any case of possible anti-Semitism involving a Jewish government worker, whatever branch of government and regardless of whether he or she is actually a civil service worker. The organization is also interested in social workers and teachers working for institutions funded by some branch of government.

Leadership Council
341-1470

Anyone—Jewish or not—who believes he or she has been denied a housing opportunity because of religion, race, sex, or national origin should call the Leadership Council.

For a somewhat dated history of anti-Semitism in Illinois, see *A History of Civil Liberty in Illinois, 1787–1942*, Chicago and Illinois Civil Liberties Committees, 1942. Pages 120–29 are devoted to the history of anti-Semitism in Illinois.

Ethnicity and Group Identity

Anti-Defamation League of B'nai B'rith
222 W. Adams, Rm. 1449, 60606; 782-5080

ADL has many audiovisuals and publications, including bibliographies, on individual ethnic groups.

Institute on Pluralism and Group Identity
55 E. Jackson Blvd., 60604; 663-5400
David Roth, Director

The Midwest office of a national center established by the American Jewish Committee. A resource center on and for the study of ethnicity in our society. Includes operations of the Illinois Consultation on Ethnicity in Education and its newsletter, *Heritage*, as well as the Chicago Coalition on Group Identity and Mental Health, which attempts to prepare mental-health professionals to understand the needs of ethnically diverse communities. The IPGI office has available many publications of studies not only of ethnic groupings but also of other identity groups, such as working-class women.

Spertus Museum of Judaica
618 S. Michigan Ave., 60605

Participated with other ethnic museums in the Ethnic Cultural Preservation Council in the creation of an exhibit, The Wedding, at the Chicago Public Library Cultural Center. The Chicago Public Library has received a major grant to develop ethnic programming.

Falashas

Falashas are the Black Jews of Ethiopia, who are under threat of extinction because of suppression, slavery, annihilation, disease, and poverty. Israel's chief rabbis have called them authentic Jews, and so Falashas are eligible for the Law of Return, unrestricted immigration to Israel.

■ **Jed Abraham**
8914 N. Central Park, Evanston 60203; 675-3335

Former Peace Corps volunteer in Ethiopia who spent time visiting Falashas and personally knows Yonah Bogele, Falasha leader. Abraham is available for lectures, with or without slides.

■ **LaDena Schnapper**
2522 W. Fitch, 60645; 262-1455

Former Peace Corps member who lived three years in Ethiopia and learned to speak Amharic, the language of that country. She presents a slide lecture on Falashas for all ages.

- **Nathan Shapiro**
  Chapter President, National Board Member, American Association for Ethiopian Jews
  831-4315
A resource and speaker on efforts in behalf of Falashas.

- **Ruth G. Silverman**
  837 Lehigh Lane, Buffalo Grove 60090; 398-2019
A resource on Falashas in general.

- **Gail Winston**
  Vice President, American Association for Ethiopian Jews
  P.O. Box 925, Ravinia Station, Highland Park 60035; 432-1736
A slide lecture on Falashas.

  SURJE (Students United to Rescue the Jews of Ethiopia)
  Chicago Chapter
  P.O. Box 925, Ravinia Station, Highland Park 60035; 432-1736

Housing

The North Shore Interfaith Housing Council
1125 Wilmette Ave., Wilmette 60091; 256-4780
Rayna Miller, Director

This ecumenical council represents 40 congregations, 8 of which are Jewish, in nine different suburbs. NSIHC is part of the fair-housing network and serves as an information and advocacy agency for moderate- and low-income housing customers of all faiths, colors, and national origins. It combats discrimination in housing whenever evidence is brought to its attention. Literature about avenues of recourse is available. The North Shore Housing Center, operated by NSIHC, offers direct house-search services to persons of low and moderate income and members of minorities. This service covers housing opportunities in fifteen North Shore communities.

Human Rights

Helsinki Monitoring Committee
55 E. Jackson Blvd., Rm. 1870, 60604; 663-5500

Established by the American Jewish Committee, the HMC's chief concern is to monitor the human rights set forth in the historic Helsinki Conference of 1975 and to increase public awareness of the Helsinki Final Act. This committee gathers and publishes information about human-rights violations and serves as a liaison with individuals and organizations concerned with human rights. Representatives from captive nations' organizations (Lithuania, Ukraine, Poland, etc.) are also included.

- **Claire Roberta Aronson**
4300 Marine Dr., 60613
A lawyer, journalist, and publicist, Aronson's many areas of expertise include the legal aspects of human rights.

Interfaith Programming

American Jewish Committee
55 E. Jackson, Rm. 1870, 60604; 663-5500
The AJC's concern with interfaith programming and intergroup relations is manifested in the work of one of its four operating departments, the Interreligious Affairs Commission. The Chicago Institute of Interreligious Research was established by AJC.

Anti-Defamation League of B'nai B'rith
222 W. Adams, Rm. 1449, 60606; 782-5080
Rabbi Yechiel Eckstein, Director of Interreligious Activities
Sponsors interfaith programs such as the annual seder at Mundelein, of which B'nai B'rith and the Catholic Archdiocese are cosponsors. Issues extensive bibliographies and program guides pertaining to intergroup and Jewish-Christian relations. Rabbi Eckstein is available to speak on other religions and on interfaith matters. He maintains a current list of Christian groups interested in Jewish programming. He frequently speaks to Christians about Jews and Judaism.

Catholic-Jewish Dialogue Group
Patty Crowley, Contact
175 E. Delaware, 60611
A group of Catholic and Jewish couples who have been meeting for about twelve years. Rabbi Robert Marx and Father John Pawlikowski are the resource people.

Center for Jewish Christian Studies
Chicago Theological Seminary
5757 University Ave., 60637; 752-5757
Dr. André Lacocque, Director

Chicago Conference on Religion and Race
111 E. Wacker Dr., Rm. 510, 60601; 565-1100
Dr. William White, Chairman
Cosponsored by the Chicago Board of Rabbis, the Church Federation of Greater Chicago, and the dioceses of the Catholic and Episcopalian churches.

Christian Friends of Israel
Zionist Organization of Chicago
6328 N. California, 60659; 973-3232

Clergy and Laity Concerned
542 S. Dearborn, 60605; 922-8234
Ronald Fruend, Midwest Director

Some of the clergy and some of the laity in this organization are Jews. Clergy and Laity Concerned confronts issues that challenge the morality of Jews and Christians. Major areas of concern are international human rights, world hunger and the politics of food, human security and disarmament, and limiting corporate power. The most recent additions to the CLC agenda have been the dangers of nuclear power and concerns about draft registration.

Common Ground
770 Deerfield Rd., Highland Park 60035; 432-6240
Dr. Ronald Miller, Director

This nonprofit membership organization offers opportunities for the study of the world's religions in order to promote better understanding. Sponsors classes, workshops, and travel led by professors or professionals in intergroup relations. A recent tour of Israel and Rome was led by an Orthodox rabbi and a Catholic sister. A resource for adult-education programming on the world's religious and spiritual traditions.

Council of Hyde Park and Kenwood Churches and Synagogues
5236 S. Blackstone, 60615; 324-5300
Werner H. Heymann, Executive Director

A prototype of the interreligious councils operating in city and suburban neighborhoods. Community Thanksgiving services and efforts to develop accord among religious groups are among the council's most important activities.

Institute on Pluralism and Group Identity
55 E. Jackson Blvd., 60604; 663-5400
David Roth, Director

Magen David Adom Chicago Chapter
6952 N. California, 60645; 465-0664

Sponsors an annual interfaith dinner with special ties to the Chicago Italian community.

National Conference of Christians and Jews
Chicago and Northern Illinois Region
203 N. Wabash, 60601; 236-9272

An advocacy organization that seeks to promote understanding and respect among all religious groups. The major sponsor of Brotherhood Week. NCCJ conducts workshops for police in community relations and disseminates literature and information about programs and resources available for intergroup and interfaith work. A Holocaust memorial service, Yom HaShoah, has been created for Christian use.

North Shore Interfaith Housing Council
1125 Wilmette Ave., Wilmette 60091; 256-4780
Rayna Miller, Director

Operation Friendship
B'nai B'rith Council of Greater Chicago
8 S. Michigan, Rm. 2301, 60603; 346-8555
Gerald M. Dicker, Executive Director

Putting its concern for interfaith relations into action, Operation Friendship seeks out Jewish volunteers among police and firemen who will man their departments on the major Christian holidays of Christmas and Easter.

Iranian Jewish Needs and Concerns

Rabbi Yehiel Poupko
c/o Jewish Federation
1 S. Franklin, 60606; 346-6700

When Rabbi Poupko himself cannot supply answers to questions and problems, he will refer those who consult him to other resources.

Labor

Jewish Labor Committee Chicago Office
127 N. Dearborn, 60602; 641-5086
David Schacter, Executive Director

The JLC represents Jewish concerns within the labor movement and relates labor's concerns to the Jewish community.

Politics

Chutzpah
P.O. Box 60142, 60660

Chutzpah is a source for lectures, classes on Jewish Socialism, Jews in Socialism, etc.

Jewish Caucus of the New American Movement
3244 N. Clark, 60657; 871-7700
Harvey Feldman, Contact

The New American Movement is a democratic socialist organization, and the Jewish Caucus was formed by its Jewish members in 1979 at the national convention, which focused on the Palestinians, Israel, and the Middle East. The Jewish Caucus is currently developing its platform, but it is committed to calling attention to anti-Semitism and to working toward a position on anti-Semitism at the NAM national level.

Jewish Council for Good Government
6734 N. Mozart, 60645; 262-6493
Dale Draznin, President

Fought successfully in 1978 to alter the date of election registration, which fell on Yom Kippur eve. This organization has the following goals: to elect to public office progressive, independent-minded candidates who will respond to the needs of the community; to keep the public aware of the activities of its elected representatives; and to involve the community in the solution of its own problems.

Jewish Labor Bund
Maurice Shafran
973-6377

The full name of this group is Coordinating Committee of the Jewish Labor Bund and Related Organizations, Chicago Chapter. It meets eight to ten times a year at the Workmen's Circle headquarters, 6506 N. California. Meetings are usually conducted in Yiddish. Funds are raised for organization publications. The Bund was founded in 1897 (the same year Theodor Herzl founded political Zionism) as a political party in Czarist Russia. It identifies itself as a socialist international organization, concerned with political issues and social aspirations for Jews and others in whatever nation they live. The Bund is cool (at best) to the principle of Zionism and is supportive of the Israeli people but not of Israel as the center of world Jewry.

Jewish War Veterans of the United States
176 W. Adams St., Rm. 2011, 60603; 372-0262
Maurice Lepavsky, Adjutant

The JWV takes political stands, especially with regard to veterans, war on crime, and so forth. In the Illinois Senate, Senator Karl Berning, Republican spokesman on the Veterans Committee, has been the liaison between the committee and the JWV.

■ Dr. Edward Mazur
2923 W. Birchwood, 60645; 274-7720

Lectures on the Jew in Politics. His doctoral thesis at the University of Chicago is entitled "Minyans for a Prairie City: The Politics of Chicago Jewry 1850–1940" (1974).

■ **Stanley Rosen**
Professor of Labor and Industrial Relations
University of Illinois–Chicago Circle
P.O. Box 4348, 60680; 996-2623 or 274-0464 (home)
Lectures on the history of the ideologies, often left-wing or radical, that motivated Jews during past generations.

Proselytizing

Throughout the history of the Chicago Jewish community, there have been attempts to convert Jews to Christianity through Missions to Jews, which were usually set up in neighborhoods of greatest Jewish population. Today, at least one of these missions is directing its slick propaganda toward the newly arrived immigrant from the Soviet Union. The 1980 Chicago Telephone Directory lists the following:

American Association for Jewish Evangelism
5860 N. Lincoln Ave.; 275-2133

American Board of Missions to the Jews (Beth Sar Shalom)
6057 N. Kedzie; 338-5959

Hebrew Christian Alliance of America
3601 W. Devon; 478-7136

■ **Rabbi Yechiel Eckstein**
Director of Interreligious Activities
Anti-Defamation League of B'nai B'rith
222 W. Adams, Rm. 1449, 60606; 782-5080
Rabbi Eckstein is a resource person on the subject of proselytizing.

Soviet Jewry

Chicago Action for Soviet Jewry
474 Central, Highland Park 60035; 433-0144
Pamela Cohen, Carole Boron, Marillyn Tallman, Cochairmen

Sponsors programs, publishes information, conducts letter-writing campaigns to the Soviet Union and to Washington. Works throughout the state of Illinois on behalf of Refuseniks still in the Soviet Union. Publishes *Refusenik*, a newsletter. Wants to be informed of anyone planning to visit the Soviet Union. Some of the group's 700 members write to Refuseniks and others who have become political prisoners, but the group steers away from dissidents. Member of the Union of Councils for Soviet Jews, a nationwide confederation. CASJ places long-distance calls to Moscow. Assists synagogues and Jewish organizations with adopting families and with telephoning expenses. The film *Ida Nudel in Exile*, filmed in Siberia and showing conditions under which Ida Nudel is forced to live, is available for a $35 rental fee. The 16mm color sound film is fourteen minutes long.

Chicago Interreligious Task Force on Soviet Jewry
55 E. Jackson Blvd., Suite 1870, 60604; 663-5500

Established by the American Jewish Committee; works with Chicago Action on Soviet Jewry, etc.

Community Council of Jewish Organizations
Committee on Mideast and Soviet Jewry
33 N. LaSalle, 60602; 782-2201
3750 N. Cicero, 60641; 725-8476

The source for the Save Soviet Jewry signs displayed by congregations and other Jewish institutions. A political-action organization with ties to Washington.

National Interreligious Task Force on Soviet Jewry
1307 S. Wabash, 60605; 922-1983
Sister Ann Gillen

Works closely with organizations such as Chicago Action for Soviet Jewry, locally and nationally, on behalf of Soviet Jewry.

Solidarity Day for Soviet Jewry held in Chicago on Sunday, September 20, 1981. Sponsored annually by several organizations, this Loop demonstration usually begins with a rally at the Daley Center. For information, call the Public Affairs Committee of JUF, 346-6700.

Women's Plea for Soviet Jewry
Local participation in the annual national observance that coincides with the anniversary of the United Nations Declaration on Human Rights. About one dozen Chicago Jewish women's organizations join with the Public Affairs Committee of JUF and the Chicago Action for Soviet Jewry.

■ **Joel J. Sprayregen**
3400 Xerox Centre, 55 W. Monroe St., 60603; 726-5700

A member of the Executive Committee of the National Conference on Soviet Jewry, author of articles on Soviet Jewry that have appeared in *Christian Century* and *Congress Bi-Weekly,* and 1979–80 chairman of the Public Affairs Committee of JUF. Sprayregen will speak to groups on Soviet Jewry as well as on other matters before the Jewish community.

Axelrods for Axelrod
Les and Leah Axelrod
432-7003

Les and Leah Axelrod and others with the name of Axelrod make continuing efforts on behalf of Dr. Ernst Axelrod, a Refusenik in Moscow.

■ Dawn Schuman
1302 Forest Ave., Highland Park 60035; 433-3380

Adult-education speaker and lecturer will speak on her trip in 1980 to the Soviet Union and visits with Refuseniks.

Efforts in behalf of Soviet Jews in Chicago are listed in Chapter 2, "Community Life."

Women's Concerns
Abortion Counseling

AFTA
338-2575

Agudath Israel
539-4241 (between 7 and 9 P.M.)

Contact for interpretation of Jewish law on the subject of abortion.

Chicago Board of Rabbis
72 E. 11th St., 60605; 427-5863

Contact for referral for pastoral counseling.

Michael Reese Hospital and Medical Center
791-2000

Provides a full range of pregnancy testing, birth-control counseling, and alternatives, including abortions, through its Family Planning Department.

The Response Center
338-2292

Provides counseling, crisis intervention, and clinical testing for teens who may be pregnant.

For abortion pro-choice advocacy, contact
  The National Council of Jewish Women, 663-9400
  American Jewish Congress, 332-7355
  Illinois Religious Coalition for Abortion Rights, 386-7165

ERA (Equal Rights Amendment)

Pro-ERA

COJO-ERA (Coalition of Jewish Organizations for Equal Rights Amendment)
c/o American Jewish Congress
22 W. Monroe, Suite 2102, 60603; 332-7355

A coalition of over twenty Jewish organizations based in Chicago has fought for passage of the ERA. Chairman is Rabbi Arnold Rachlis, whose advisory board includes 40 rabbis representing all Jewish movements. Information and speakers available.

Anti-ERA

Agudath Israel
3540 W. Peterson, 60659; 588-5078

This organization has taken a position against passage of ERA. Call for information and possible speaker.

Programming Resources

Anti-Defamation League of B'nai B'rith
222 W. Adams, Rm. 1449, 60606; 782-5080

A good source for programming materials (including multimedia presentations) on women's issues.

Chutzpah
P.O. Box 60142, 60660

Chutzpah has come out strongly in behalf of women's rights and the women's movement and has links to the Women's Caucus. Several years ago, Chutzpah joined other groups in sponsoring a women's liberation seder.

Daughters of Israel Speakers' Bureau
Cyndee Meystel, President
973-6955

The topics presented by these women all reflect the confrontation between traditional Orthodox Judaism and the modern women's movement. Examples: The Jewish Woman in the Women's Lib World, The Jewish Woman in 1981, The Torah's View of Women's Liberation, and The Orthodox Woman in Contemporary Society.

Institute on Pluralism and Group Identity
55 E. Jackson Blvd., 60604; 663-5400

This office has extensive literature on women's issues and concerns. Judaica women's classes are presented by Brisk Rabbinical College,

Hebrew Theological College, Lubavitch Chabad of Greater Chicago, and Yeshivah Migdal Torah.

- **Dr. Ellen S. Cannon**
  468 W. Melrose, Apt. 455, 60657
  A member of the Department of Political Science, Northeastern Illinois University. Speaks on Jewish Feminism and Jewish Women.

- **Chaya Borenstein Hirshman**
  743-8921
  Speaks on The Jewish Woman and on other topics related to Jewish education and Judaica. She has spoken on The Traditional Jewish Woman Faces Contemporary, Historical, Legal, and Social Issues.

- **Dr. Judith-Rae Ross**
  8725 Springfield, Skokie 60076
  Dr. Ross speaks on topics relating to Jewish history. Subjects relevant to women are Feminism and Judaism and The Evolution of the Jewish Mother. Dr. Ross is Executive Director of the Chicago Zionist Federation.

- **Holly Rozner**
  766 LaCrosse, Wilmette 60091; 251-7395
  Leads classes and group study on various topics, including The Jewish American Woman in Literature.

- **Dawn Schuman**
  1302 Forest Ave., Highland Park 60035; 433-3380
  An adult-study leader who has conducted scholar-in-residence seminars on Jewish Women in History.

- **Dr. June Sochen**
  Professor of History
  Northeastern Illinois University
  5500 N. St. Louis Ave., 60625; 583-4050
  Author of books and articles on women and ethnic groups in the United States, including *Herstory: A Woman's View of American History* and *Movers and Shakers: American Women Thinkers and Activists*. Lecture topics include Jewish American Women: Past and Present, and Jewish Women Writers.

- **Emily D. Soloff**
  2325 W. Greenleaf, 60645; 262-7721
  Writer and editor; lecturer on The Role of Women.

■ **Norma Spungen**
9011 N. Kildare, Skokie 60076; 676-0715

Among her many topics within the framework of the American Jewish Experience, this lecturer and educator includes a lecture on Where There's a Woman—Jewish Clubwomen in America.

■ **Marillyn Tallman**
514 Jackson Ave., Glencoe 60022; 835-2688

A popular educator, historian, study-group leader. Presents educational programs on various topics, including The Chain of Tradition of Jewish Women.

11
Israel and Zionism

Persons in Chicago who have telephones with overseas direct dialing may dial Israel directly. Those who do not have this service as yet may pay for operator-placed calls at the lower direct-dialing rate, according to the Illinois Bell Telephone Company.

Consulate General of Israel
111 E. Wacker Dr., 60601; 565-3300
The Honorable Moshe Gilboa, Consul General
Handles all consular services to Israelis who are in the Chicago area and provides information to Americans traveling or moving to Israel. Consular department handles passports. Press and Information Department provides programming resources to organizations. Hours: 9 A.M. to 12:30 P.M. Mondays through Fridays. No hours Saturdays or Sundays.

Commerce, Business, and Investment

American-Israel Chamber of Commerce and Industry Inc.–Midwest
180 N. Michigan, 60601; 641-2937
Roberta Lipman, Executive Director
Founded in 1958 by a group of businessmen to further business and commercial ties between Israel and the U.S. (especially the Midwest). Acts as a clearinghouse for information on economic opportunities and conditions. Sponsors programs about and business missions to Israel.

Bank Hapoalim
174 N. Michigan Ave., 60601; 621-0800
The local branch of one of the largest commercial banks in Israel. At the close of 1979—eighteen months after opening—the balance sheet showed $100 million in footings. Lobby space provided for exhibits of Jewish organizations. Moriah Room available at no charge to groups needing a meeting place. There's a kosher kitchen, and the bank will supply beverages, napkins, and tables. Speakers provided on various subjects, including banking and the economy of Israel.

Bank Leumi Le-Israel B.M.
100 N. LaSalle St., 60602; 781-1800
A full-service branch of Israel's first and largest bank. Located under the Hebrew clock at the northwest corner of LaSalle and Washington, Bank Leumi buys and sells Israeli pounds and issues Israeli-pound traveler's checks. Runs seminars for key clients concerning Israeli economics and investments; also provides travel information on Israel. Three lecture rooms and a kosher kitchen available (capacity up to 125).

Buy Israeli Goods
708 Church St., Rm. 233, Evanston 60201; 864-1502
Pearl Harand, Executive Director
Sulie Harand, Chairman
Where to Buy Israeli Goods: A Chicagoland Directory, published by the Harands in 1977, remains an excellent source for Chicago shops and merchants carrying Israeli goods. The Harands will issue updated materials in bulletin form and are available for programs on the purchase and use of Israeli products, "Thinking B.I.G."

Israel Government Investment and Export Authorities
174 N. Michigan Ave., 60601; 332-2160
Bert Danzig, Regional Trade Commissioner
Provides help to Chicago-area persons interested in investing in or otherwise dealing with trades and businesses of Israel.

Chicagoans to Israel—Travel, Study, Aliyah

American Jewish Committee
55 E. Jackson, Rm. 1870, 60604; 663-5500
Sponsors an Academician Program in Israel, a winter seminar open to Chicago-area college or university faculty members. Preference given to faculty members under 45 who have never been to Israel. No limitation in terms of academic field. Call for information.

American Jewish Congress
22 W. Monroe St., Suite 2102, 60603; 332-7355
Offers many tours to Israel through its extensive travel service. Special age-grouped tours for singles.

American Zionist Youth Foundation
c/o Israel Aliyah Center
205 W. Wacker Dr., Rm. 516, 60606; 332-2709
Sponsors many college and postgraduate courses and study programs at various locations in Israel. Summer plans also available.

Association of Parents of American Israelis
c/o Audrey Goldblatt
2734 W. Greenleaf, 60645; 764-6243
The Chicago chapter, founded in 1977, includes about 100 families, and membership is open. The association keeps communication going between separated families, sponsors and assists in travel arrangements and group charters (through the APAI Travel Service), and maintains contact with local Israel Aliyah office concerning housing and employment in Israel. Monthly meetings with speakers. Roster of members' children enables fellow members to act as couriers on their trips to Israel. Rabbi Jay Karzen, a member, available for supportive counseling. New project: ham-radio communication with Israel. Attention: local ham-radio operators are needed as volunteers in receiving calls from Israel. Call Al Goldblatt, 764-6243.

Chicago Chug Aliyah
c/o Bill Weisel, Chairman
2614 W. Fitch, 60645; 764-5969
One of three clubs sponsored by Israel Aliyah Center promoting immigration (aliyah) to Israel. This chug (club) is composed of young, religious Jews. Membership open.

Chicago Community Israel Program
1 S. Franklin, 60606; 346-6700
Coordinates Israel travel and study programs for high school students—for long-term or summer study. For information, contact CCIP or any of the sponsoring organizations—Associated Talmud Torahs, Board of Jewish Education, Jewish Community Centers, and Chicago Jewish Youth Council. Scholarships available.

Chicago Jewish Youth Council
3003 W. Touhy, 60645; 761-9100
Beverly Fox, CJYC Worker
In addition to helping coordinate the Chicago Community Israel Program, this office also issues a descriptive guide to all Israel travel plans

available to high school students. Included are the many tours, study programs, and other travel packages sponsored by the Zionist youth organizations.

Chicago Zionist Federation
220 S. State, Rm. 604, 60604; 922-5282

A good resource for travel/tours to Israel—its own programs and those of other Zionist organizations.

El Al Israel Airlines
174 N. Michigan Ave., 60601; 236-7264
For travel information and reservations call (800) 223-6280

El Al has no direct passenger flights between Chicago and Israel. Does have film presentations and speakers available to interested groups. Telephone number for air cargo sales at O'Hare: 686-5850.

Hebrew University Study Programs
American Friends of the Hebrew University–Midwest Regional Office
1 N. LaSalle, 60602; 236-6395

Call for information on college and university exchange programs with the Hebrew University and available scholarships. Chicago-area colleges and universities participating in the year abroad with the Hebrew University are noted in the sections on institutions of higher learning in Chapter 6.

Israel Aliyah Center
205 W. Wacker Dr., Rm. 516, 60606; 332-2709

A resource for a wide selection of opportunities in Israel, for permanent and temporary residence, for adults and students. Particularly helpful in reorienting and training professionals in Israel in the fields of social work, psychology, education, hotel administration, travel and tourism, and banking. Information also available on a variety of living facilities and life-styles. Sponsors ongoing clubs (chugim) locally for future immigration to Israel for young singles, couples and families, and young religious Jews. Membership open.

Israel Government Tourist Office
5 S. Wabash Ave., 60603; 782-4306

Information on Israel tourism and travel through brochures and programs for interested organizations.

Israel Information Center
3539 Dempster, Skokie 60076; 267-2900 or 679-4800

A travel agency that plans travel to Israel.

Israel Scholarship Foundation
P.O. Box A3101, 60690
c/o Steve Rhodes, 781-1800

Founded in 1980 to establish scholarships to assist people in their travels to Israel. Particularly aimed at college-age people. Will serve as a clearinghouse for available funding from other sources. Expected to start awarding scholarships in the spring of 1981.

Jewish United Fund Missions
1 S. Franklin, 60606; 346-6700

Sponsors missions to Israel for different kinds of groups. During 1980-81 travel year, trips organized for singles, young leadership groups, families, and trade-industry and professional workers.

Marc Sommer's Israeli Connection
3123 W. Chase, 60645; 338-6966

Sommer is an Israel-travel specialist who arranges group and individual travel. Persons interested in joining an already arranged tour group should contact Sommer for placement opportunities. Jewish, Christian, and interfaith tours offered. Bat/bar mitzvah and wedding celebrations in Israel arranged. Film and slide presentations for interested groups can be arranged.

Pearl White
Rama Vacations
188 W. Randolph, 60601; 641-1272

A travel agent who for many years has promoted family travel to Israel for important happy events, including bar/bat mitzvah and wedding anniversaries.

Union of American Hebrew Congregations
100 W. Monroe, Rm. 312, 60603; 782-1477

Anyone interested in joining a group of American Reform Jews in the development of a kibbutz devoted to Progressive Judaism may obtain information from this office. Settlement will begin in 1981. A first annual singles trip to Israel was offered in February 1981.

ZIM Israel Navigation Lines
10600 W. Higgins Rd., Rosemont 60018; 298-9700

This office will arrange for bookings and supply shipping containers (both personal and commercial) for transport to Israel or elsewhere in the world. The Israeli shipping line no longer comes into Chicago's harbor, but the Chicago office will process freight through New York.

Israelis in Chicago

American Friends of Israel War Disabled Foundation
6649 N. Maplewood, 60645; 262-5192
Roselyn Kraus, Contact

Sponsors a visit to Chicago each summer for ten disabled veterans of Israel's wars who are brought here for a 2½-week vacation. In 1981, the fourth annual visit will take place. Everything is handled by volunteers and more are needed—to be hosts, to furnish local transportation, and to help plan the program.

Association of Israeli Students and Faculty in Metropolitan Chicago
Yeshayahu Har-El, 565-3319

Social organization providing assistance.

Israel Boy and Girl Scout Federation Caravan
70 Lakeside Pl., Highland Park 60035; 433-0250
Louis Weinberg, Chairman

The Jewish Committee on Scouting, with representation from the Chicago Metropolitan Jewish Girl Scout Committee, plans the local summer visit of the Israel Boy and Girl Scout Federation Friendship Caravan. Each summer the caravan of ten boys and girls presents Israel through song and dance at several local sites. Delegations from the Israel Scouting movement are also sent to work in American Boy and Girl Scout camps and in some camps associated with National Young Judaea. The Israel Boy and Girl Scouts Federation, founded in 1953, has membership covering all segments of Israel's population: Arab, Moslem, Orthodox Jew, Catholic, Druze, etc. The largest group is called Hebrew Boy and Girl Scouts. Local programming provides hospitality.

Sabra School
Board of Jewish Education
5050 Church St., Skokie 60077; 675-2200

A weekend school for Israeli children whose families are living in the Chicago area for temporary periods, sometimes lasting several years. The school has been accredited by Israel's Ministry of Education. Teachers are Israeli teachers, and curriculum materials are those used in Israeli schools.

Fund Raising

State of Israel Bonds
230 N. Michigan Ave., 60601; 558-9400

A major capital investment program on behalf of Israel, which is promoted through religious and secular segments of the community. The Rabbinic Cabinet coordinates efforts of all religious movements. The Women's Division has several functions, but the highlight is the annual Ambassador's Ball on behalf of Israel Bonds. The 25th annual ball will be held in 1981. Young women who are presented socially at the ball must be sponsored by a purchaser or seller of $25,000 in Israel Bonds, and escorts pay a minimum of $2,500. Presentations are made to the Israel Ambassador to the United States. Most foreign consuls serving Chicago attend.

Israel Histadrut Campaign
220 S. State St., 60604; 427-4086
Julius R. Cogen, Director

Full name is the Israel Histadrut Campaign of the National Committee for Labor Israel, which raises money for a network of health services in Israel: vocational training programs of Amal, a network of 40 schools; youth centers; cultural centers; synagogues for religious workers and immigrants; athletic facilities; and children's villages and residential communities for retirees. Israel Histadrut Campaign is the major fund-raising effort for Labor Israel and as such is closely allied with the Labor Zionist Movement. The Labor Zionist Movement in the United States consists of the Labor Zionist Alliance, Pioneer Women, and Habonim, the Labor Zionist youth movement. However, there are many organizations outside the Labor Zionist Movement that support IHC as well, including labor unions, folk groups, and others sympathetic to Labor Israel. A special project allied with IHC that lies outside the Labor Zionist Movement is CASE (Community Assistance for Secondary Education in Israel), an effort to provide high school scholarships for underprivileged Israeli youths.

Jewish National Fund Council of Chicago
230 N. Michigan, 60601; 236-9100

The JNF is the only major fund-raising organization that raises funds for land development in Israel—reclamation, reforestation, road construction, and major site preparation. Through the sale of trees, JNF brings to all, to synagogues and organizations, and especially to the young in Jewish schools, a sense of loyalty and responsibility to the *land* of Israel.

Walk With Israel
Chicago Jewish Youth Council, Coordinator
3003 W. Touhy Ave., 60645; 761-9100

The 10th annual walk scheduled for 1981; between 6,000 and 7,000 walkers, joggers, and volunteers expected. In this event sponsored by the Jewish United Fund, it is the CJYC that coordinates the events of the day. In 1980 Walk With Israel events included the Greater Chicago Walk through Rogers Park and nearby suburbs; the North Suburban Walk through Glencoe and Highland Park; the Hyde Park/Kenwood Walk; the South Suburban Walk through the Homewood, Flossmoor, and Park Forest area; Jog in Lincoln Park; and two mini-walks for senior adults and preschoolers and their parents—one in Rogers Park and the other in Highland Park. Added a Northwest Suburban Walk for 1981.

Political-Action Groups

Most Zionist organizations support particular political parties or philosophies in Israel. These loyalties are noted in the list of Zionist Organizations. Listed immediately below, however, are organizations that are concerned with the broad political scene in Israel and with American foreign policy concerning Israel and the Middle East.

American Professors for Peace in the Middle East
3601 W. Devon, 60659; 588-1484

A nonsectarian, nonpartisan organization of academicians from many religious affiliations and academic disciplines. The group is dedicated to seeking a just and lasting peace between a secure Israel and her Arab neighbors. Open only to persons with academic standing, APPME will provide speakers to interested organizations. National chairman of the APPME is Prof. Fred M. Gottheil of the University of Illinois–Urbana.

Chicago Friends of Peace Now
P.O. Box 25675, 60625

Attached to the Shalom Achshav—the Peace Now Movement—of Israel. CFPN is concerned with Israel's secure and continued existence while supporting the goals of the Peace Now Movement: finding a way for Israel to live in peace and mutual respect with Palestinian Arabs. Activities include public events presented at synagogues and Hillels in the Chicago area. A speakers' bureau will provide persons able to speak in English, Hebrew, or Yiddish and who represent the network of Peace Now organizations in Israel and the United States. To contact the speakers' bureau, call P. Gray, 871-3598, or J. Aronson, 761-0844.

Community Council of Jewish Organizations
Committee on Mideast and Soviet Jewry
33 N. LaSalle, 60602; 782-2201

Warren Krinsky, President
3750 N. Cicero, 60641; 725-8476
Sol Silverstein, Contact
A political-action organization founded in the early 1970s to work on behalf of the State of Israel and Jews who are living under oppression throughout the world. Serves as Chicago's link with AIPAC (American Israel Public Affairs Committee), which is the only lobbying organization for Israel in Washington, D.C. A good general resource for any group wanting to engage in political action.

ISRANEWS
Americans for a Secure Israel of Illinois
P.O. Box 25174, 60625; 539-3733
Advocates Jewish rights to entire Eretz Yisrael, both sides of the Jordan, Yarmuk, and Harman; opposes the Camp David agreements; and sponsors recorded programs by telephone. For a lecture on the position of ISRANEWS, dial J-E-W-T-R-U-E. For a message in Hebrew, call 539-5334.

Programming Resources

American Jewish Committee
55 E. Jackson, Rm. 1870, 60604; 663-5500
Issues *Israel Press Highlights,* a weekly summary of articles from the Israeli press.

American Jewish Congress
22 W. Monroe St., Suite 2102, 60603; 332-7355
Sponsors some programs pertaining to Israel.

American Zionist Youth Foundation
University Service Department
c/o Israel Aliyah Center
205 W. Wacker Dr., 60606; 332-2709
This organization has published the best of all possible resources on Israel programming, *Israel on the Campus: A Source-Book for Activists.* Over 100 oversize pages crammed full of organization pointers, available films, nationwide contacts, descriptions of all groups sympathetic to Israel, etc. AZYF also has shorter, more specific bibliographies and ideas for such topics as Zionist Teach-ins and Israel Independence Day. These resources are not necessarily limited to campuses. If not available locally, order from the New York office, 515 Park Ave., New York, NY 10022.

■ **Prof. Eliezer B. Ayal**
2948 W. Birchwood, 60645; 743-0469
Professor of Economics at the University of Illinois–Chicago Circle and a native of Israel whose major academic expertise is in the economic and social development of Third World countries. Prof. Ayal speaks on Israel's history and foreign relations and on Jewish rights and interests and how to promote them.

■ **Nancy Gabriela Carroll**
377 Walnut St., Winnetka 60093; 446-4577
Slide programs and lectures—extensively and exclusively about Israel. Travelogues are helpful in planning itinerary for organizations contemplating group tours to Israel. Some of her illustrated lectures—all photography is her own—include Children of Israel: At Home, at School, at Play; Gardens in Israel: Jerusalem Gardens; Sculpture Gardens; Israel as an Art Experience; and New Amim and Yad Hashmona: Christian Villages in Modern Israel.

■ **Dr. Robert Goodman**
Board of Jewish Education
72 E. 11th St., 60605; 427-5570
Dr. Goodman is the Israel curriculum expert with the Board of Jewish Education. He has prepared many units for use in Jewish schools, most of which deal with Israel.

Israel Information and Resource Center
Yeshayahu Har-El, 565-3319
Pearl Karp, 675-2200
Volunteer organization cosponsored by Consulate General of Israel and the JCCs, with the purpose of providing resources and programs on all aspects of Israel to the general public. Provides lecturers and films. Hopes to operate a hot line for answers to questions about Israel. The telephone number will be 677-1948.

ISFI (Institute of Students and Faculty on Israel)
Yeshayahu Har-El, Midwest Regional Director, 565-3319 or 470-1031
A source for speakers, exhibits, literature, films, and professional advice on public relations to college campuses. No membership, no fund raising—rather, a basic resource for Israeli programming, social, cultural, and political. ISFI is run by Israeli students and faculty on local campuses. Formerly called the Israel Information Foundation.

Israel Perspectives
Students for Israel
752-1127

This publication of Students for Israel, sponsored by the Hillel Foundation at the University of Chicago, may soon be available at other Chicago-area campuses as well. Publication is fortnightly, and copies are available free at the U of C Hillel. Covers news of Israel primarily, but also some local stories, especially if they concern the Middle East.

■ **Mel and Pearl Karp**
P.O. Box 8, Highland Park 60035
Slide-lecture program available, Jewish History through Israeli Stamps and Coins—35 minutes long, good for all ages.

MEIR (Mid-East Information Resource)
P.O. Box 925 Ravinia Station, Highland Park 60035; 432-1736
Gail Winston, Executive Director
MEIR is both an acronym for Mid-East Information Resource and a Hebrew word meaning "enlightener." MEIR attempts to fight against anti-Israel and anti-Jewish propaganda by the following means: providing audiovisual presentations to Jewish and non-Jewish audiences; organizing and conducting seminars and workshops that train people to respond effectively to propaganda; and providing an ever-growing library of materials, information, and expertise to continue the fight against propaganda. MEIR also raises funds to provide for a professional public-relations campaign to promote Israel's image.

Neot Kedumim Filmstrips
4080 Morrison Dr., Gurnee 60031; 662-4400
A series of filmstrips, slides, and posters for use in schools covers Israel's biblical gardens from different angles, including the holidays, Jewish history, and the ecology of the Bible. Hebrew-English guides and cassettes for narration are available to teachers. Call or write for brochure.

■ **Geraldine Stern**
2311 Paulsen Rd., Harvard 60033; (815) 338-4791
The author of *Daughters from Afar, Profiles of Israeli Women* (New York: Abelard-Schuman, 1958) and *Israeli Women Speak Out* (Philadelphia: Lippincott, 1979) speaks on Israeli Women, Then and Now (1948–80), as well as on her own life as a writer and painter. Stern's books on Israeli women were based on extensive oral histories.

United Synagogue of America Midwest Region
72 E. 11th St., 60605; 939-2351
Publishes *Israel Newsletter*, a critique and digest of news relating to Israel.

For a whale of a good time, observe Israel Independence Day by joining in the annual joyous celebration at the Bernard Horwich JCC—complete with Israeli entertainment, folk dancing, food, films, and exhibits—and balloons!

Zionist Organizations

The early history of Zionism in Chicago is summarized in an article by Anita Libman Lebeson, "Zionism Comes to Chicago," which appeared in *Early History of Zionism in America,* edited by Isidore S. Meyer, published by the American Jewish Historical Society and Theodor Herzl Foundation (New York, 1958). The article covers three very important parts of that history: (1) the founding of the Knights of Zion, the first official Zionist organization in the United States; (2) a summary of antecedent Zionist-minded groups, including literary societies; and (3) the story of the Reverend William E. Blackstone, a lay Protestant preacher who may be regarded as Chicago's first Zionist, and the loyalty and distrust he drew from different elements of the Chicago Jewish community.

American Mizrachi Women, Inc.
3018 W. Devon Ave., 60659; 973-0688

This is the Religious (Orthodox) Women's Zionist Organization, which raises money for the education of Israeli children, education that is offered in a traditionally religious environment. AMW, founded in 1925, promotes and supports social services, child care, and vocational-educational programs in Israel. In connection with the 50th anniversary of AMW, a national oral history project collected the reminiscences of senior members to prepare local chapter histories. American Mizrachi Women is an independent organization whose local chapter is represented on the Public Affairs Committee of JUF.

American Zionist Youth Foundation
c/o Israel Aliyah Center
205 W. Wacker, Rm. 516, 60606; 332-2709

A major resource for programming regarding Israel and Zionism, for all ages but particularly for high school and college students.

Americans for Progressive Israel
Thelma Padawer, Contact
831-9520

A Socialist Zionist organization affiliated with Kibbutz Artzi, a network of over 70 kibbutzim in Israel. API believes that Zionism is the National Liberation Movement of the Jewish people. It is affiliated with the youth group Hashomer Hatzair.

ARZA (Association of Reform Zionists of America)
100 W. Monroe, Rm. 312, 60603; 782-1477
Jerry Kaye, Contact

B'nei Akiva
6500 N. California, 60645; 338-6569
Orthodox Zionist youth movement that is affiliated with the Religious Zionists.

Chicago Zionist Federation
220 S. State, Rm. 604, 60604; 922-5282
Dr. Judith-Rae Ross, Executive Director
This is an umbrella for many of the Zionist organizations in Chicago. The CZF attempts to speak and act on behalf of affiliated organizations and sponsors citywide events such as the annual Israel Independence Day Celebration.

Habonim
4155 Main, Skokie 60076; 679-4061
Labor Zionist youth movement.

Hadassah WZO of America
Hadassah-Chicago
111 N. Wabash, 60602; 263-7473
Hadassah–North Shore
1710 First St., Highland Park 60035; 433-6350
Women's Zionist Organization of America, which supports medical services, schools, and Youth Aliyah in Israel. The Chicago chapter was founded in 1913 when Henrietta Szold visited the city and met with the women's "gate" of the Knights of Zion. Within ten years there were 750 members in 4 local branches. Today there are thousands of members in 38 local groups, including 4 founded within the last year or two. Hadassah–North Shore operates separately, with its own chapters and fund-raising activities. Hashachar and Young Judaea are the youth groups associated with Hadassah in the United States. Locally, represented on the Public Affairs Committee of JUF.

Hashachar
4155 Main, Skokie 60076; 676-9790
Youth group attached to Hadassah WZO and incorporating Young Judaea.

Hashomer Hatzair
c/o Israel Aliyah Center
205 W. Wacker Dr., 60606; 332-2709
Youth group attached to Americans for Progressive Israel.

Israel Aliyah Center
205 W. Wacker Dr., Rm. 516, 60606; 332-2709
A central resource agency for all individuals and organizations interested in moving to Israel or having aliyah as a central purpose.

Israel Histadrut Campaign
220 S. State St., 60604; 427-4086
Raises money for a network of Histadrut services and agencies. Closely allied with the Labor Zionist Movement.

Labor Zionist Alliance
6122 N. California, 60659; 973-3924
2600 W. Peterson Ave., 60659 (during construction)
Roy Shlagman, Executive Director
Formed in 1971 through the merger of two related groups—the Farband, the fraternal insurance organization originally called the Jewish National Workers Alliance, and the Labor Zionist Organization-Poale Zion, the political arm of the Farband. There are fifteen or sixteen branches in Chicago. Most of the branches were founded on Labor Zionist lines or were related to trade unions. LZA sponsors a number of annual events, including a Chanukah party, a third seder, and High Holiday services, all interwoven with the purposes of the Labor Zionist movement. The Chicago headquarters building, the Dolnick Center, was demolished in the fall of 1980, and construction is under way for a new center/residence complex to be completed before the end of 1981 or by early 1982. The new center will include 21 units for senior-adult housing.

Masada
6328 N. California Ave., 60659; 262-5949
Youth movement of the Zionist Organization of Chicago and Zionist Organization of America.

Pioneer Women-Chicago Council
220 S. State, 60604; 922-3736
Pioneer Women-Suburban Council
466 Central, Northfield 60093; 446-7275
Pioneer Women is the Women's Labor Zionist Organization of America, working in close cooperation with Na'amat, a sister organization in Israel. Their efforts support a network of educational and social

services for children, youth, and women in every part of Israel. In America, Pioneer Women promotes Jewish education and culture and actively participates in furthering social legislation especially affecting the well-being of women and children. In Chicago, Pioneer Women is represented on the Public Affairs Committee of JUF and COJO-ERA. Chicago metropolitan area has thirty chapters of Pioneer Women with women from all walks of life. Many of the chapters have their own interest groups or membership is predominantly of common interest, such as Menorah Pioneer Women for singles.

Religious Zionists of Chicago
6500 N. California, 60645; 338-2871
Hebrew name is Mizrachi-Hapoel-Hamizrachi. This organization is dedicated to building the Jewish state on the principles of Orthodox Judaism. Nationally and locally, RZ supports B'nei Akiva for youth and NOAM, a young-adult organization. There is a women's group within the organization. Member of Public Affairs Committee of JUF.

TELEM Movement for Zionist Fulfillment
c/o Israel Aliyah Center
205 W. Wacker Dr., 60606; 332-2709
New to the Chicago area, TELEM places aliyah as the highest priority of the Zionist movement. Without endorsing any particular political philosophy, TELEM strives to assist, aid, and be an advocate for all groups and individuals concerned with aliyah.

United Zionist Revisionists Herut-USA
Barbara Maniloff, Secretary
3845 W. Greenleaf, Lincolnwood 60645; 675-3844
Supports the policies of the Herut in Israel, the political party founded by Prime Minister Menachem Begin in 1948. UZR itself began in 1925, under the leadership of Vladimir Jabotinsky, whose centennial was celebrated in 1980. The Chicago office will supply information and speakers.

Zionist Organization of Chicago
6328 N. California, 60659; 973-3232
Frank Isaacs, Executive Director
ZOC is technically the descendant of the Knights of Zion, the first American Zionist organization. Its headquarters, the Beth Am building, is the focal point for many activities central to the Chicago Jewish community. Masada, the youth organization, and a Women's Division are two of the arms of ZOC. The non-Jewish Christian Friends

of Israel is also affiliated. The annual Chanukah Festival—held for over 40 years—dramatically demonstrates ZOC's support for and association with the Masada youth movement. The candlelighting begins with a torch brought from Israel and conveyed by members of Chicago Masada. Central to the work of ZOC is a constant effort to safeguard the independence and integrity of the State of Israel and to assist Israel economically, culturally, and philosophically.

Support Groups for Specific Projects

AKIM
Israel Association for the Rehabilitation of the Mentally Handicapped
6952 N. California, 60645; 465-0664
Anne Serota, President

Organized in 1980, Chicago chapter AKIM is devoted to aiding Israel's mentally handicapped children and adults through rehabilitation and improvements in the quality of life. Also attempts to provide for better understanding of the special needs of disabled people. Chapters are in formation throughout the world. In Israel AKIM has a network of day-care centers for infants, kindergartens, sheltered workshops, social clubs, and residential homes.

America-Israel Cultural Foundation, Inc.
33 E. Cedar St., 60611; 280-1684
Esther Garduk, Regional Director

Supports Israel's major cultural institutions and provides scholarships in the arts for Israeli students. Makes available traveling exhibits, including the work of contemporary Israeli artists and craftsmen. These exhibits are available to community centers and synagogues and may be shown at special Israel-centered events.

American Committee for Shaare Zedek Hospital in Jerusalem, Inc. Midwest Region
79 W. Monroe, Rm. 1314, 60603; 236-5778

Includes a Women's Division. Handles fund raising for the hospital. Provides speakers and films on the hospital.

American Friends of Bar Ilan University
Mrs. Herzl Rosenson, Contact, 266-0371

Provides information about and support for Bar Ilan University.

American Friends of Gush Emunim
505 N. Lake Shore Dr., Apt. 2706, 60611
Irving Taitel, Executive Director

Not specifically allied with any political party in Israel, the Gush Emunim movement aspires to broader territorial limits. Promotes settlement in areas of dispute and calls for the right of Jews to settle in historic Eretz Yisrael, including Golan, Gaza, Judea, and Samaria. Provides information and speakers from Gush Emunim to speak to interested organizations.

American Friends of the Hebrew University
1 N. LaSalle, 60602; 236-6395
David Koren, Midwest Regional Director
Manuel Silver, Executive Director, Chicago Chapter

Provides information concerning the Hebrew University and its programs, supports the university by fund raising and public information, and supervises student and professor exchange programs with the United States.

American Technion Society
327 S. LaSalle, 60604; 939-0911
Barry Axler, Executive Director

Official fund-raising organization supporting Technion Israel Institute of Technology in Haifa—Israel's major scientific university. The Chicago chapter is composed mainly of men. There is a Women's Division that contains a North Shore Chapter. A Young People's Division has also been formed that holds its own functions on occasion. Visiting professors from Technion often take part in symposia and programs for local chapters in order to attract membership.

AMHAI (Association for Mental Health Affiliation with Israel)
P.O. Box 357, Wilmette 60091; 251-0065

Founded immediately after the Yom Kippur War by Chicago psychoanalyst Dr. David Roth, AMHAI has an international membership of 1,000 psychoanalysts, psychiatrists, psychologists, social workers, and other professionals dedicated to improving the quality of life in Israel by supporting mental-health training, research, and delivery of services. Annual seminars in Chicago usually center on one topic (1980 theme was The Holocaust Family), and participants may receive continuing medical education (CME) credit. Has set up Committee for the Study of the Psychological Effects of the Holocaust.

Amishav, Israel
This suburb of Petach Tikvah is Chicago's partnership community in the Israel Project Renewal. Through contributions, Chicagoans support social and welfare services for the disadvantaged people of this distressed area. Contributions are handled by the Jewish United Fund.

CASE (Community Assistance for Secondary Education) in Israel
c/o Israel Histadrut Campaign
220 S. State, 60604; 427-4086

Provides scholarships in secondary education for underprivileged Israeli youths.

Friends of Neot Kedumim
770 Elder Ct., Glencoe 60022; 835-3472
Joyce Saffir, Chairman

This organization supports the historic Neot Kedumim gardens in Israel and demonstrates through this support how Jews, Judaism, and the land of Israel interrelate. Now under development, the gardens consist of 500 acres in the region of Mod'in, birthplace of the Maccabees, between Jerusalem and Tel Aviv. With full restoration and reclamation, the gardens will contain all the flora and fauna known to have existed in biblical and talmudic times. Audiovisual programs, using slides, cassette, and lecture, tell the story.

Maccabi Sports Club
6237 N. Sacramento, 60659; 338-7597
Isaac Glickstein, President

Supports Jewish and Israeli sports, with special emphasis on the Maccabiah Israeli Sports Movement.

Magen David Adom, Chicago Chapter
6952 N. California, 60645; 465-0664

The Chicago chapter is primarily interested in raising funds for Magen David Adom, the Israeli equivalent of the Red Cross. Information may be received by calling or writing. From time to time MDA has speakers available. MDA has a twenty-minute, 16mm color and sound film for organizations to use, called *The Team*, that tells the work of the agency. It is available upon reservation directly from the office. Some other projects include an annual interfaith dinner and greeting cards for Rosh Hashannah.

Weizmann Institute of Science
79 W. Monroe, 60603; 641-5700

The fund-raising office for the Weizmann Institute, especially for cancer, health, and genetic research.

12
Publications and Media

Chicago Jewish Print Media

Chicago Jewish Post and Opinion
4948 Dempster, Skokie 60077; 677-5451
Bertha Berman, Business Manager and Contact
A weekly local and national publication. Accepts news releases from local organizations.

JUF News
1 S. Franklin, 60606; 346-6700
Saree Halevy, Editor
The official publication of the JUF and the Jewish Federation of Metropolitan Chicago. Published ten times annually. Although the primary purpose of the *News* is to inform readers of the activities of the JUF, the Federation, and their agencies and beneficiaries, the paper has very good coverage of local and world Jewish events. News releases accepted.

New Jewish Times
1930 N. Hudson Ave., 60614; 565-0272
Michael C. Markovitz, President and Copublisher
Planned local edition of new national publication will include local calendar of events.

The Sentinel
323 S. Franklin, 60606; 663-1101
J. I. Fishbein, Editor and Publisher
Celebrating its 70th anniversary in 1981. In format, not so much a newspaper as a weekly newsmagazine. Regular columnists include

Rabbis David Polish, Morris Gutstein, and Irving Rosenbaum. Sheryl Leonard's column for singles is a must for Chicago Jewish singles who wish to be part of the Jewish community. Columnist and longtime Jewish radio broadcaster Libby Olar will keep you posted on who's doing what, where, and when. See the paper for information on where to send news releases and to whom. Some of the columnists have addresses that differ from that of the paper.

Broadcast Media

Radio

"Ask the Rabbi," featuring Rabbi Arnold G. Kaiman, a program of Jewish interest, is heard from 11 P.M. to midnight Sundays on WIND-AM (560).

"Federation Forum" is broadcast 11 to 11:30 P.M. Sundays on WCLR-FM (101.9). Send releases to Zan Skolnick, Producer, 1 S. Franklin, 60606.

"FREE—Program for Soviet Jews in Chicago" is broadcast 3 to 4 P.M. Sundays on WEEF-AM (1430). Features Yiddish and Russian music, interviews, discussion of Jewish holidays, history, Torah study, and community news. Includes Russian-language "Ten Minutes to Israel" programs from the Jewish Agency.

"Israel on the Air" is on from 12:30 to 2 P.M. Sundays on WNIB-FM (97.1). This program includes music by the Israel Philharmonic and a Jewish community calendar. Send releases to WNIB, 12 E. Delaware, 60611.

"Jewish Community Hour," featuring Bernie Finkel, begins at 11 A.M. Sundays on WONX-AM (1590). Includes music, commentary, special features, local news. Send releases to WONX, 2100 Lee, Evanston 60202.

"Jewish Sound" is presented by the Lubavitch Chabad of Evanston from 9:30 to 10 A.M. Sundays on WEEF-AM (1430). Rabbi Daniel Moscowitz is host. Includes Jewish music, "Jewish thoughts," and current events.

Television

Rabbi Allen Secher
Director of Broadcasting
Chicago Board of Rabbis
72 E. 11th, 60605; 427-5863

Rabbi Secher directs the following programs that are produced by the CBR. He is also Media Coordinator for the Jewish Federation.

"Some of My Best Friends," hosted by Bonnie Remsberg, is aired 9:30 A.M. Sundays on Channel 5 (WMAQ-TV), with replay at approximately 1:15 A.M. Mondays. Programs feature guest personalities.

"Of Cabbages and Kings," hosted by Rabbi Herman Schaalman, is produced in February, May, August, and November. Aired Sunday at noon, Channel 7 (WLS-TV), for four consecutive weeks in each of the designated months. Deals with issues of importance to the Jewish community.

"What's NU?" is a community calendar and news program hosted by Rabbi Mordecai Simon and Grace Grossman, 7:45 A.M. Sundays on Channel 9 (WGN-TV).

"Magic Door," the only weekly Jewish children's program in the country, is shown at 7:30 A.M. Sundays on Channel 2 (WBBM-TV).

Since 1972 the annual Selichot evening service is taped live for rebroadcast the following morning. Each year a different congregation is featured with an interview with the host rabbi. Rabbi Mordecai Simon does the voice-over. On Channel 9 (WGN-TV).

WTTW (Public Broadcasting)
Channel 11
5400 N. St. Louis, 60625; 583-5000

Memories, a documentary produced by Jane Kaplan, first shown in 1978, is occasionally repeated. This moving program is an interweaving of the reminiscences of three elderly Jewish people who grew up in Chicago and came from widely varied backgrounds. Although they are never specifically identified as Jewish in the script, the program, nonetheless, has content of local Jewish interest, particularly in the contrasts of the German-Jewish and immigrant Yiddish cultures. Featured were Burt Hamburg, then 94; Sophie Hecht, 98; and Hedwig Loeb, 95.

■ **Neal Sabin**
1946 W. Touhy, 60626

A consultant on media use, especially Jewish-content broadcasting. Can give advice on how to get on TV and radio. Has expertise in production and voice.

■ **Harlan Loebman**
1114 Pfingsten, Glenview 60025; 998-0093

A resource person regarding radio broadcasting.

Secular Media Contacts

Roy Larson
Religion Editor, *Chicago Sun-Times*
401 N. Wabash, 60611

Bruce Buursma
Religion Editor, *Chicago Tribune*
435 N. Michigan, 60611

The Reader
P.O. Box 11101, 60611

The best bargain in town for publicizing good causes. To find out how to place an ad, consult the paper, which is given away on Thursdays at various locations in Chicago. Classified ads for nonprofit groups and free events may be placed without charge.

Films and Audiovisual Resources

Anti-Defamation League of B'nai B'rith
782-5080

ADL has a catalog of its own audiovisuals and films.

Audio Brandon
8400 Brookfield Ave., Brookfield 60513; 485-3925

A national distributor of films. Request catalog, *The Jewish Heritage on Film*, which includes descriptive synopses of each title presented. Israeli and Yiddish films included.

Chicago Public Library
78 E. Washington St., 60602; 269-2910

Films on many subjects are available on loan.

Film Availability
University of Illinois–Chicago Circle
996-2543

Maxwell Street Blues, a 60-minute documentary by Raul Zaritsky and Linda Williams, was produced in 1980 and shot in 1978 and 1979. The film depicts the street today, integrates the history of the street and the market, and shows the transition from the former Jewish to the present Black dominance.

The Lawson Boys, produced by Herbert DiGioia, is a sympathetic portrait of the Jewish men who grew up on the Lawson School Playground, how they were influenced by their early athletic endeavors and by their coach, Frank Heidenreich, and how they still meet for a biennial banquet. Sixty minutes.

Films Incorporated
733 Green Bay Rd., Wilmette 60091; 256-3200 (national sales)
1144 Wilmette Ave., Wilmette 60091; 256-4730 (rental library)
16mm films for rent or sale and video cassettes for sale on subjects pertaining to Jewish history, Israel, and Nazi Germany.

Suburban Audio-Visual Service
352-7671
This service supplies 16mm films and videotapes to all the suburban library systems in the area. Catalogs—which include many features, children's films, documentaries, and biographical portraits of Jewish interest—are at member libraries. Films are available to anyone with a suburban system library card; the only charge is 50¢ for insurance.

TJC Inc. Productions
Mike Kamen and Myrna Ravitz
611 Ridge Road, Highland Park 60035; 831-2344
Producers, writers, and directors of independent films including three of Jewish content: *Benjamin and the Miracle of Chanukah*, which aired on network national TV; the Holocaust film that is part of the Zell Holocaust exhibit at the Spertus Museum; and their latest, *Sons of Zebulon*, filmed on location in Israel. The latter is based on a book by the same title, written by George T. Radan, about Jewish maritime history.

■ **Joseph Ben-Israel**
Director, Frank G. Marshall Multi-Media Center
Board of Jewish Education, 72 E. 11th St., 60605; 427-5570
6967 N. Bell, 60645; 274-1983 (home)
Expert in producing multimedia presentations. Available for freelance assignments and consultations. Native of Israel, speaks Hebrew, Yiddish, Hungarian, as well as English. Master's degrees in Jewish Communal Service and Instructional Media/Educational Technology. He is the editor of *Or V'Kol*, media publication of the Board of Jewish Education.

■ **Merle Kaminsky and David Obermeyer**
Producers of *Thirty-Nine Leagues from Home*
475-7766
Thirty-Nine Leagues from Home is a 1980 film funded by the Illinois Humanities Council based on interviews with Soviet Jewish immigrants in East Rogers Park. It is a 28-minute documentary available to local organizations.

■ Miriam Rosenbush
6033 N. Sheridan Rd., Apt. 43D, 60660; 271-2339

Filmmaker and lecturer. Her film *The Legacy: Children of the Holocaust Survivors*, a 23-minute documentary, has been shown on Channel 11, at the Art Institute of Chicago, and for organizations. Based on interviews with Chicagoans.

■ Neal Sabin
1946 W. Touhy Ave., 60626

Sabin has an extensive rental library of Jewish films.

■ Israel Signer
505 Fifth St., Northfield 60093; 724-7647

All-around film resource person. Shows films from Consulate General of Israel and other sources. Books films, repairs films if necessary, and operates machinery.

■ Gerald Temaner
7206 S. Oglesby, 60649; 363-5112

Filmmaker with wide experience in ethnic content films, including some of Jewish content. One film, *Home for Life* about Drexel Home, is available through the Suburban Audio-Visual Service.

13
Goods and Services

Goods

A very helpful, though slightly dated, guide to shopping sources is the soft-cover *Where To Buy Israeli Goods: A Chicagoland Directory*, published in 1977 and still available from the Buy Israeli Goods Council, 708 Church St., Rm. 233, Evanston 60201; 864-1502. Although the "goods" covered are strictly imports from Israel, the book is filled with lists of Judaica shops, synagogue and hospital gift shops, boutiques, etc., that usually carry products of Jewish interest. Anyone interested in merchandising a Jewish product will find a nearly up-to-date list of Jewish stores.

Sisterhood gift shops are indicated in the section on Congregations in Chapter 3. They carry a wide variety of Judaica, gift items, jewelry, ritual objects, holiday items, books, art, and greeting cards.

Art

For the work of individual Chicago artists, see Chapter 8, "The Arts."

Art from the Kibbutz
Presented by Marcus Fine Arts
5816 S. Blackstone Ave., 60637; 363-4479

Cilla and Joseph Marcus present the work of Israeli kibbutz artists—represented by the Association of Painters and Sculptors of the Kibbutz Artzi Federation. Included are works by Haim Bargal, Ronny

Rechev, Yuval Danieli, Yona Gur, and others. Marcus Fine Arts will help set up exhibits of kibbutz art or will sell directly, by appointment only.

Art Gallery Inn
7514–7520 N. Skokie Blvd., Skokie 60077; 676-0111
Auctioneer Len Rubin will conduct fund-raising auctions for Jewish organizations that may include the art of Jewish and Israeli artists.

Bernard Horwich JCC
3003 W. Touhy, 60645; 761-9100
An annual art fair and auction has been held in the spring for sixteen years. This is an invitational art fair with a fine selection. A special feature is a children's fair with works, all under $20, especially aimed at very young collectors. The Horwich JCC also has a gallery with changing exhibits.

B'nai Torah Art Panorama
2789 Oak St., Highland Park 60035; 433-7100
Congregation B'nai Torah Sisterhood's twelfth annual exhibition and sale of fine art was held in May, 1981. Featured among a wider selection were artists whose works have Jewish content.

Festival of the Arts
North Suburban Synagogue Beth El Sisterhood
1175 Sheridan Rd., Highland Park 60035; 432-8900
An annual top-flight art show that includes a wide variety of artists and media: paintings, photography, sculpture, jewelry, glass, graphics, ceramics, fibers, etc.

Hakol Yafeh
433-1013 or 446-3380
Quality Judaica ceremonial objects sold on a retail basis. Sources are Israeli and American artists. Call for appointment.

In the Beginning Ltd.
Distinctive Israeli Crafts
916 Maple Rd., Flossmoor 60422; 646-4500 or 748-2900
A labor of love run by three south suburban couples—the Arthur Starks of Flossmoor, the Max Adlers of Homewood, and the Michael Kulakovskys of Park Forest. Sales of fine Israeli arts and crafts through a catalog, private showings, and art shows. Included are cloth and silver tallitim by Malka Gavrieli, weaver; biblical thematic sculpture in gold, silver, and stone by Yaacov Heller; caricature lithographs by Martin Holt (such as basketball-playing rebbes); watercolors by

Gila Holt; and primitive, flowered ceramic candlesticks, menorahs, plaques, mezuzot by Chaya Magal, a Soviet Jewish "Grandma Moses" working in Israel. In the Beginning also handles the work of Frank Meisler, one of Israel's most noted sculptors.

Museum Store
Spertus Museum of Judaica
618 S. Michigan, 60605; 922-9012
Jeffrey Kraft, Manager

Offers a wide selection of Israeli paintings, sculpture, graphics, crafts, posters, jewelry, and ceremonial art. Jewish holiday gift items, books, and gift certificates are available. Members of the museum receive a discount. Shop by phone if you wish.

Books

Bais STaM
6343 N. California, 60659; 973-1311
Rev. Yochanan Nathan, Proprietor

An Orthodox Jewish bookstore, limited to books in keeping with Orthodox traditions and to religious ceremonial garments and objects. Rev. Nathan is a scribe (a sofer). He sells, repairs, and creates Sifrei Torah, *T*efillin, and *M*ezuzot—thus the acronym STaM.

Bob's News Emporium
5100 S. Lake Park Ave., 60615; 684-5100
Bob Katzman, Proprietor

This has the best selection of Jewish titles (at least 300 of them) south of the Loop and one of the best in the metropolitan area. Sells hardcovers, paperbacks, and periodicals. Open every day of the year, 7 A.M. to 6 P.M. Mondays through Fridays; 9 P.M. Saturdays; and 6 A.M. to 5 P.M. Sundays. Katzman also owns Bob's In Newtown, 2810 N. Clark, 60657; 883-1123, which also carries Jewish titles. Open 11 A.M. to 9 P.M. Mondays through Fridays; shorter hours on weekends.

Brandeis Book Sale
Brandeis University National Women's Committee
North Shore Chapter
Book Pickup, 251-0690

The Brandeis Book Sale, which claims to be the largest used-book sale in the world, is held each year under a tent at Edens Plaza Shopping Center, Wilmette, on Memorial Day weekend and through the following weekend. The 22d annual sale will be held in 1981. Opening night starts at 6 P.M., but the line starts forming at 6 A.M. Free admission except for the first night. The second weekend is the bargain weekend. There's a silent auction on selected titles and editions held from the opening night through Thursday. Volunteers work year-round at the depot in Highland Park (call for book pickup).

Brisk Rabbinical College Book Store
9000 Forest View Rd., Skokie 60203; 674-8920

Chicago Hebrew Book Store
2942 W. Devon Ave., 60659; 973-6636

Besides books, this store carries a full line of religious and ceremonial articles, greeting cards, and gifts.

Hamakor-Judaica, Inc.
6112 N. Lincoln, 60659; 463-6186

Books plus religious and ceremonial articles, gift items, household items, festival decorations, jewelry, novelties, even T-shirts. Good selection of Jewish music and records. Hamakor periodically issues catalogs filled with pictures and information about the items they stock.

Jewish Book Mart
127 N. Dearborn, 60602; 782-5199
Benjamin Fain, Proprietor

Used and new, rare and unusual Judaica are handled by Fain in this small second-floor shop in Chicago's tilting office building. Fain will appraise books and libraries, search for bibliographic treasures, and lecture on the great literature of the Jewish tradition. Open 9:30 A.M. to 5 P.M. Mondays through Fridays.

ORT Alley Book Shop
1905 Sheridan Rd., Highland Park 60035; 432-9625

A charming rear shop, accessible through an alley only, containing a wonderful collection of used-book bargains. Half-price sales from time to time. Visit and get on the mailing list. Book donations are accepted.

Schwartz-Rosenblum Hebrew Book Store
2906 W. Devon, 60659; 262-1700

The granddaddy of Jewish bookstores in Chicago, with roots going back to the old West Side and later to Albany Park. Besides books, there are religious and ceremonial articles, garments, gift items, music, records, greeting cards, holiday decorations, even chupah frames. The store also carries some of the Hebrew calligraphy done by the artists listed in Chapter 8 under Artists and Artisans. Also in the market for used sifrei Torah and silver ornaments.

Spertus College of Judaica
618 S. Michigan Ave., 60605; 922-9012
In behalf of the Asher Library, Spertus held its first annual Judaica book sale during the summer of 1980. The sale included many rare or out-of-date Hebrew, Yiddish, and English books, most of which were donated to Spertus over the years but were duplicates or, for some reason, outside the sphere of the library's own collection. New books are sold year-round in the museum store.

JCCs and congregations have book sales throughout the year—of both used and new books—the latter sometimes tied up with National Jewish Book Month or the Chanukah season.

Flowers

Mayer Kaplan JCC Teens
5050 Church, Skokie 60077; 675-2200
National Conference of Synagogue Youth
6716 N. Whipple St., 60645; 761-2188
Both of these youth groups participate in Israflowers, a nationwide program that delivers flowers from Israel within 24 hours after they have been cut. Especially popular at Passover time are Israeli spring flowers for the seder table.

Michael Reese Hospital and Medical Center
Auxiliary of the Dysfunctioning Child Center
2915 S. Ellis Ave., 60616; 791-4233
Sells roses for Mother's Day.

Food

Kosher supervision in Chicago is not centralized. Most of the supervision is done by the Chicago Rabbinical Council, though it does not supervise meat markets. The CRC does issue a periodic list of its endorsed products, restaurants, caterers, etc. The Merkaz Harabonim, the Chicago Orthodox Rabbinate, issues no similar list for the meat markets under its supervision. In addition, there are independent rabbis and even one rebbetzen, a rabbi's wife, supervising kashrut in Chicago. (Rebbetzen Rosa Ziemba is the kashrut supervisor for Carmel Kosher Food Products.) Because *all endorsements are subject to cancellation,* persons are urged to look for the sign ⓒRⒸ, Ⓤ, or K on products and for the well-displayed hechsher, or seal of endorsement, of the United Kashruth Commission in meat markets.

Bakeries and Bagels

The following is a list of kosher bakeries endorsed by the Chicago Rabbinical Council:

Gross Kosher Bakery
2546 W. Devon, 60659; 465-2144

North Shore Kosher Bakery
2919 W. Touhy Ave., 60645; 262-0600

Tam Tov Kosher Bakery
3909 W. Lawrence, 60625; 267-3383

The following bakeries may or may not be kosher, but all cater to a Jewish clientele:

Brooklyn Bagel Boys
9179 Gross Point Rd., Skokie 60077; 674-0488
1456 Lee St., Des Plaines 60018; 297-3579
c/o Ackermen's Delicatessen, Dundee Rd. and Arlington Heights Rd., Buffalo Grove 60090; 259-5700

Wide variety of pareve bagels: egg, onion, poppy seed, etc. For orders of two dozen or more, call ten minutes ahead and pick up the order hot.

Karen's Pastry Shop
3113 N. Broadway, 60657; 525-5700

Pareve pastries and candy; only kosher ingredients are used.

Kaufman's Bagel Bakery
4411 N. Kedzie Ave., 60625; 267-1680
4905 Dempster St., Skokie 60077; 677-9880

The Dempster store also has a deli.

Leonard's Bakery
2651 W. Devon, 60659; 743-0318

Specialty is a cheese chala.

Levinson's Bakery
2856 W. Devon, 60659; 761-3174

New York Bagels and Bialys
4714 W. Touhy Ave., Lincolnwood 60646; 677-9388

3556½ W. Dempster, Skokie 60076; 673-9388
133 Old Skokie Rd., Northbrook 60062; 835-0940
8794 W. Dempster St., Des Plaines 60016; 296-4198

Simon Brothers Bakery
3548 W. Lawrence, 60625; 267-5005

All baked goods are pareve and follow kosher recipes. Simon Brothers sells retail, but also caters to restaurants and delicatessens.

Tel Aviv Kosher Bakery
2944 W. Devon, 60659; 764-8877

Candy

Barton's candies are carried in many retail stores, including Marshall Field's, Goldblatt's, Carson's, and independent drugstores. The gift shop, North Suburban Synagogue Beth El, Highland Park, sells Barton's candies year-round.

Ash Sales Association
3635 Winnetka Rd., Glenview 60025; 480-0420

The fund-raising division of Barton's Candy Corp. Minimum orders are $250.

Barton's Candy and Cards
2816 W. Devon, 60659; 274-1273

Breezes
2813 W. Touhy, 60645; 764-4084

Also a Barton's candy and card store.

Karen's
3113 N. Broadway, 60657; 525-5700

Division of the House of Fine Chocolates that sells pareve candy as well as pastries.

Fish Markets

Chicago Fish House
1250 W. Division, 60622; 227-7000

The first and only wholesale-retail fish market to be certified to sell kosher fish by the Chicago Rabbinical Council.

Fannie's Old Fashioned Fishery and Delicatessen
4718 Touhy Ave., Lincolnwood 60646; 676-4000

Carries kosher products.

Fish Factory
5545 N. Kedzie Ave., 60625; 539-1188

Smoked fish and lox.

Fish Market of Highland Park
1843 Second St., Highland Park 60035; 432-6605

Owner Louis Green's father, Sam, ran the Hollywood Fisheries in Chicago. The market will skin, bone, and grind fish.

Northtown Fisheries
2318 W. Devon, 60659; 764-9552

Lou and Ethel Kaufman

Will fillet, wash, and grind fish for gefilte.

Robert's Fish Market
2916 W. Devon, 60659; 761-3424

Robert Schuffler, Proprietor

Closed Saturdays and after 3 P.M. Fridays.

St. Louis Fish Market
3537 W. Lawrence, 60625; 478-4424

This market's roots are on the old West Side. Will also skin, bone, and grind fish.

Groceries and Delicatessens

The following markets, delis, and carryout places are endorsed by the Chicago Rabbinical Council:

Hungarian Kosher Meat Market and Deli
2613 W. Devon, 60659; 973-5991 or 973-5977

Delicatessen and sausage products, salami, hot dogs, corned beef, and other smoked beef products; knishes, kishke, soaked and salted kosher meats.

Kosher City—Nosh-o-Rama
3355 W. Dempster, Skokie 60076; 679-2850 or 679-4030

Full line of TV dinners, kishke, pizza.

Kosher Karry
2828 W. Devon, 60659; 973-4355

A complete carryout deli plus cafeteria.

Kosher Zion Sausage Co.
5529 N. Kedzie Ave., 60625; 463-3351

An outlet store and delicatessen for the Kosher Zion sausage manufacturing company. Discounted prices on sausages.

The Meal Market
2915 W. Touhy, 60645; 761-4131
A sit-down kosher deli with complete carryout. Also makes up party trays, fish trays, meat trays.

New York Kosher
2900 W. Devon, 60659; 743-1664
Really a fully kosher supermarket and deli that also handles imported Israeli foods.

The Stiebel Pantry
Mayer Stiebel Organization
679-7000, x335
Take-home meals. Minimum order, 16 dinners. Call for a brochure.

The markets in the following list that are kosher and have the approval of a rabbi or board other than the Chicago Rabbinical Council are so indicated. Others listed here are not kosher but serve "kosher-style" foods.

Al's Delicatessen and Restaurant
18677 Dixie Highway, Homewood 60430; 798-4399
Sells only kosher foods but is not supervised.

Dilly of a Deli
8353 Golf Rd., Niles 60648; 470-1888
Kosher-style; hand-carved belly lox.

Goldie's S & S Deli and Bakery
594 Roger Williams, Highland Park 60035; 432-0775
Kosher-style counter with kosher foods from the freezer case. Delivers Sunday mornings to neighboring suburbs. Chala from Simon Brothers Bakery.

Kaufman's Delicatessen
4905 Dempster St., Skokie 60077; 677-6190
Attached to Kaufman Bagel Bakery. Carries kosher products.

Kosher Gourmet
3552 Dempster, Skokie 60076; 679-0432
Supervised but not by the CRC. Carryout hours are limited. Call for information.

Lazar's Deli
1272 E. Dundee, Palatine 60067; 359-7500
Third-generation descendants of Lazar Kosher Sausage Company (now called Kosher Zion Sausage), which started on W. Roosevelt Rd. Kosher-style.

Romanian Kosher Sausage Company
7200 N. Clark St., 60626; 761-4141

Strictly kosher, supervised by Rabbi Karno of Congregation Mishne Ugmoro. Besides sales in the shop, Romanian will take orders on a regular basis for delivery throughout the greater Chicago area.

Rosen's Finer Foods
3419 W. Lawrence Ave., 60625; 588-2756

Complete line of kosher products, including special Passover foods. Will deliver in the immediate areas of Albany Park, Hollywood Park, and Peterson Park.

Salami & Gomorrah
1931 Central, Evanston 60201; 864-1491

Kosher-style deli, catering. Ask for owner Martin Smith, who calls himself the Deli-lama!

Sam & Hy's
3438 Dempster, Skokie 60076; 674-8560

Kosher-style delicatessen, restaurant, and catering. Fish, dairy trays, vegetarian submarine up to six feet long.

Shel-Mar Delicatessen
2637 W. Devon, 60659; 262-7810

Fishery, delicatessen, lox, smoked fish, corned beef. Closed Saturdays.

Sheridan Deli
6574 N. Sheridan Rd., 60626; 764-3354 (764-DELI!)

Kosher-style deli and caterer. Forty-five flavors of cheesecake. Box lunches for large groups, including pareve boxes for kosher clients.

Sinai Kosher Sausage Corp.
1000 W. Pershing Rd., 60609; 927-2810

Wide variety of delicatessen products. All kosher. Sells prepackaged kosher sandwiches available at retail store 7 A.M. to 4 P.M. Mondays through Thursdays and 7 A.M. to 3 P.M. Fridays. Also sold at various locations in Chicago, including University of Chicago Bookstore, 5750 S. Ellis, and University of Illinois Medical School Bookstore, 750 S. Halsted.

Vienna Sausage Manufacturing Co.
Retail Stores
2501 N. Damen, 60647; 235-6652
1215 S. Halsted, 60607; 226-4288

All-beef products. Manufacturer's outlet stores for brand popularly sold throughout area at small hot-dog carryout stands as well as supermarkets and grocery stores.

Wally's Kosher Deli
Milk Pail
3320 W. Devon, Lincolnwood 60659; 673-9854 or 673-3459
Kosher Zion products, sausage, corned beef, Tam Tov Kosher bakery products. Kosher Deli within the larger food market. This is the place to find Jewish Chinese fortune cookies!

Ice Cream

The Chicago Rabbinical Council has endorsed two local manufacturers of ice cream.

Bresler Ice Cream Co.
4010 W. Belden Ave., 60639; 227-6700
All Bresler's ice cream is kosher excluding cones and items containing marshmallow flavoring. Besides ice cream, Bresler manufactures sherbets, Italian ices, frozen yogurt. Call for the dealer locations.

Drexel Ice Cream Co.
5201 W. Grand, 60639; 622-6700
Call for dealer locations.

Some ice cream parlors advertise themselves as kosher.

Big Scoop
6347 N. California Ave., 60659; 973-4473
Features Vala, 28 "fantastic Kosher flavors," a division of Bresler Ice Cream Co.

Bresler's 33 Flavors
6103 Lincoln Ave., 60659; 539-3322
Ask for the kosher ice cream, ices, or sherbet.

Dr. Jazz
913 Chicago Ave., Evanston 60202; 328-9795

Kosher Food Co-ops

Kosher Food Co-op
Mayer Kaplan Senior Adults
3003 W. Touhy, 60645; 761-9100 x56
Oscar Levine, Morris Gilford, Contacts (Wednesday and Thursday mornings)

This co-op is officially part of the Mayer Kaplan Senior Adults at the Horwich Center, but actually only five persons handle the whole operation. Open to the public 9 A.M. to 12:30 P.M. Wednesdays and Thursdays. Estimated saving is 10 to 15 percent. This co-op carries produce, baked goods, candles, eggs, and sandwich meats. Everything is kosher. Any money left over goes to the Senior Center, but the co-op is run as a nonprofit organization with the lowest possible prices. Founded in 1976.

Kosher Meat Co-op
B'nai B'rith Hillel Foundation–University of Chicago
5715 S. Woodlawn, 60637; 752-1127

Work and finances shared by participants. Orders must be placed by noon Tuesday for delivery Thursday. Bylaws, order blanks, and the names and numbers of the people in charge are available at Hillel.

Meat

Because there is no central agency supervising kashrut in kosher meat markets, the following list is a compilation from several sources. Most of the kosher meat markets listed appeared on a customer list kindly offered by United Poultry, Inc., supplier of kosher poultry to the retail market. All listed meat markets have been identified as kosher. But *all kosher endorsements are subject to change*. Kosher meat markets must display a sign of approval issued by the "United Kashruth Commission." Although there is in fact no such commission, the rabbis who individually supervise meat markets uniformly use that certification label. Many of these meat markets deliver.

Bryn Mawr Kosher Meat Market
3305 W. Bryn Mawr, 60659; 463-6590

Cohen & Horwitz Kosher Market
3341 W. Broadway, 60657; 528-6565

Dempster Kosher Meat Market
4918 Dempster St., Skokie 60077; 676-0950

Devon Kosher Market
2913 W. Devon, 60659; 274-6198

Ebner's Kosher Meat Market
2649 W. Devon, 60659; 764-1446

Fine's Kosher Meat Market
3310 N. Broadway, 60657; 248-5599

Highland Park Kosher Meat Market
1813 St. Johns, Highland Park 60035; 432-0748

Ed Hobfoll Kosher Market
3550 W. Lawrence, 60625; 588-6778

J. and M. Kosher Meat Market
1009 W. Argyle, 60640; 561-4551

Jacob M. Miller and Sons Self Service Meat and Poultry
2727 W. Devon, 60659; 761-4200
Deliveries as far as the South Side of Chicago.

Jack's Kosher Meat Market and Poultry
3253½ W. Bryn Mawr, 60659; 539-9621

Lipman Kosher Meat Market
2255 W. Devon, 60659; 338-6120

Main St. Kosher Meat and Poultry Market
4004 Main, Skokie 60076; 677-5188

One Stop Fleishig Shop
(Romanian Kosher Sausage Co.)
7200 N. Clark, 60626; 761-4141

Rapoport Kosher Market
3920 W. Lawrence, 60625; 463-2434

Savitzsky & Millstein Kosher Meat Market
2604 W. Devon, 60659; 274-0430

Shaevitz Kosher Market
2907 W. Devon, 60659; 743-9481

Skokie Valley Kosher Meat Market
3945 Dempster, Skokie 60076; 674-3440

Slovin & Solomon Kosher Meat Market
4023 Dempster, Skokie 60076; 673-3737

Touhy Kosher Meat Market
2811 W. Touhy, 60645; 274-3305

Poultry

Odes Live Poultry and Egg Market
4741 N. Kedzie Ave., 60625; 539-4685
Chicago's only remaining strictly kosher retail live-poultry market.

Wines and Beverages

International Wine Cellar
9800 Balmoral, Rosemont 60018; 671-7700
A distributor of Carmel and Mogen David wines.

Kosher Wine Corp.
4751 N. St. Louis, 60625; 478-6869
Sells kosher wine to congregations.

Mogen David Wine Corporation
3737 S. Sacramento, 60632; 254-6300
444 N. Michigan Ave., 60611; 836-1650

Montreal Beverages
3691 W. Grand, 60651; 772-5600
A variety of flavors, all kosher for Passover.

Wholesalers, Manufacturers, and Distributors

B. Manischewitz Sales Corp.
4040 W. Belmont, 60641; 283-3336

Best Kosher Sausage Company
207 W. South Water Market, 60608; 738-2100

Carmel Kosher Food Products
4840 S. Kedzie, 60632; 254-5335
A broad line of grocery products that includes soup mixes, potato-pancake mixes, kugel mixes, gelatin, and schmaltz. Kosher and wholesale only.

Central Kosher Sales
3740 W. Lawrence, 60625; 478-1755

Schwartz Pickle Company
160 N. Loomis, 60607; 738-1772
Under rabbinical supervision, processor of kosher pickles and kosher tomatoes. Wholesale only.

United Frozen Food
1843 W. 16th, 60608; 243-1683
Lov-em Frozen Kosher Potato Pancakes, etc.

United Kosher Food
711 W. Grand, 60610; 733-3961
Frozen poultry specialties.

United Poultry Inc.
1016 W. Fulton St., 60607; 421-6500

Greeting Cards

The following four organizations sell Jewish New Year cards or cards for other occasions:

Hadassah-Chicago
111 N. Wabash, 60602; 263-7473

Jewish Children's Bureau Auxiliaries
1 S. Franklin, 60606; 346-6700

Magen David Adom
6952 N. California, 60645; 465-0664

Michael Reese Hospital and Medical Center
Dysfunctioning Child Center
2915 S. Ellis Ave., 60616; 791-4233

Artforms
3150 Skokie Valley Rd., Suite 7, Highland Park 60035; 433-0532
Bluma Marder
A commercial greeting card company manufacturing greeting cards with Jewish themes—humorous, serious, children's special occasion, Jewish holidays, and even one with a proven latkes recipe. Marder sells to stationery stores throughout the country, but may sell overruns or last year's line at a discount to nonprofit organizations and gift shops. Founded in 1976, Artforms had ten artists in its employ in 1980 and is still growing. Marder is always on the lookout for new artists. Call for a catalog.

Irene Baer
6101 N. Sheridan Rd., Apt. 10C, 60660; 274-4531
Primarily known for oil painting and linoleum-block prints of Jewish subjects; sells original cards made from block prints to individuals and gift shops.

Henry Jelen
262-7296
Creates greeting cards for Jewish occasions from original drawings. Sells to gift shops, bookstores, and groups.

Mike's Specialty Shop
4014 Main St., Skokie 60076; 679-4313
Greeting cards with Jewish themes, Jewish holiday decorations, party goods, novelties.

Shalom Gifts & Boutique
2707 W. Devon, 60659; 262-0543
Greeting cards, gifts; also some Jewish ceremonial articles.

Hair Goods

Leah Ray
973-3982

Sells hair goods to Orthodox women. She is a certified wig stylist, with formal training, specializing in cutting and styling. Call for an appointment.

Records and Tapes

Michael Katz
325 Prospect, Highland Park 60035; 432-3844

Katz has created tapes for the chanting of magillot, including Ruth, Lamentation, Song of Songs, and Esther.

Living Archives, Ltd.
P.O. Box 86, Barrington 60010; 381-3736

Rozhinkes mit Mandlin ("Raisins with Almonds") produced and narrated by Rita Jacobs Willens, is a two-hour montage-documentary that has received three national broadcast awards. Contents and information are available from Gamut Productions Inc., Route 2, Spring Creek Rd., Barrington 60010. A double album or double cassette is available from Living Archives for $25 each. Included are voices and music of Jewish actors, authors, and musicians from all over the world.

Musique Internationale
3111 W. Chase Ave., 60645; 761-3111
Barry Serota

Has a catalog of about 60 LP records of Jewish cantorial music from the past 50 years. Also recently issued two albums of Russian Jewish pre-Revolutionary twentieth-century composers. Serota is a one-man preservation committee for nearly lost Jewish music.

Resale and Thrift Shops

Ark Thrift Shop
4703 N. Kedzie, 60625; 267-5578 or 463-4545

Donations accepted 11 A.M. to 6 P.M. Sundays through Thursdays.

Association of the Jewish Blind Resale Shop
3603 W. Lawrence, 60625; 539-2209

Dollars & Sense KAM–Isaiah Israel Thrift Shop
1312 E. 53rd, 60615; 363-1100

Esther Clamage Auxiliary Thrift Shop
3228 N. Clark, 60657; 525-9837

Benefits the Jewish Children's Bureau.

Hadassah House
1710 First St., Highland Park 60035; 433-6352
Open 10 A.M. to 5 P.M. Mondays through Fridays; 1 to 4 P.M. Sundays. Closed Saturdays.

Hadassah House
725 Madison, Oak Park 60302; 386-9898

Infants Aid
821–23 Dempster, Evanston 60201; 475-9182

Johanna's Bargain Boutique
1031 Davis St., Evanston 60201; 328-5775
10 A.M. to 4 P.M. Thursdays through Saturdays.

Michael Reese Service League Thrift Shop
54 W. Chicago, 60610; 664-8164 or 337-8266
Daily 10 A.M. to 4 P.M.

National Council of Jewish Women Thrift Shop
1524 W. Howard, 60626; 743-9500

Bargains Unlimited
2552 N. Clark, 60614; 525-8595
National Council of Jewish Women is one of ten beneficiary agencies.

National Council of Jewish Women Thrift Shop
41 Highwood, Highwood 60040; 433-6560

Price Is Right Thrift Shop
2450 Western Ave., Park Forest 60466; 481-4220
Operated by the Lincolnway and South Cook sections of the National Council of Jewish Women. Check the address; this thrift shop may be moving.

ORT Value Center
1905 Sheridan Rd., Highland Park 60035; 432-9860

ORT Resale Shop
3326 N. Lincoln, 60657; 525-4969

ORT Thriftique Shop
920 Chicago Ave., Evanston 60202; 491-6099

Parkview Home Thrift Shop
3503 W. Lawrence, 60625; 583-5118

The Right Place Resale Shop
5205 N. Clark, 60640; 561-7757
Open daily except Saturdays; Sundays, afternoons only. Benefits the Anshe Emet Day School.

Three-Corner Thrift Mart
1508 W. Howard, 60626; 465-3393
Operated by Dvorah Chapter, American Mizrachi Women. Open 10 A.M. to 5 P.M. Sundays through Thursdays; 10 A.M. to 3:30 P.M. Fridays; closed Saturdays.

When You Have Items to Give Away, Give . . .
Discarded Fisher Price, Playskool, and wooden puzzle toys to AKIM, Israel Association for the Rehabilitation of the Mentally Handicapped, 465-0664. Other toys in good condition, to Masada, 6328 N. California, 60659, 262-5949, for Israeli War Orphans.
Kosher food and grocery coupons to The Ark, 3509 W. Lawrence Ave., 60625, 463-4545. Food goes into the emergency food pantry.
Technical books on all aspects of engineering and business to the Jewish Vocational Service, 1 S. Franklin, 60606, 346-6700, for Soviet immigrants.
Old minutes, photos, programs of your congregation or club to the Chicago Jewish Archives, 922-9012, or call the Chicago Jewish Historical Society, 663-5634, for a pickup.
Household items including furniture to FREE, 274-5123, for Soviet immigrants.
Judaica books to the Associated Talmud Torahs, 2828 W. Pratt Blvd., 60645, 973-2828, for the new Leonard Mishkin Historical Resource Library.
General books to Brandeis, 251-0690, for the book sale, or to Women's American ORT for their Alley Book Shop, 432-9625.
Salable used or unused goods of all kinds can be donated to any of the resale shops mentioned in this book.

Trophies

KEMCO Trophies
7211 N. Western, 60645; 262-1468
Hebrew and Yiddish engraving for trophies or any other gift items in the store.

Typewriters

International Typewriter Exchange, Inc.
1229 W. Washington Blvd., 60607; 733-1200
Has Hebrew and Russian typewriters for sale and for long-term rental.

Services
Caterers

The following kosher caterers are supervised and approved by the Chicago Rabbinical Council:

Danziger Kosher Caterers
2932 W. Greenleaf, 60645; 743-4325

Goldman-Segal Kosher Caterers
6814 N. Sacramento, 60645; 338-4060

Kosher Karry
2828 W. Devon, 60659; 973-4355

Polski Kosher Catering
6553 N. Kimball, Lincolnwood 60645; 539-2288

Mayer Stiebel Organization
9599 Skokie, Skokie 60076; 679-7000 x335

Meal Market
2915 W. Touhy, 60645; 761-4131

Turner Kosher Caterers by Jack and Myra Rosenbloom
721-8017 or 764-5161

These two caterers have rabbinic endorsement other than the CRC:

Continental Caterers
242-1208 (Chicago); 432-5770 (Highland Park); 355-1208 (Naperville)
Caters at Navy Pier with seating to 2,000.

Kosher Gourmet
3552 Dempster, Skokie 60076; 679-0432
Joel and Eileen Jacobs

The following caterer is without rabbinic supervision:

From Soup to Nuts
6712 N. Fairfield Ave., 60645; 761-1335
Barbara Rosen and Gloria Schanks

Caterers who will, upon request, prepare kosher meals in kosher homes, including traditional Shabbat dinners, one of their specialties.

The CRC endorses the kosher catering facilities at these hotels:
Belmont Hotel, 248-2100
Conrad Hilton Chicago, 922-4400

Holiday Inn of Evanston, 491-6400
Hyatt Regency Chicago, 565-1000
Palmer House, 726-7500
Pick Congress, 427-3800 (ask for Michael Page or Sherry Smith)
Sovereign Hotel, 274-8000 or 274-4448

Most of the above caterers who have CRC approval serve additional hotels, as well as specific restaurants and clubs, where they are accustomed to catering kosher meals.

Cleaners

Lake City Cleaners
1740 First St., Highland Park 60035; 433-4800
Will clean any religious garment or ceremonial fabric at no charge.

Collecting

AAA Stamp Co.
P.O. Box 99, Wilmette 60091; 256-3990 (evenings only)
Buys and sells Israeli stamps at the following bourses (markets) only:
  Third Sunday of the month, Holiday Inn of Highland
      Park–Northbrook
  Fourth Sunday of the month, Holiday Inn, 5300 Touhy, Skokie
Both markets are held from 10 A.M. to 4:30 P.M. Both markets have free admission and free parking.

■ Dr. Louis A. Berman
928 Asbury, Evanston 60202; 475-3148
Collector of Jewish postcards; has put together a slide program showing postcards from his collection, from the Spertus Museum, and from several private collections.

Chicago Society of Israel Philatelists
Israel Palestine Philatelic Society of America, Chicago Chapter
Dr. Robert B. Pildes, 30 N. Michigan, Rm. 1009, 60602;
    782-0503
Irv Holland, P.O. Box 99, Wilmette 60091
Meetings on the second Thursday of each month, 7:30 P.M. at Irving Park YMCA, 4250 W. Irving Park Rd., 60641. Each meeting includes a slide show and lecture. Generally slide shows are available only to member clubs. However, persons interested in a possible private showing might contact Dr. Pildes. Membership must be one of the great bargains of the 1980s: $4 a year and $2 for students.

■ **Rabbi Hillel Gamoran**
Beth Tikvah Congregation
300 Hillcrest Blvd., Hoffman Estates 60195; 885-4545
Has prepared an exhibit of ancient Jewish coins, with accompanying teaching machines, available for loan to synagogues, Jewish centers, schools, etc. A flyer is available upon request.

Israel Numismatic Society of Illinois
P.O. Box 427, Skokie 60076; 673-8514
Peggy Goldsmith, President
Meets at 8 P.M. the fourth Wednesday of each month at the Skokie Public Library, 5215 Oakton.

■ **Philip Pinsof**
41 Oakmont Rd., Highland Park 60035
Presents lectures on Collecting Judaica and on Judaica Art—ceremonial objects, manuscripts, books, and Jewish art forms.

Communications

Iris Barchechat
4522 N. Ashland, 60640; 769-4529
Graphic arts, publicity, Jewish arts and crafts.

Steve Grubman
442 N. Wells St., 60610; 787-2272
Photographer.

Charles Chi Halevi
Combined Communications
410 N. Michigan Ave., 60611; 527-5200
Public relations, free-lance writing on Chicago Jewish subjects.

John G. Heimovics
P.O. Box 524, Highland Park 60035
Custom photographic services, including archival printing, reproductions, and enlargements. Specialty area: Chicago Jewish historical photographs.

Rachel B. Heimovics
P.O. Box 524, Highland Park 60035
Public relations, free-lance writing. Specialty areas: Chicago and American Jewish subjects, including historical commemorations, special events, and other celebrations.

Marion E. Kabaker
4800 S. Chicago Beach Dr., 60615; 548-6267
Free-lance writer.

Dr. Elliot Lefkovitz
1001 Hull Ter., Evanston 60202
Writer and researcher available for projects of Jewish interest. Author of *A History of Anshe Emet Synagogue.*

Al Lieberman
9525-E Gross Point Rd., Skokie 60076; 676-9347
Free-lance photographer.

Photography Group
Lincoln Park–Lakeview JCC, 871-6780
Singles group made up of photography buffs; some may be available for free-lance assignments.

Beverly Siegel
465-4544
Free-lance writer: articles, organizational brochures, newsletters, etc.

Ruth G. Silverman
837 Lehigh Lane, Buffalo Grove 60090; 398-2019
Public relations and free-lance writing about Jewish subjects such as Falashas, Spertus College and Spertus Museum, and Olin-Sang-Ruby Union Institute.

Herb Slobin
433-1459
Graphic designer: brochures, books, posters, etc.

Emily Soloff
2325 W. Greenleaf, 60645; 262-7721
Free-lance writer, editor of books and magazine articles on such subjects as Jewish history, education, and women.

Convention Planning and Leadership Training

The Convention Planners Inc.
200 E. Delaware Pl., Suite 11A, 60611; 944-0910 or 649-0989
Roz Silverman, President

This longtime executive director of B'nai B'rith Women in the Midwest has established her own convention-planning business with special expertise in meeting needs of Jewish organizations. Handles all details of convention, meeting, and conference management; provides consultative services and will undertake individual fund-raising events. Has also developed leadership-training workshops for organization officers, executive boards, and key chairmen. Not limited to the Chicago area.

Cooking and Baking

- **Cynthia Berland**
  2729 W. Lunt, 60645; 274-0928
  Cooking classes and food demonstrations with special emphasis on Jewish holiday cooking and kashrut (kosher observance).

- **Eenie Frost**
  1386 Orleans Circle, Highland Park 60035
  Specializes in Jewish cooking and editing cookbooks. Editor of several cookbooks for Women's American ORT, *Tradition in the Kitchen* by the Sisterhood of North Suburban Synagogue Beth El, and others.

- **Rosaleah Goland**
  8641 Harding Ave., Skokie 60076; 674-7321
  Cooking and baking teacher and demonstrator. Programs include The Chala Baker—a 45-minute demonstration of chala baking with enlightening and entertaining stories of its history and folklore; and Wok's Up Dot!—a 45-minute demonstration of wok cooking, applied to the kosher kitchen, when requested. Suitable for organizations and bridal luncheons. Also a two-hour class on many uses of the wok.

- **Dr. Yaacov Selhub**
  363-0321
  Professionally a chemist at the University of Chicago hospitals, Selhub is a member of the University of Chicago Hillel faculty, where he teaches North African Jewish cooking as he remembers it from his native Libya.

- **Elaine Sherman**
  The Complete Cook
  405 Lake Cook Plaza, Deerfield 60015; 729-7687 (SAY-POTS)
  A complete resource for Jewish cooking information. Cooking demonstrations available to sisterhoods and other organizations.

- **Sarah Stiebel**
  432-0156
  Teaches a kosher cooking and baking class at North Suburban Synagogue Beth El. Nonmembers may enroll in the class by making a contribution to the synagogue.

Some of the organizations that provide cooking demonstrations and have a cookbook for sale are American Mizrachi Women, Hannah Senesh Chapter (973-0688); Beth Hillel Sisterhood (256-1213); Neshei Chabad (869-8060); Beth Shalom Sisterhood (498-4100); and North Suburban Synagogue Beth El Sisterhood (432-8900).

Dating Service

Jewish Singles Dating Directory
Chutzpah Unlimited, Inc.
P.O. Box 2400, 60690

Matchmaking with a modern twist. Men and women submit information about themselves to Eleanor Heather Siegel, who publishes coded descriptions without specific names, addresses, or telephone numbers. Siegel coordinates the matchmaking for subscribers who send in requests from the current issue of the directory. Participants do not have to be from the Chicago area. Write for details.

Entertainment

Musicians and other entertainers for hire are listed in Chapter 8, "The Arts."

Jewish Student Union
Gabe Saltan, Contact
6400 N. Sacramento, Suite 101, 60645; 262-8029

JSU is an independent, nonprofit organization that sponsors monthly programs of Jewish entertainment for singles and married couples in their twenties. Locations vary.

Fund Raising

The Convention Planners Inc.
200 E. Delaware Pl., Suite 11A, 60611; 944-0910 or 649-0989
Roz Silverman, President

Among the many services to Jewish organizations provided by this office are fund-raising events and total fund-raising packages.

■ Manuel Silver
236-6395 (days) or 869-0737 (evenings)

Professional fund raiser with knowledge of all aspects of the Jewish community, but special expertise in areas of Israel, Jewish education, public relations, and community organization.

Rental Facilities

Park District field houses, congregations, Jewish Community Centers, and summer camps are some of the sources for halls, meeting rooms, and auditoriums for rent. With camps, of course, you also get sleeping accommodations.

Spring Grove Camp of the Prairie Club
Harold Kiehm, Contact
478-2960 or 327-5848 (home)
Camp phone number is (815) 675-2527

This is a lodge, heated and available year-round, located 55 miles northwest of Chicago in the town of Spring Grove. The kitchen may be koshered easily because one range is reserved for kosher use only. Bunk beds accommodate up to 40, and there's room for as many as 60 in sleeping bags. There are ten acres of surrounding camp grounds with water and electrical hookups. Use of this facility must be arranged through a member of the Prairie Club. Jewish groups may contact Harold Kiehm.

The following organizations rent rooms in their own headquarters buildings:

Free Sons of Israel
6335 N. California, 60659; 338-9810

Workmen's Circle
6506 N. California, 60645; 274-5400

Zionist Organization of Chicago
6328 N. California, 60659; 973-3232

The two Israeli banks with branches in Chicago have rooms available to organizations at no charge:

Bank Hapoalim
174 N. Michigan, 60601; 621-0800

Bank Leumi Le-Israel
100 N. LaSalle, 60602; 781-1800

Restaurants

Kosher Restaurants Supervised and Endorsed by the Chicago Rabbinical Council

Kosher endorsements are subject to change.

Cafe Hanegev
6407 N. California, 60645; 761-8222
Meat restaurant. Serves delicious falafel, shish kabobs. Carryout.

Falafel King
4507 W. Oakton, Skokie 60076; 677-6020
Wonderful falafel. Meat restaurant.

Kosher Karry
2828 W. Devon, 60659; 973-4355
Meat. Restaurant, catering, carryout deli; a fantastic emporium of old-world tastes and smells, including soups, gefilte fish, meat blintzes, and chicken.

Meal Market
2915 W. Touhy, 60645; 761-4131
Meat. A sit-down kosher deli with carryout and catering. Advertises itself as "more than just a deli"; offers a Sunday night buffet from 4 to 8 P.M., with all you can eat for a flat $5.99.

O.K. Corral Restaurant
3144 W. Devon, 60659; 465-6400
Meat. On the order of a kosher McDonald's, this is unlike the other restaurants. Not a Jewish-style deli, not a European Jewish restaurant, not an Israeli-style one. This is American food—hamburgers, BBQ ribs, Italian beef, and pareve milk shakes—and all of it kosher.

Sabra Kosher Restaurant
2712 W. Pratt, 60645; 764-3563
Meat. *Chicago* magazine once called this the best of the meat-only restaurants.

Tel Aviv Kosher Pizza Restaurant
6349 N. California, 60659; 764-3776
The only dairy restaurant of the lot.

Other Restaurants—Either Kosher, Kosher-Style, or Jewish-Style

Al's Delicatessen and Restaurant
18677 Dixie Highway, Homewood 60430; 798-4399
Formerly on 75th St. in South Shore, now probably the only place in the south suburbs serving and selling nothing but kosher food. Closed during Passover.

The Bagel
3000 W. Devon, 60659; 764-3377
Popular Jewish-style restaurant, once located in Albany Park. Stuffed whitefish, blintzes, etc.

Bagel Nosh
Willow and Pfingsten Rd., Glenview 60025 (Plaza Del Prado Shopping Center); 272-9420

Bagel Nosh
1135 N. State, 60610; 266-6369

Two separately owned franchises serving a bagel smorgasbord—something of everything on nine varieties of bagels.

Braverman's Cafeteria Restaurant
441 N. Wabash, 60611; 421-3979
Historic; famous for its kosher-style corned beef sandwiches.

Fluky's
6821 N. Western, 60645; 274-3652
Originated on Maxwell St. in the 1920s.

Bernard Horwich JCC
3003 W. Touhy, 60645; 761-9100
A nonprofit kosher lunch counter is operated by the senior adult center. Open Sundays through Fridays during the lunch hour until 1 P.M. Hot lunches prepared by an on-premises caterer. Open to the public.

Lippy's
3114 W. Devon, 60659
Kosher-style hot dogs.

Manny's
1141 S. Jefferson St., 60607; 939-2855
Kosher-style kugel, kreplach, kishke.

Zweig's
8630 Golf Rd., Des Plaines 60016; 297-4343
The Zweig family used to be kosher caterers. Grandpa Alex and Grandma Bella owned Zweig's Banquet Hall, 3146 W. Roosevelt. Current generation runs this kosher-style deli.

Vegetarian Restaurants That Use Absolutely No Meat or Poultry Products

Chicago has a number of vegetarian restaurants that never use any meat or poultry products. The following are a few examples:

Blind Faith Cafe
800 Dempster St., Evanston 60202; 328-6875

Blue Gargoyle
5655 S. University, 60637; 955-4108
Operates during the U of C school year.

New Earth
3339 N. Halsted, 60657; 525-4150
211 W. Front St., Wheaton 60187; 665-5255

For a more complete list of vegetarian restaurants in Chicago—and for a broad survey of nonvegetarian restaurants that safely serve vegetarian meals and meatless foods such as those that are available in ethnic cuisines—see *The Chicago Green Pages* by Lori Lippitz (Chicago: Chicago Review Press, 1980).

■ **Dr. Louis A. Berman**
928 Asbury, Evanston 60202; 475-3148

This psychologist, writer, and lecturer is also a resource on vegetarianism. His book, *Vegetarianism and the Jewish Tradition*, was published in New York by KTAV Publishing House, 1980.

Scribe (Sofer)

A Jewish scribe, or sofer, is certified, based upon his education and piety, to write the sacred texts of Judaism, including preparing (and repairing) Torah scrolls and mezuzot parchments.

■ **Rev. Yochanan Nathan**
Bais STaM
6343 N. California, 60659; 973-1311

Rev. Nathan is the only full-time scribe working in Chicago. He can be found at his religious bookstore, Bais STaM.

Shaatnes Testing

A shaatnes lab analyzes fibers to detect whether shaatnes—the mixing of linen and wool in the same garment, a practice prohibited by Jewish law—exists.

■ **AFTA (Association for Torah Advancement)**
2852-D W. Touhy, 60645; 338-2575

AFTA supervises the shaatnes labs in Chicago and has an up-to-date listing of places that will provide this service. AFTA also has been conducting an educational program in the Jewish day schools demonstrating by use of a microscope how to detect shaatnes. Throughout the year, AFTA sponsors a shaatnes-testing drop-off service at The Cleaning World, 3049 W. Devon. Testing takes approximately one week.

In 1980, the following men's clothing stores were providing free shaatnes testing for garments purchased or rented at the store: all Baskin stores in Chicago and the suburbs; Capper and Capper, downtown Chicago and Old Orchard; Eric Salm, Lincoln Village; Gingiss Formal Wear, Lincoln Village; Monitor Tuxedo Rental, 1422 W. Wilson, 60640; Turner North, 3425 W. Devon, 60659.

Shopping Services

The Ark and the Council for Jewish Elderly provide shopping and transportation services for clients who need assistance.

National Council of Jewish Women North Shore Section
P.O. Box 234, Glencoe 60022

Shopping and transportation services for elderly housebound people living in Highland Park and Deerfield. Volunteers pick up the shopper and drive her or him to the grocery store; assistance in the actual purchasing of groceries is available if necessary.

Tours

Chicago Jewish Historical Society
Leah Axelrod, Tour Coordinator
2100 Linden Ave., Highland Park 60035; 432-7003

The Chicago Jewish Historical Society will assist organizations in presenting tours of Jewish Chicago. CJHS also offers bus tours through the summer on a first-come, first-served basis.

Jewish United Fund
1 S. Franklin, 60606; 346-6700

JUF sponsors a series of Mini-Missions, tours of local beneficiary agencies. For information about scheduling such a tour or participating in a planned one, call the JUF office.

Travel Assistance

JUST (Jewish United Singles Travel) For You
P.O. Box 2400, 60690

A travel-partner matching service for Jewish singles, by Eleanor Siegel and her nonprofit Chutzpah Unlimited, Inc.

Marcia Schreibman
Travel Magic Ltd.
2200 Waukegan Rd., Glenview 60025; 729-9191

Tours to Israel and Jewish-content travel throughout the world.

Pearl White
Rama Vacations
188 W. Randolph, 60601; 641-1272

Kosher travel arrangements throughout the world.

For Future Editions

Send additions, deletions, changes, or suggestions (include your name, address, and telephone number) to

Chicago Jewish Source Book
P.O. Box 524, Highland Park IL 60035

Index

Adolescence, 64–68, 73–74, 82.
See also Drug abuse; Runaway youth counseling
Adoption, 17
Adult education, 177. See also Colleges; Congregations
Agencies. See also College organizations; Educational associations and boards; Hospitals; Senior adult resources; Youth resources; and other specific subjects
   Ark, 69
   Council for Jewish Elderly, 45–46
   Jewish Children's Bureau, 73–74
   Jewish Community Centers, 46–47, 74–76
   Jewish Family and Community Service, 76–77
   Jewish Federation of Metropolitan Chicago, 77–78
   Jewish United Fund, 79
   Jewish Vocational Service, 79–80
   Response Center, 82
Aging, 49, 50
Alternative minyanim, 114, 115–16
Alumni, 40–44
Am Chai–Chutzpah network, 129–30

Arabs and Arabic, 178
Arbitration, religious, 28, 117
Archaeology, 178–79
Architecture and architectural landmarks, 212–14, 241–43
Archives, 233–37
Armed forces, 259–62
Art, 201–14, 301–3. See also Gift shops; Landmarks
Artists and artisans, 201–10
Audiovisual resources, 298–300

Bagels, 306–7
Bakeries, 306–7
Banks, Israeli, 278
Bar and bat mitzvah, 147
Bible, 179
Birth, 145–47
Black-Jewish relations, 262
Blind and visually handicapped, 18–19
Books, 303–5
Brides, 148
Broadcasting, 296–97
Burial, 149–55

Calligraphers. See Artists and artisans; Scribe
Camps, 19–23
   day, 22–23
   overnight, 19–21
   special overnight, 21

Candy, 307
Cantors, 229
Caterers, 319-20
Cemeteries, 151-54
Central area resources, 13
Chanukah, 119-20
Chaplaincy services, 116-17. See also Armed forces
Chavurah groups, 114-15
Chicago Jewish bibliography, 237-40
Chicago Jewish demography, 11
Chicago Jewish history, 233-40. See also Labor history; Landmarks; Oral history
Chicago Jewish population, 11
Child abuse, 23-24
Children's concerns, 73-74, 77
Choirs. See Performing arts
Circumcision, 146
City clubs, 24-25
Civil rights and liberties, 262
Civil War, 262
Cleaners, 320
Coin collecting, 321
Collecting and collectibles, 320-21
College organizations, 70. See also Colleges
Colleges, 168-77
Communications, 295-300, 321-22
Community organizations, 262-63
Congregations, 89-113
Conservative Judaism, 85-86
Convention planning, 322-23
Conversion, 117
Cooking and baking demonstrations, 323-24
Correspondence courses, 183
Country clubs, 25
Couples clubs, 25
Crafts. See Artists and artisans
Cults, 26

Dance, 229-32. See also Performing arts
Dating service, 324
Day-care centers
  for children, 26-27
  for senior adults, 49

Day schools, 165-66
  elementary, 165
  high schools, 166
Deaf and hearing impaired, 27-28
Death and dying, 149-55
Defense organizations, 257-59
Delicatessens, 308-11
Discrimination recourse, 263-64
Diseases, Jewish, 196-97
Divorce, 28
Donating, 318
Dramatics, 225. See also Performing arts
Driving services. See Shopping services
Drug abuse, 28-29

Early childhood education, 161-64
Educational associations and boards, 157-59
Educators' resources, 159-61
Emergency food, 29
Emergency shelter, 78
Employment
  agencies, 29-30, 79-80
  services, 29-30, 79-80
  training, 79-80
English language lessons, 179-80
Entertainment, 324. See also Performing arts
Ethnicity, 265

Falashas, 265-66
Families, 30, 76-77. See also Support groups
Family planning, 31
Festivals, 119-25, 201
Films, 298-300
Financial assistance, 31-32
Fish, 307-8
Flowers, 305
Folk dancing, 230-32
Folk groups (landsmanshaften verein) 130-33
Food, 305-14
  bagels, 306-7
  bakeries, 306-7
  candy, 307
  demonstrations, 323-24

emergency, 29
emergency, for Passover, 29, 59
  fish, 307-8
  groceries and delicatessens, 308-11
  ice cream, 311
  kosher food co-ops, 311-12
  Kosher Meals-on-Wheels, 29
  kosher supervision, 305-6, 312
  meat, 312-13
  poultry, 312-13
  restaurants, 325-28
  wholesalers, manufacturers, and distributors, 314
  wines and beverages, 313-14
Foster care, 32
Fraternal organizations, 32
Fraternities and sororities, 32-33
Free-lance writers, 321-22
Free loans, 31-32
Fund raising, 324
Funeral directors, 149-50
Funerals, 149-51

Gay Jews, 33
Genealogy, 248-51
Geography of Chicago, 11-13
Gift shops. See Agencies, Jewish Community Centers; Books; Congregations; Hospitals; Neonatology support
Greeting cards, 314-15. See also Artists and artisans; Gift shops
Grieving, 62, 63, 155. See also Mental health; Pastoral counseling
Groceries, 308-11

Hair goods, 316
Halacha (Jewish religious law), 117-18
Handicapped, 33-34
Havdalah candles, 209. See also Gift shops
Health agencies and services, 192-94. See also Hospitals
Health clubs, 194

Health-support organizations, 194-96
Hebrew, 180-82
High Holidays, 118-19
Historical societies, 233-37
Historic landmarks, 241-43
Holidays, 118-25
Holocaust, 251-56
Home-care services, 34-35
Hospitals, 191-92
Hotels. See Caterers
Housing, 45-46, 48-49, 266
Human rights, 266-67

Ice cream, 311
Illinois, early Jewish history in, 240-41
Immigrants and immigration, 35-36, 56-61
Indiana, 113
Infant and new mother's aid, 145
Institutions of higher learning
  Jewish, 168-70
  other, 170-77
Interfaith programming, 267-69
Intermarriage, 149
Iranian Jews, 138, 269
Islam, 178
Israel. See also Zionist organizations
  aliyah, 278-81
  banks, 278
  commerce, business, and investment, 277-78
  consulate general of, 277
  fund raising, 282-84
  political-action groups, 284-85
  programming resources, 285-88
  specific support groups, 292-94
  study in, 278-81
  travel to, 278-81
Israeli folk dancing, 230-32
Israelis, in Chicago, 282

Jewelry. See Artists and artisans; Gift shops
Jewish communal service, 36

334 *Index*

Jewish diseases, 196–97
Jewish Effectiveness Training, 183–84
Jewish history, 243–46. *See also* Chicago Jewish history
Jewish humor, 133
Jewish institutions of higher learning, 168–70
Jewish literature, 134–36
Jewish Marriage Encounter, 36
Jewish mysticism, 127–28
Jewish philosophy, 127–28
Jewish schools, after-school and weekend, 166–67. *See also* Day schools; Jewish institutions of higher learning; Preschools
Jewish theology, 127–28
Judaeo-Arabic, 138

Karaites, 36
Kashrut Hotline, 118
Ketubot (Jewish marriage contracts). *See* Artists and artisans; Books; Scribe
Kosher bakeries, 306
Kosher caterers, 319–20
Kosher delicatessens and groceries, 308–11
Kosher fish, 307
Kosher food co-ops, 311–12
Kosher ice cream, 311
Kosher laws, 118
Kosher meat and poultry, 312–13
Kosher restaurants, 325–27
Kosher supervision, 305–6, 312
Kosher wine, 313–14

Labor, 269
Labor history, 246–47
Labor Zionist Movement. *See* Zionist organizations
Ladino, 138
Landmarks, architectural and historic, 241–43
Landsmanshaften folk groups, 130–33
Leadership training, 36–37, 322–23

Learning disabilities resources, 184–85
Legal resources, 37–39
Libraries, 185–88. *See also* Archives; Congregations
Literature, 134–36
Loop and North Michigan Avenue resources, 13
Lubavitch Chabad, 87–88

Maps, 14–15
Marriage, 148–49
  mixed, 149
Meals for senior adults, 49
Meals-on-Wheels, 29
Meat markets, 312–13
Media, 295–98
Medical services, 191–94
Men's clubs, 39. *See also* Congregations
Mental health, 127, 197–99
Mentally retarded, 39–40
Mezuzah, 125–26
Mikvah, 126
Military, 259–62
Minyanim, 114, 115–16. *See also* Congregations
Mixed marriage, 149
Mohelim (persons qualified to perform circumcisions), 146
Monuments, 154
Museums, 188–90
Musicians. *See* Performing arts
Music resources, 226–29
Mysticism, 127–28

Naming ceremony, for baby girls, 146–47
Neonatology support, 146
Newcomers to Chicago, 13, 16
Northwest Indiana, 113
Numismatic resources, 321
Nurses, 34–35
Nursing homes. *See* Health agencies and services; Senior adult resources

Oral history, 247–48
Orchestras. *See* Performing arts
Organizations, a miscellany of, 68–84
Orthodox Judaism, 86–88

Passover, 120–23
    products for, 120
    seder observances, 121–23
Pastoral counseling, 127
Performing arts, 214–29. *See also* Israeli folk dancing
    performers, 214–25
    resources, 225–29
Philatelic resources, 320
Photographic resources, 321, 322. *See also* Archives; Artists and artisans; Audiovisual resources
Politics, 269–71
Population statistics, 11
Prenatal care, 145
Preschools, 161–64
Prisoners, 40
Proselytizing, 271
Public art and sculpture, 210–12. *See also* Landmarks
Publications, 295–96
Public relations, 321, 322
Puppetry, 221
Purim, 123–24

Rabbinical organizations, 85–87, 89
Rabbis, 178. *See also* Congregations; Rabbinical organizations
Reconstructionist movement, 88
Recordings, 316
Reform Judaism, 88–89
Religious articles and supplies. *See* Art; Books; Gift shops; Holidays; Scribe
Religious organizations, 85–89
Religious services, 89–116
Rental facilities, 324–25
Resale shops, 316–18
Resettlement. *See* Immigrants and immigration; Soviet Jews in Chicago

Restaurants, 325–28
Reunions, 40–44
Runaway youth counseling, 44
Russian Jews. *See* Soviet Jewry; Soviet Jews in Chicago
Russian language, 182

Scholarships, 184
Schools. *See* Colleges; Day schools; Jewish institutions of higher learning; Jewish schools; Preschools; Special education; Universities
Scouting, 44–45, 282
Scribe, 328
Sculptors. *See* Artists and artisans
Secular Judaism, 136–37
Seder observances, 121–23
Self-help groups, 61–63
Senior adult resources, 45–50. *See also* Employment
Separation, 28
Sephardic resources, 137–38
Shaatnes testing, 328
Shelter, 78
Shofar instruction, 119
Shopping, 301–18. *See also* Gift shops
Shopping services, 329
Simchat Torah, 124
Single parents and single-parent families, 50–51. *See also* Self-help groups
Singles, 51–56, 324, 329
Sisterhoods, 56. *See also* Congregations
Social and political-action agencies, 257–59. *See also* Discrimination recourse; Israel; Soviet Jewry; and other specific subjects
Soviet Jewry, 271–73
Soviet Jews in Chicago, 56–61. *See also* Immigrants and immigration
Special education, 184–85
Sports, 61
Stamp collecting, 320
Storytellers. *See* Performing arts

Sukkot, 125
Support groups, 61–63
Synagogue art and architecture, 212–14. *See also* Congregations; Landmarks
Synagogues. *See* Congregations; Landmarks; Synagogue art and architecture

Talmud, 183
Tapes, 316
Targum (modern Aramaic dialect), 138
Teachers' resources, 159–61
Theater. *See* Performing arts
Thrift shops, 316–18
Tours, in Chicago, 329
Traditional congregations, 89, 90
Travel, 329
    to Israel, 278–81
Travelers assistance, in Chicago, 13
Trophies, 318
Typewriters, Hebrew and Russian, 318

Universities, 168–77

Vegetarianism, 328
Vegetarian restaurants, 327–28
Veterans, 259–62
Visiting the sick, 17–18
Visitors, to Chicago area, 13, 16
Visually handicapped, 18–19
Vocational resources, 29–30, 59

Weddings, 148
Wedding supplies (chupah canopies, frames, ketubot, rings). *See* Artists and artisans; Books; Gift shops; Scribe
Widows and widowers. *See* Grieving; Self-help groups
Wines and beverages, 313–14
Women's business and professional organizations, 63–64
Women's concerns, 273–76
Writers, 321, 322

Youth organizations, 64–68. *See also* Congregations
Youth resources, 44, 73–74, 82

Zionist organizations, 288–92
ZIP code key, 16